Servant Leadership

Servant Leadership:

Attitudes, Skills and Behaviours

By

Larry W. Boone

Cambridge
Scholars
Publishing

Servant Leadership: Attitudes, Skills and Behaviours

By Larry W. Boone

This book first published 2019

Cambridge Scholars Publishing

Lady Stephenson Library, Newcastle upon Tyne, NE6 2PA, UK

British Library Cataloguing in Publication Data
A catalogue record for this book is available from the British Library

Copyright © 2019 by Larry W. Boone

All rights for this book reserved. No part of this book may be reproduced, stored in a retrieval system, or transmitted, in any form or by any means, electronic, mechanical, photocopying, recording or otherwise, without the prior permission of the copyright owner.

ISBN (10): 1-5275-2080-3
ISBN (13): 978-1-5275-2080-6

This book is dedicated
to Betty and Natalie
for a lifetime of love and support.
There could be no greater gift.

TABLE OF CONTENTS

FOREWORD ix
CHAPTER ONE: SERVANT LEADERSHIP 1
    Servant leadership and characteristics of servant leaders 4
    Leadership and power 12
    Leadership and service 15
    Virtues, values and traits 16
    Leadership styles 18
    Critiques and early bumps in the road 22
    How servant leadership is addressed in this book 24
CHAPTER TWO: ATTITUDES 28
    Think and say "We" not "I" 29
    Value statements are meant to be practiced 30
    Vision isn't everything, but it's the beginning of everything ... 32
    Everyone is good at something 37
    I am committed to your success 37
    It's useful to give my power away 39
    I don't have to be right all the time 43
    Listening is hard work 44
    Feedback is a gift 47
    I am a community builder 49
CHAPTER THREE: SKILLS 52
    Knowing and sharing personal values 53
    Listening 57
    Communicating 62
    Visioning 86

Managing time 95
Running a meeting 117
Forgiving 128
CHAPTER FOUR: BEHAVIOURS 132
Being proactive 135
Establishing credibility 141
Building trust 148
Building networks 160
Empowering others to act 172
Embracing change 180
Planning the future 193
Reflecting 208
BIBLIOGRAPHY 219
INDEX 235

Foreword

Like many workers my early career consisted of several different jobs with several different organizations. Before, during and after college I was a concession stand attendant, road repair worker, telephone company driver, steel mill pipefitter's helper, production engineer, quality assurance engineer and quality assurance manager. Some of my personal work experiences were highly satisfying and enjoyable; others were decidedly not. I became very curious about what made the difference between the places I wanted to work and the places I didn't. The environment of work became such a personal interest that after my first graduate degree in Engineering Management I decided to pursue doctoral studies in business management and organization behaviour.

Upon attaining my Ph.D. and beginning my teaching career I came to know many college students searching for their first job, and I have had the pleasure of staying in touch with many of them through their early careers. I noticed that they had very similar experiences to my own. Some were very happy, comfortable and motivated with their work situations while others realized they had made a poor job choice and soon resumed their employment search. In general, I believe it is fair to say, many simply accepted the highest paying position offered to them or the one with the employer of highest reputation or perhaps the one closest to their "dream" location, assuming all job environments were pretty much the same once they entered their employer's door. Large numbers of these former students came to know that compensation, employer reputation and geographic landing spots were not the most important contributors to their satisfaction with work. This is no surprise to many experienced workers, of course. But it was enlightening to see how many early career workers thought money, prestige or location were the answers in their search for satisfaction and motivation at work.

Through my own teaching and research I focused on what I thought was the true differentiator between good places to work and poor ones–the quality of leadership.

At the Peter J. Tobin College of Business at St. John's University in New York I enjoyed wonderful opportunities to teach both graduate and undergraduate students in courses on leading, planning and venturing as well as other management topics. I also had the great fortune to associate with the university's Vincentian Center for Church and Society. Through the Center many opportunities emerged to conduct workshops with religious and lay leaders in a variety of Church organizations. Numerous occasions to work with leaders in for-profit enterprises also developed through the Tobin College of Business.

Throughout my decades of teaching I came to know and appreciate some highly meaningful and useful books on leadership and management. Some of the earliest that captured my attention were by Peter Drucker and Stephen Covey. They helped me understand what leadership, management and working with and through people was really about.

Then I discovered the work of James Kouzes and Barry Posner through books such as *The Leadership Challenge*. Their work became a mainstay of my leadership teaching. The practitioners and students with whom I have worked truly enjoyed discussing their Five Practices of Exemplary Leadership and putting their ideas to use.

One day a small book titled *Christian Reflections on The Leadership Challenge* came to my attention. Through it I became more familiar with the writings of John Maxwell because he was the sponsor of the Catalyst Leadership Conference from which this little book emanated. Maxwell's work also impressed me greatly and became part of any leadership course outline I created. Through this *Christian Reflections* book I also became more familiar with Ken Blanchard and Patrick Lencioni, although their prestigious works had been well known to me previously. But two other *Christian Reflections* contributors, David McAllister-Wilson and Nancy Ortberg so enthused me that I began a concerted effort to learn more about visioning, enabling others to act and servant leadership. At that point I dug into materials by Robert Greenleaf, James Hunter and James Autry and by James Sipe and Don Frick.

Each book on servant leadership left me more inspired than the last and helped me come to personally important conclusions about what really makes the difference between the places I wanted to work and those where I just felt I had to work. Leadership is indeed the difference, and especially leadership by one who serves others first. I hadn't realized it at the time, but I was fortunate enough to come into contact with real servant leaders during my early business career. They made work environments stimulating. They made me want to get out of bed and go to work because I knew I could do my best and that my contributions were appreciated. They facilitated, educated and coached me. They were the difference.

Ideas about leading and working taken from the writers I have named led to the best classroom and workshop experiences I have had, and, referencing the feedback I have received from large numbers of practitioners and students, they also affected many others in very significant, positive ways.

Based on the reactions I have received from my numerous workshop colleagues and students, I believe I recognize the servant leadership concepts and practices they have found to be most useful, inspiring and implementable. Also, with the assistance of those I have engaged in conference rooms, training rooms and classrooms, I have organized these concepts and practices into the categories of servant leader attitudes, skills and behaviours that readers will encounter in this book.

So I heartily express my gratitude to all the talented researchers and writers whose intellectual contributions form the basis of my servant leadership teaching and to the leaders and students who have helped derive the contents and organization of this book!

Also, thanks to Sr. Margaret John Kelly, DC, founder and former Executive Director of the Vincentian Center for Church and Society at St. John's University. She recruited me for the service work in which I have participated for over twenty-five years. Her leadership, professionalism and charism inspired me and modelled the way for me. My great appreciation is also extended to Mary Ann Dantuono, former Associate Director of the Center, with whom I have worked collegially across the New York metropolitan area and the U.S. as well as in Africa. We continue to do our best to help administrators lead a bit better. I also thank heartily Rev. Patrick Griffin, CM, current Executive Director of the Center, who has continued the institution's great work and introduced new initiatives that enthuse me and others to do the work that helps leaders serve others well. In no small measure I owe thanks as well to Rosemarie McTigue and Kimberly Hoppe-Hernandez, whose administrative support has been so helpful to me over many years.

Certainly, I owe my thanks to the many graduate assistants with whom I worked at St. John's over the years. Two of these former assistants, now well-established and outstanding professionals in their own fields of accounting and marketing, served as valuable co-authors on servant leadership articles. Monica Peborde was co-author of "Developing Leadership Skills in College and Early Career Positions" and Sanya Makhani served as co-author of "Five Necessary Attitudes of a Servant Leader." Not only was it a pleasure exploring servant leadership concepts with these intellectually challenging graduate students (at the time of co-authorship) but also the successful and enjoyable completion of these pieces made it easy for me to commit to writing this book.

During my teaching career I have been supported by numerous guest professionals who enter my classroom with outstanding enthusiasm to share their knowledge, experiences and advice with students. I want to express my sincere appreciation to all of them. They have enriched my students' learning experiences immeasurably.

Among the many guest professionals who have educated my students, a few, in particular, stand out. I thank John and Florence Tutunjian as well as Angie Parlionas for generously sharing their talents, time, passion and humour with generations of St. John's business students pursuing their personal interests in becoming better entrepreneurs, leaders and managers. They went beyond imparting their considerable expertise for starting and leading successful business ventures by stressing the importance of doing the right things while running a business, all the while exciting students and bringing a large measure of fun into the classroom. There are no greater ambassadors for business and business education–so a special thanks to John, Florence and Angie!

I conclude this foreword by offering a simple and profound idea about servant leadership that is taken from previous authors on the topic and will be found in several sections of this book. My hope is that it will encourage those with a servant's heart (and I am sure there are many of you) to read through this material and conclude that it is okay to think this way.

In my many years as a management professor I read a lot of text books on management, leadership and associated topics. In none of them did I run across the word "love." When I started to read about servant leadership, I did.

Leaders should love their followers. That is, leaders should be patient with others and treat them with kindness and respect. In their dealings with others, leaders should be honest, humble, selfless and forgiving (another word not often found in management text books). Leaders should listen to others and be committed to high principles based on their own personal values as well as their organization's values. Finally, leaders should love others by expecting them to achieve great things and hold them accountable for doing so while seeing their own leadership role as facilitating their followers' success. Is this not the way people express love for each other outside the workplace? When leaders love their followers, work environments become places where people want to do their best knowing their work is important and their contributions will be appreciated.

Chapter One

Servant Leadership

Servant leaders do many special things for their organizations. One of their major contributions is setting the stage for other people to succeed. Because high numbers of followers achieve success, servant led organizations accomplish great things.

This book is about the attitudes servant leaders adopt, about the skills they develop and apply, and especially, about the behaviours they practice over time to create the environment for others to succeed. It's about the way servant leaders establish and maintain a supportive, facilitative climate where people strive together to enact a compelling shared vision of a better future, where people simultaneously accomplish tasks and build relationships and where leaders empower others to meet high expectations while holding them accountable for their performance and behaviours.

Different terms and approaches are used by many authors to describe the environment servant leaders create. For example, Ken Blanchard describes a climate where people willingly contribute their hearts, minds, creativity and excellence toward mutually beneficial goals–an environment where workers commit to the mission and to becoming the best they are capable of becoming.

James Kouzes and Barry Posner write about enabling others to act through fostering collaboration and strengthening them. Collaboration is fostered by building trust and facilitating relationships while followers are strengthened by enhancing self-determination and supporting development of their competence and confidence.

Nancy Ortberg writes that servant leaders release others to do their work by trusting them as they trust themselves to accomplish outstanding results.

James Hunter describes the servant-led environment as one in which leaders are driven by the institution's mission and where their followers simultaneously accomplish goals and build relationships. It is a climate where excellence is demanded, people are held accountable for performance and community is built.

John Maxwell says leaders empower people in the workplace. His Law of Empowerment states that leaders themselves have a strong sense of self-worth, and they believe not only in themselves but also in their mission and their people. To Maxwell empowering followers means leaders help others reach their potential by being on their side, encouraging them, giving them power and helping them to succeed.

James Autry says servant leadership is concerned with creating a place in which people can do good work while finding meaning in their efforts. It's a place where followers are free to bring their spirits to work.

Of great interest here is how servant leaders affect others through who they are and what they do. That is, how followers' satisfaction, commitment, productivity and creativity are improved through the environment servant leaders create. This is where servant leadership shines. This environment is applicable to the workplace, the community, the congregation, the family, the sports team or whatever particular unit may be guided by the servant leader.

Creating such a climate is attractive to many leaders. It's not hard to imagine that it should be. It is an environment where people "want to" work instead of feeling like they "have to" work. It's an environment that supports participants' dedication to mission, personal fulfilment, pride in accomplishment, sense of responsibility for achieving results, desire to be both effective and efficient and willingness to create new methods and relationships.

However, acting as servant leader for one's enterprise, agency, community, family or team is not a simple matter. It's a way of behaving one adopts over the long term. It's individual as well as organizational. Servant leadership is based on values, both personal and institutional, as well as relationships. The servant leadership style can be learned and applied by people who possess the intent to change, grow and improve. That is, servant leadership involves the type of person you are as well as the style you apply to lead others.

Generally speaking, leadership is a process through which a leader influences the behaviours of others toward a common goal. A vast amount of research informs us that an enterprise's performance is related directly to its leadership quality. Leadership accounts for the difference between long-term success and failure no matter how performance is assessed–in terms of growth, quality of service, financial results, innovativeness or any other means.

Because leadership is so important to people and institutions, the topic has been the subject of much interest and research for many decades. The contingency approach dominates the extensive literature on the subject.

The appropriate style of leading others depends upon the situation. Some contexts call for autocratic leadership, some for democratic or participative leadership. Best results are attained in other situations by using transformational or transactional approaches, and still others call for bureaucratic, charismatic or laissez-faire leadership styles–and so on.

Organizations seeking servant leaders (small sample)

7-Eleven	Nordstrom
Balfour Beatty Construction	Opportunity International
Broetje Orchards	Organisations That Matter
Catholic Relief Services	Rally Software Development
Cengage Learning	SAS
Container Store (The)	ServiceMaster
Darden Restaurants	Southwest Airlines
Evergreen Freedom Foundation	Starbucks
Federal Express	SunDurance Energy
Heartland Health	Synovus Financial
Herman Miller	TD Industries
Hess Corporation	Toro Company
Insperity Business Solutions	U.S. Cellular
Landry's Bicycles	U.S. Air Force, Army,
Liberty Dialysis	Marine Corps, Navy
Luna Data Solutions	Vanderbilt University
Marriott International	Wal-Mart Stores
Matrix Information Consulting	Wegmans
McKinney Capital & Advisory	Whole Foods
Medtronic	Yum Brands
Men's Warehouse	Zappos.com

Primary source: Lichtenwalner, Ben. "Servant Leadership Companies List," last modified April 29, 2017. https://www.modernservantleader.com/featured/servant-leadership-companies-list/. Other sources supplemented the list.

Servant leadership's timeless relational and values-based principles help to address many of the myriad challenges facing those in leadership positions today. Organizations around the globe are revamping their approaches toward people, relationships and leadership. And servant leadership is emerging as a preferred practice as demonstrated by its adoption at numerous successful and admired business enterprises across all industries and cultures as well as at many government agencies and multitudes of not-for-profit organizations and religious institutions. (See the figure on organizations seeking servant leaders for a small sample.) Many enterprises are including the practice of servant leadership principles as necessary or desired on the job descriptions they are posting when recruiting for various leader, manager and administrator positions.

Servant leadership and characteristics of servant leaders

Let's now explore the background of servant leadership as well as what it takes to be a servant leader.

The servant leadership approach is not new; it has been used for thousands of years. However, the term *servant leadership* was introduced into the modern leadership literature in 1970 when Robert Greenleaf published his seminal essay "The Servant as Leader." Greenleaf spent a long and highly successful career at AT&T working in the fields of management, research, development and education. His essay was based on his personal experiences and offered a unique insight into the nature of leadership and a holistic slant to the behaviours distinguishing excellent leadership.

He believed the effective leader leads with a compelling vision shared with all who contribute to an organization's efforts, sets clear behavioural expectations and serves as an authentic practitioner of the values proclaimed.

Among its many features Greenleaf's approach to leading included a dedication to the value of service, a call to personal transformation and an emphasis on community. He recognized the need to produce high-quality work, achieve challenging goals and hold people accountable for their results and behaviours. But his relational and communal emphasis distinguished his ideas from prevailing leadership practice by emphasizing more about the power of love and less about the love of power, more about listening and connecting to others and less about watching and correcting and more about finding out what people want, less about telling people what to do.

There is broad agreement that Greenleaf's "servant as leader" approach draws upon and fosters the best within individuals and organizations. Primarily, servant leadership focuses on the growth and well-being of people and the communities in which they operate. At its core is respect for the human person and for the dignity of work. Servant leaders place the needs of others first, share power, involve others in decision-making and help people reach their full potential.

Larry Spears, President and CEO of the Robert K. Greenleaf Center for Servant-Leadership from 1990-2007 as well as author and editor of hundreds of articles, books and other publications on servant-leadership, has identified ten characteristics of critical importance to servant leaders. This set of attributes provides a valuable overview of the effective, caring leadership provided by those who see themselves as serving others.

Characteristics of Servant Leaders

Listening
Servant leaders strive to identify the will of a group and also help clarify that will. Servants listen receptively to what is said and unsaid. They also listen to their own inner voices. Listening, combined with self-reflection, is necessary for the growth and well-being of servant leaders.

Empathy
Servant leaders are skilled empathetic listeners. They accept and recognize people for their special, unique spirits. Co-workers' and colleagues' good intentions are assumed. They are not rejected as people even when leaders must refuse to accept their certain behaviours or performance.

Healing
Many people possess broken spirits and emotional hurts. This is part of being human. Servant leaders recognize the potential for healing self and relationships to others. They seek opportunities to make whole those with whom they interact.

Awareness
While servant leaders have their own inner serenity, their keen awareness of general conditions awakes and disturbs them to action. It helps them to understand ethical, power and values issues. Awareness helps servants observe situations from an integrated and holistic perspective.

Persuasion
Servant leaders do not coerce others into compliance by relying on the traditional authoritarian model of leading within organizations. Rather, they rely upon persuading, convincing others. They are effective consensus builders within their groups.

(Continued on next page)

> **Characteristics of Servant Leaders (continued)**
>
> **Conceptualization**
> Servants lead by visioning. They dream great dreams. They balance their necessary focus on day-to-day issues and problems with a conceptualizing perspective on what can be. Opportunities matter. Servant leaders call others forward to a grand future none could be capable of achieving alone.
>
> **Foresight**
> Rooted within the intuitive mind, foresight enables servant leaders to integrate past lessons, current realities and the likely future consequences of their decisions. Foresight is the hard-to-define ability to anticipate potential outcomes of a situation. It is closely related to the conceptualization characteristic.
>
> **Stewardship**
> Since above all servant leaders recognize and attend to the needs of others, they view their role as holding their organizations in trust for the greater good of society. Leaders do so by emphasizing openness and persuasion, not control.
>
> **Commitment to the Growth of People**
> A belief that people have intrinsic value beyond their tangible contributions as workers drives servant leaders' strong commitment to every constituent's personal and professional growth. Servants nurture others' development through funding for training, taking personal interest in their ideas, encouraging participative decision-making and many other practices.
>
> **Building Community**
> Servant leaders strive to build community within their institutions. Emphasizing common pillars, like mission, vision and values, helps create shared identity and unity of direction and expected behaviour.
>
> Spears, Larry C. 2010. "Character and Servant Leadership: Ten Characteristics of Effective, Caring Leaders." *The Journal of Virtues & Leadership*, Volume 1, 25-30.

Fundamentally, Greenleaf discussed leading others not from the pedestal-style sources of authoritative power, control or dominance but as an attitude and perspective about self, about others and about a meaningful, fulfilling life. His message's simplicity has reverberated in people of different generations and across many cultures. Greenleaf believed that by first learning to be a good follower, a servant leader acquires "habits"–ways of *being with* others and *for* others–or what ethicists would term "virtues."

The other-centred personal habits of a servant leader emanate from strong self-awareness and social consciousness, and they translate into positive organizational behaviours and leadership approaches. They meld into a distinctive posture that allows a person to be both leader-servant and servant-leader simultaneously. From this dual position questions of "For whom do I work?" or "Whom do I serve?" and "Why do I work?" or "For what purpose do I serve?" are active continuously to keep leaders on track, that is, focused on a better future for the organization and all its constituents.

Servant leaders
- lead with a compelling vision shared with all who contribute to an organization's efforts
- set clear behavioural expectations
- serve as authentic practitioners of the values proclaimed

Servant leadership includes
- a dedication to the value of service
- a call to personal transformation
- an emphasis on community

With personal humility servant leaders place themselves at the service of others. The servant leadership approach focuses on the needs and interests of others. Leaders serve followers, not the other way around. The personal needs of the servant leader are subservient to the desire to help followers grow both personally and professionally. According to Greenleaf, servant leadership begins by demonstrating integrity, creating relationships based on trust and assisting others in learning, growing and developing into leaders themselves. Because leaders are committed to developing their followers, they encourage the freedom to experiment and take risks as well as to make mistakes without fearing punishment.

Some of Greenleaf's intriguing people-growing and community-building tenets of servant leadership may be expressed as:

- leaders and leadership can emerge from any place in any enterprise, agency, congregation or community; leaders are not necessarily those with formal position and authority
- the best leaders are dedicated followers (servants) first, then emerge as leaders, and
- most group members realize intuitively who their real leaders are.

What led Greenleaf to develop this concept that has been embraced by practitioners, academics and consultants over the years and has been adopted by hundreds of organizations as their leadership philosophy? Two stories help to relate his motivation.

First, in Greenleaf's (2002, 21) own words we come to understand the genesis of his realization:

> The idea of the servant leader came out of reading Hermann Hesse's *Journey to the East*. In this story we see a band of men on a mythical journey, probably also Hesse's own journey. The central figure of the story is Leo, who accompanies the party as the *servant* who does their menial chores, but who also sustains them with his spirit and his song. He is a person of extraordinary presence. All goes well until Leo disappears. Then the group falls into disarray and the journey is abandoned. They cannot make it without the servant Leo. The narrator, one of the party, after some years of wandering, finds Leo and is taken into the Order that had sponsored the journey. There he discovers that Leo, whom he had known first as *servant*, was in fact the titular head of the Order, its guiding spirit, a great and noble *leader*. ... to me, this story clearly says that *the great leader is seen as servant first,* and that simple fact is the key to his greatness. Leo was actually the leader all of the time, but he was servant first because that was what he was, *deep down inside*.

Second, while a student in a college course titled "Sociology of the Labor Problem," Greenleaf accepted a challenge issued by his professor to develop a way to make the world a better place. His particular professor wasn't charismatic or dynamic, personal traits often mistakenly associated with leadership. Instead, Greenleaf's teacher was advanced in years and a quiet man who asserted that social change occurs only when people within organizations, not outside them, choose to make their institutions themselves forces for public good. Greenleaf accepted the professor's challenge. He became such a force during his AT&T career.

The wise teacher's advice is still applicable today. A few brief passages from Greenleaf's writings illustrate his insights into human nature and the prudence of servant leadership.

On who the servant leader is:

The servant-leader is servant first ... It begins with the natural feeling that one wants to serve, to serve *first*. Then conscious choice brings one to aspire to lead. That person is sharply different from the person who is *leader* first, perhaps because of the need to assuage an unusual power drive or to acquire material possessions ... The leader-first and the servant-first are two extreme types. Between them there are shadings and blends that are part of the infinite variety of human nature.

The difference manifests itself in the care taken by the servant-first to make sure that other peoples' highest priority needs are being served. The best test, and difficult to administer, is: do those served grow as persons; do they, *while being served*, become healthier, wiser, freer, more autonomous, more likely themselves to become servants? *And* what is the effect on the least privileged in society; will they benefit, or, at least, will they not be further deprived? (2008, 15)

On considering what one is trying to do:

A mark of leaders, an attribute that puts them in a position to show the way to others, is that they are better than most at pointing the direction. As long as one is leading, one always has a goal. It may be a goal arrived at by group consensus, or the leader, acting on inspiration, may simply have said, "Let's go this way." But the leader always knows what it is and can articulate if for any who are unsure. By clearly stating and restating the goal the leader gives certainty to others who may have difficulty in achieving it themselves (2002, 29).

On seeking, listening to others, hope and optimism:

But if one is *servant*, either leader or follower, one is always searching, listening, expecting that a better wheel for these times is in the making. It may emerge any day. Any one of us may find it out of their own experience (2008, 11).

On power and authority:

A fresh critical look is being taken at the issues of power and authority, and people are beginning to learn, however haltingly, to relate to one another in less coercive and more creatively supporting ways. A new moral principle is emerging which holds that the only authority deserving one's allegiance is that which is freely and knowingly granted by the led to the leader in response to, and in proportion to, the clearly evident servant stature of the leader (2008, 11-12).

Transforming from conventional leader to servant leader is not a simple task. It requires conscious effort to change one's ways of thinking, acting and reacting. It means ensuring one has the requisite attitudes, skills and behaviours of a servant leader.

James Autry, author of *The Servant Leader: How to Build a Creative Team, Develop Great Morale, and Improve Bottom-Line Performance*, writes that it is easier to develop an attitude of service if leaders develop ways of being authentic, vulnerable, accepting, present and useful to others.

Authenticity means being who you really are in all circumstances, practicing the same values in whatever role you fulfil. Being vulnerable requires courage because it entails giving up some traditional notions of a leader always being in control. Vulnerability means being open and honest about your feelings in the work environment. It means expressing candidly your doubts, fears or concerns about personal ideas or a constituent's performance. Also, vulnerability includes admitting your mistakes to others and being able to say, "I was wrong" and "I am sorry." Acceptance requires embracing disagreement as part of the work process. Humans will disagree. Acceptance doesn't imply that you agree with others' ideas merely because they have been expressed. Rather, it means that you accept ideas as valid for discussion, review and critique and that you focus on the ideas themselves and not on the individual who offers them. Being present means applying your values at all times to tasks and decisions at hand and being fully available to others as you react to their issues or problems. Finally, by being useful Autry means providing service to others, seeing yourself as a resource to them and for them.

Those who lead as servants put the needs of their organization and people before their own; conceptualize what "can be" and lead with an inspiring vision for the future; listen to, understand and empathize with others; and accept others with tolerance for their imperfections but may refuse to accept some of a person's effort or performance as sufficient, that is, they hold people accountable for their performance and behaviour. Also, servant leaders persuade rather than coerce; appreciate the value of learning; adapt to change readily; work hard to gain trust; help others reach their potential; encourage others to try new things and new ways; support people in healing when necessary; and withdraw regularly to renew themselves through reflection.

Servant leaders do not lead from the top. They do not always visualize themselves at the peak of an organizational pyramid. Instead, servants see themselves in various flexible positions within any hierarchy. As servant leaders they do not force people to follow through authoritarian means but walk among followers, helping them move in a direction that unites all in a common vision by facilitating, educating and coaching them.

> **Servant leadership**
> **Newly-appointed leader's introduction**
>
> Marie was recently appointed to her first leadership position in a very large technology company. She is to serve as director of western region operations even though she worked in the eastern region since starting with the firm just four years ago. Only a few people in the west have met her, and it's fair to say none feel they really know her well.
>
> Upon being introduced for the first time to a large gathering of western region employees, she took microphone in hand and began, *"I learned early in life from my mother and father, my Granny Mildred and my fifth grade teacher, Charlotte Weems, that the most important things I should remember are: #1 always do my best no matter what I do, #2 be concerned personally about the welfare of others and #3 be smart enough to listen to people who are smarter than me. That advice has served me very well through two college degrees, an exciting early career entrepreneurial venture that failed but taught me a lot about business and going for what I believe in, four different jobs with three different firms, two inspiring terms as a board member of a children's hospital, one wonderful 20-year marriage and raising two great children right up to today in their early teenage years. I have tried my best and am still trying to instill those same values in our kids.*
>
> *During my time with our firm I have appreciated the way my leaders have given me opportunities to do my best in several projects I was able to initiate, and I have met many colleagues who have taught me a great deal. Also, I'm proud to be part of an organization whose concern for the welfare of others within the company and people in the community is just as strong as my own."*
>
> Servant leaders reveal their personal values to followers and, whenever possible, link them to organizational values. When followers know what's important to their leaders, trust builds.

Several researchers have developed scales for measuring servant leadership. Some of the behavioural dimensions identified are: accountability, altruistic calling, authenticity, behaving ethically, conceptual skills, courage, creating value for the community, emotional healing, empowering, forgiveness, helping subordinates grow and succeed, humility, interpersonal acceptance, organizational stewardship, persuasive mapping, putting subordinates first, relationships, standing back and wisdom.

From these results it can be seen that servant leaders give first priority to the interests of others while delivering necessary support and affording credit to others for accomplished tasks. They demonstrate genuine concern for others' career growth and professional development by providing encouragement and aid, even mentoring. Servant leaders use their deep organizational knowledge to facilitate others, especially immediate followers, in identifying and solving problems as well as determining when and how to complete tasks. They interact openly, fairly and honestly with others, make genuine efforts to know, understand and support others in the institution and emphasize building long-term relationships with close followers. Importantly, servants foster a proactive, self-confident attitude among followers and engender in them a sense of personal power. They hold others accountable for performance they can control while keeping their own accomplishments in perspective and, when appropriate, admit their own fallibility and mistakes. They take reasonable risks and embrace new approaches to problems and situations. Servant leaders take responsibility for the organization's well-being, acting as caretakers for their institution and role models for others. They have a conscious and sincere concern for helping the community as well as demonstrate sensitivity to others' personal concerns.

The servant leader employs a powerful shared vision to inspire others to work enthusiastically and to be committed to a brighter future which benefits the collective interests of the group, the organization and/or society. Among widely diverse constituents servant leaders build community by emphasizing unity as defined by common mission, values and vision.

Leadership and power

Greenleaf points out that leaders' influence over others necessarily involves power. Power is the ability to act. It moves people and organizations. Power is to leadership what energy is to physics; it makes things happen.

Servant leadership
Visioning

Paul, a newly appointed Chief Executive Officer was making his first remarks to his constituents when he asked for questions from the assembled group. One of the questions was, "What do you see ahead for us?"

Paul had been discussing and considering his vision for the enterprise for quite some time so without hesitation he started to speak about what he envisioned in the future and how he expected to inspire his followers.

"I see an organization that will support families and individuals in achieving health and happiness through the products and services we create and deliver to them. They will come to us with excitement because they are confident that we will provide what they need to support their dreams and solve their most meaningful problems. They will see us as partners in building fulfiling lives.

I see a work family that consists of colleagues who respect and trust each other and value each member for who they are and what they are capable of doing. We will view each other as teammates who share the responsibilities and rewards associated with achieving grand things and celebrate together as we attain success.

I see an organization that contributes radically to the improvement of society and the communities in which we work and live. We will make a difference. We will have a positive impact on our world."

Servant leaders envision the future in a manner that expresses high ideals and values, incorporates followers' as well as the leader's hopes and aspirations and serves as a call to action for working together to create a better tomorrow. Visions are meant to inspire. Vision isn't everything, but it's the beginning of everything.

What organization do you think Paul heads?

However, Greenleaf describes very different types of power. Servant leaders may influence others through persuasion and example. In these approaches "power is used to create opportunity and alternatives so that individuals may choose and build autonomy" (Greenleaf 2002, 55). Followers' behaviours may be influenced by leaders' articulation of superior organizational knowledge derived from their "closer to the ground" position within the enterprise; leaders hear, see and know things others may not.

Another potential power source for leaders is coercion. Greenleaf writes that coercive power is used "to dominate and manipulate people ... into a predetermined path" (Greenleaf 2002, 55). Coercive power derives from leaders' positions of formal authority and their ability to sanction the actions of others by providing or withholding effort, support or money. The author warns of negative consequences when coercive power is exercised; it strengthens resistance among followers. Accordingly, servant leaders avoid the exercise of coercive power.

Referent power is another source of influencing behaviour, and it is afforded to people to whom others naturally refer when leadership is necessary. This type of influence does not depend on the authority that accompanies a formal position of organizational leadership. Rather, referent power emerges from a voluntary relationship between leader and followers. Others sense that their referent leader possesses personal characteristics and appeal, inspiration, wisdom or expertise. Seeking guidance and direction, followers are drawn to them even though they are not formal leaders within their enterprise. Servant leaders tend to be high in referent power.

It is interesting, perhaps fascinating, to view power as possessing something of a mystical quality. Under certain conditions power is not depleted when it is used. Rather, power multiplies. When leaders' power is applied for the purpose of meeting the needs of the institution or advancing the capacity of followers to accomplish work, power is not an exhaustible resource or even a zero-sum game among powerholders. The more power is shared, given away by leaders, the more it accrues back to them. Sharing power increases followers' willingness to work toward organizational goals as well as the resources (connections to authority) they need to make things happen. Thus the effectiveness of workers increases. When followers accomplish more, organizations thrive and leaders are recognized as effective. Effective leaders garner more responsibility and power.

What does this power multiplication look like in day-to-day operational terms? Leaders share power with everyone, including those closest to where organizational action takes place–for example, where well-trained, self-confident and clearly-directed nurses care for patients, faculty teach students, attendants serve passengers, mechanics repair equipment, designers create products, salespersons sell to customers and so forth. At all points where followers contact clients they may be far removed in place and time from their hierarchical leader, but they are able to make decisions and take actions that bring to fruition the organization's vision without checking all the way back through the chain of command. In other words, followers are empowered.

As we shall examine in closer detail throughout this book, servant leaders' attitudes and skills are applied to develop many specific behaviours that contribute directly to workplace environments where followers feel empowered to act. This is the real "magic" of servant leadership.

Should leaders be perceived as using power to satisfy their own personal needs, followers judge them to be self-serving leaders, not servant leaders. In that case, followers tend to limit leaders' power to the formal authority they have to tell people what to do on the job. Workers will do what is necessary to keep their jobs, and that's about all. Self-serving leaders see their power to affect workers' behaviours dwindle over time.

But power used effectively, as it is by servant leaders, can be viewed as demonstrating a mystical quality. When it is used to meet the legitimate needs of the organization and its workers, power multiplies.

Leadership and service

While servant leadership involves the exercise of power, as do all forms of leadership, it also is about service, caring about others' needs and interests and about the organization's well-being. Like power, service can be viewed as having a mystical quality.

Leaders serve others by advancing their capacities for achieving success. Because servant leaders facilitate, educate and coach their followers, people grow in self-awareness, abilities, organizational knowledge, connections and self-confidence. They feel capable because they are aware of vision and values–what the institution wants to accomplish and how they are expected to behave. They are motivated because they believe their work is important. They feel valued and supported. Leaders serve others by creating this environment for success. Also, servant leaders model their leadership style for others. They educate and inspire through example. And service multiplies when followers being served are inspired to serve others. As Greenleaf suggests, one of the results of servant leadership is that followers are more likely to become servant leaders themselves.

**Servant leadership
Emergency room doctor**

Here is a great story from Nancy Ortberg. It demonstrates many aspects of a servant leader's approach.

... I worked as a registered nurse in the emergency room of a busy hospital. One ER doc was such an incredible leader that when he was on your shift, you knew things were going to go smoothly. You thought, 'Today I'm going to be part of a team, I'm going to learn something, and I'm going to be a better nurse for it.'

Other doctors would tell us what to do, and we just did it. But this guy orchestrated the emergency room. He asked questions while he was calling for procedures. He wanted to know, 'Why are we doing this?' He would say to his staff, 'What do you think?' as he worked with a patient. He never lost control of the situation, but he conducted the team like a fine-tuned orchestra, because he involved everybody. Obviously, he stayed the leader; he made the calls. But it was not uncommon for him to ask someone for an opinion, obtain a vital piece of information, and then change his mind. By working under such a leader, I felt like I was part of saving lives, not just working a shift. He gave us critical tasks to do, and we rose to the challenge. He called us by our names and asked for feedback. And at the end of the shift, he always thanked everybody. Who wouldn't want to follow a leader like that? (Ortberg 2004, 90-91)

Servant leaders are educators. They ask questions, involve and challenge others and let people influence their decisions when appropriate. They solicit feedback because they want to improve. They address followers by their names and acknowledge their contributions to success.

Virtues, values and traits

Effective leaders and their followers practice virtues and act on their shared values. Practicing virtuous behaviour, which entails acting with courage, wisdom, justice, patience, humility or other virtues, builds *character* in leaders and others. Practicing values, such as the espoused core values of an organization, builds *community* among leaders and their followers.

No one is born with character. Rather, it is developed through an inward journey supported by virtuous living, honest reflection and self-discipline. That is why it is often said that great leadership starts with *self-awareness*, realizing what is important to us, and *self-knowledge*, such as recognition of our personal motivators, strengths and weaknesses.

Applying ideas emanating from the inspiring and highly practical leadership research of James Kouzes and Barry Posner as published in their book, *The Leadership Challenge: How to Make Extraordinary Things Happen in Organizations*, once we know ourselves well, we can find our own voice and start to develop effective relationships between ourselves and others. After all, in the end, leadership is not about me or about you; it's about *you and me*.

One key aspect of self-awareness related to servant leadership is a personal understanding of whether we attain satisfaction and fulfilment by serving others or by acting in more self-serving ways. The servant leader, of course, is called to serve others first. Those with different sources of satisfaction and fulfilment will most likely be more comfortable with other leadership styles.

Leadership finds its personal origins in faith. Faith in ourselves is *confidence*, a widely recognized trait associated with leadership. Faith in each other is *trust*, a critical success factor for any interdependent group, team or organization. Faith in an institution is *loyalty* and *commitment*, highly prized organizational attributes that contribute to operational stability and long-term success. Of course, it should be recognised that for many people faith begins with their relationship with God. And the stronger their faith in God, the easier they find it to have faith in themselves and each other.

Leaders become trusted by others, that is, they become *trustworthy*, by acting with *integrity*. Integrity is the integration of leaders' values and behaviours. In other words, leaders demonstrate their integrity when they practice what they preach, walk their talk and honour their promises. When followers observe integrity, they find it possible to believe in their leaders. As a result, leaders possess what Kouzes and Posner call *credibility*, the most critical trait for exemplary leadership. One will do well to attend to Kouzes and Posner's First Law of Leadership: if people don't believe in the messenger, they won't believe the message.

> **Servant leadership**
> **Commitment to growth**
>
> Albert is a baby boomer, and he's starting to consider the retirement his family claims is "long overdue." As Vice President for Sales for a large corporation, he signed off two months ago on a new training program that is expected to improve the way his firm's services are marketed to millennials. All salespeople are required to take the two-day training that will be offered over the next six weeks. The first scheduled session is today.
>
> At 9:00 Albert takes a seat in the third row of Training Room B at corporate headquarters and looks across the aisle. He extends his hand to a young woman who started to work about seven months ago. He says, "Good morning, my name is Al. I'm looking forward to learning something new. What's your name?"
>
> Servant leaders have a strong commitment to every constituent's personal and professional growth. Servants bolster organizational trust by acknowledging their own need for continuous self-improvement. They know that if it is necessary for followers, it's necessary for them.

Leadership styles

For many decades two major approaches to studying leadership have involved traits and behaviours. Trait studies consider particular elements of character or personality as well as social, physical or intellectual attributes that differentiate leaders from non-leaders. Traits describe "what leaders are made of." If all we needed to know about leadership involved traits, we could select the potentially effective leaders from among any population.

Behaviour studies describe a leader's actions, practices or performance. In other words, behaviours describe "what leaders do." If all we needed to know about leadership involved behaviours, we could readily train just about anybody to be an effective leader.

Appreciating servant leadership requires an understanding of both traits and behaviours.

Many different leadership styles have been identified and studied. Each has its advantages and disadvantages. Each tends to be effective under certain circumstances such as the types of followers being led, the structure of tasks undertaken, the relative power positions of leaders and followers, the culture within which leadership is practiced and a host of other factors. Here the purpose is to help the reader better understand the concept of servant leadership by suggesting other leadership styles that are very different from servant leadership or similar to it.

Autocratic leadership, or the classic *command-and-control leadership* style, involves exercising high levels of power over people. It is a very different approach compared to servant leadership. The autocratic leader issues commands to others and practices close control over them. Autocrats tend to make solo decisions, rely on the formal power vested in their organizational position and are likely to exercise power for personal interests and seek personal recognition and status within their enterprise. Servant leaders, on the other hand, delegate responsibilities to others, support followers' initiatives, involve others in decisions, emerge from anywhere within the organization (with or without a formal power position), access organizational power for use by team members and give credit to others instead of accepting it personally. In the long term servant leaders engage and free others while classic autocratic leaders can deaden motivation and erect barriers to progress.

The servant leadership style has often been compared to other leadership approaches such as transformational, transactional and charismatic leadership.

Transformational leaders are said to transform people and organizations through their focus on enterprise-wide change and a shared vision of the future. They are often described as demonstrating integrity and high emotional intelligence and as being self-aware, authentic, empathetic and humble. Transformational leaders are highly visible and spend much time communicating. They tend not to lead from the front, but delegate responsibilities among team members, and then expect the best from them. They are concerned that followers reach their personal potential; they challenge others to reach higher levels of motivation and performance; they listen and react to individual's needs; and they seek to inspire others to achieve extraordinary outcomes. Through these behaviours and processes, transformational leaders support followers' efforts to become leaders themselves by developing their own personal leadership capabilities. As a result, followers' self-confidence increases, and they become more concerned with their personal growth and achievement.

20   Chapter One

> **Servant leadership**
> **Walk the shop;**
> **Catch people doing things right**
>
> After his morning coffee, Xavier, head of the Service Department, took the long way from the break room back to his office through the service center. He stopped for a short while to listen to Sean, an experienced service operator, take a couple of customer calls.
>
> As Xavier prepared to leave, he complimented Sean on his implementation of the new procedures that had been established last week and thanked him for taking unexpected steps to be helpful to customers. He assured Sean that he was contributing to the agency's vision of exciting customers when calling with questions or seeking follow-up service.
>
> Servant leaders are available to their constituents and they show they care by encouraging people and thanking them for their good work.

There are many similarities between servant and transformational leadership, and differences can be somewhat subtle. Some authors observe that transformational leaders' primary focus tends to be on the organization. Thus, those applying this leadership style direct followers' commitment toward institutional objectives. Servant leaders' focus, on the other hand, is on followers. They try to find out what people need to be successful. They want to make a difference in others' lives and, in the process, impact the organization. For servant leaders accomplishing organizational objectives, while still important, is subordinate to meeting followers' needs. With followers being first in servant leadership, servant leaders do not dominate, direct or control, but instead prefer to share control and influence with their followers. This can be somewhat different in transformational leadership where leaders may act to influence and motivate their followers.

Perhaps another difference involves servant leaders' stronger emphasis on the role of personal and organizational values as guidelines or boundaries for followers' behaviours. For servant leaders results *and* behaviours are important. This leads some analysts to suggest that a strong link exists between servant leadership and ethical behaviour in institutions.

Transactional leaders are thought by many observers to be more managers than leaders. That is, they focus more on day-to-day or short term tasks. They do not attend to "bigger picture" strategic issues, such as future visions for the organization, like transformational and servant leaders. Transactional leadership begins with the premise that team members agree to do what they are told by their leader when they accept payment for their labour; the "transaction" is that the enterprise pays them and they comply with their leaders' commands. Effectiveness derives from transactional leaders' close attention to clarifying peoples' roles and responsibilities, organizing their efforts and keeping people motivated to work toward common goals through systems of rewards and consequences. This leadership style has significant limitations for knowledge-based or creative work, but it is a very widely applied style in numerous institutions.

A key point to understand here is that every organization has need for an effective mix of leaders (like servant and transformational leaders who inspire through compelling "big picture" visions) and transactional leaders or managers (who organize people, equipment, materials and other resources and motivate followers daily through rewards and punishments). Many organizations are under-led and over-managed.

Charisma can be described as a special attraction between a leader and followers. Followers at first may identify strongly with the message and later with the *persona* of the leader. Charismatic leaders can be spellbinding communicators or charming individuals on an interpersonal basis. All leaders benefit from at least a little bit of charisma. Otherwise they may attract no followers at all.

Charismatic leadership can appear similar to servant or transformational leadership in that the leader injects high amounts of enthusiasm into the team and is very capable of driving others forward. However, charismatic leaders may not be other-centred. They may not listen to others well, believing more in themselves than in their team members. They may not be "organization builders" like servant and transformational leaders. They may not create a foundation for future success by supporting team members in their own personal growth and development and may not cultivate new generations of leaders. Thus, there is real risk that a project, or even an entire organization, may collapse if its charismatic leader exits their position or the enterprise.

Around the globe today people are looking for those who stand out in front of others to conceptualize a better future, communicate it effectively to constituents and inspire all to work together in community to achieve it. They seek honest, authentic leaders who care about both results and relationships and strive to make the world a better place. And they welcome leaders who see their role as humble facilitators, educators and coaches who build strong organizations that will thrive under future generations of "home grown" leaders. Those capable of applying servant leadership fill the bill.

Critiques and early bumps in the road

Large numbers of not-for-profit organizations and religious groups were among the earliest adopters of Greenleaf's servant leadership concepts after their 1970 introduction. Most likely this was due to his quasi-religious approach marked by a scriptural value of service, call to personal transformation and emphasis on community. Business enterprises and their leaders were slower to join the swell of interest in servant leadership. Some thought that at first glance it lacked the strong control of personnel required in a commercially competitive environment. The servant approach was interpreted by some critics as simplistic, soft or upside-down (bosses not leading from the top of the hierarchy).

After further investigations into the details of the servant leadership concepts and additional explanation of its principles, it became clear that servant leadership is not simplistic. Rather, it is based upon and applies sophisticated social science principles dealing with complex human interaction. It is not just patting workers on the back and serving as cheerleader, and it is not letting the players run the team, as some harsh critics claimed. Rather, servant leadership is just as performance-based as it is relationship-based. And it's not upside-down. Most long ago got over the "shock" of hearing that leaders don't always have to lead from the top. They have come to realize that it really is helpful for leaders to possess the flexibility to lead from various positions in a hierarchy. Sometimes they are boss, sometimes co-worker, sometimes supporter. Over time many business leaders have come to appreciate that being humble and relationship-oriented doesn't mean a leader is weak.

Servant leadership
Empowering others to act

What do you think about James Hunter's Southwest Airlines story?

Just before the cabin door was closed for departure, a preteen boy jumped onto the plane, his arms filled with large boxes of candy, the type sold by schoolchildren for fund-raisers.

There may have been one or two empty seats left on the plane, and the overhead-storage availability had long been depleted ... I was sure this kid was going to get blasted with the usual 'Those boxes will need to be checked below! Can't you see we are out of room back here?'

But that is not what happened. Instead, this young flight attendant asked the boy if he would like assistance in selling his candy. Of course, the boy's eyes lit up as he said, 'Sure.'

The flight attendant then proceeded to take the candy and put it into the cockpit with the pilots! I had never seen a flight attendant put a passenger's belongings into the cockpit before, nor have I since that day.

The next thing I knew, we were at cruising altitude, and the flight attendant was on the overhead PA system announcing that candy bars were going to be passed down the aisle for $2 per bar. The flight attendant concluded the announcement by saying that she wanted to know who would be the first person _not_ to buy one so she could inform the rest of the passengers to stay clear of the grump in seat 10C! The plane roared with laughter.

Of course the candy was gone before the boxes reached the halfway point in the fuselage ...

That was an act of leadership on the part of one flight attendant who had no positional power in her company. She went the extra mile with that boy and influenced the entire airplane! I am sure I was not the only one on that airplane who would never forget the look on that boy's face as he held the empty boxes and a thick wad of cash (Hunter 2004, 36-37).

Leadership can emerge from any place in any enterprise, not only from those with formal position. Constituents feel empowered to take action when the organization's mission, values and vision are clear.

Another typical critique of servant leadership involves the potential for upper managers in highly competitive environments to underappreciate and overlook lower level leaders using the servant style in favour of those applying other styles. Perhaps servant leaders' effectiveness could be missed due to the fact that other leaders appear to be controlling followers more closely and getting better short-term results under certain circumstances. But such lack of recognition may be attributed to the upper level leaders who choose the criteria and make the observations. If you are looking for fast results and quick turnarounds, servant leadership may not be the most effective approach. If you are looking for high levels of performance over the long term, employee satisfaction, commitment and loyalty, dedication to mission and vision, innovation, consensus, community and desire to serve clients, co-workers and society, then servant leaders will stand out.

How servant leadership is addressed in this book

In this book readers will find discussions derived from great past and current writers on servant leadership, general leadership and management. Among many others, these writers are Peter Drucker, Stephen Covey, Robert Greenleaf, James Kouzes and Barry Posner, John Maxwell, Ken Blanchard, Patrick Lencioni, James Sipe and Don Frick, James Hunter, James Autry, Jim Collins and John Kotter. Based upon the reactions and inputs from a very large number of practicing leaders and students over the last three decades, the most helpful, practical and inspiring ideas put forward by these writers have been identified and arranged as readers see them here–as attitudes, skills and behaviours that people desiring to act as servant leaders can adopt, develop and practice.

The framework of servant leadership's three-legged stool adopted here–attitudes, skills and behaviours–was itself also derived over time based on feedback from practitioners and students seeking to better understand this method of leading others.

The complex concept of servant leadership is viewed as both traits and behaviours. Traits are the *attitudes* and *skills* leaders apply to serve others. They are what successful leaders have and bring to their leadership task. *Behaviours* are applications of attitudes and skills. They are what leaders do–how they practice leading others.

Servant leaders adopt the following attitudes and bring them to their relationships and tasks:

- think and say "we," not "I"
- value statements are meant to be practiced, not stored on a shelf
- vision isn't everything, but it's the beginning of everything
- everyone is good at something (and I am a talent scout helping people connect their talent to the organization's vision)
- I am committed to your success
- it's useful to give my power away
- I don't have to be right all the time
- listening is hard work–and it is worth the effort
- feedback is a gift, and
- I am a community builder.

Those who serve others through leadership develop the following skills and apply them continuously:

- knowing and sharing personal values
- listening
- communicating
    o asking questions
    o telling stories
    o being optimistic
    o saying "we"
    o stimulating informal conversations
- visioning
- managing time
- running a meeting, and
- forgiving.

Certainly, managing time and running meetings effectively are relevant skills no matter what particular style a leader may be using. However, servant leaders tend to manage time and run meetings somewhat differently since they are applying other servant leader attitudes and skills to these specific efforts.

In applying adopted attitudes and developed skills, servant leaders use the following behaviours to set the stage for others' success:

- being proactive
- establishing credibility
- building trust
- building networks

- empowering others to act
- embracing change
- planning the future, and
- reflecting.

Effort has been made to present these servant leadership attitudes, skills and behaviours in ways that make them easy to understand and apply. That is, throughout the book leadership practices are presented as tips and techniques: "think about it this way," "say this" or "do this." In other words, emphasis has been placed on putting sound, proven leadership theories and specific servant leadership concepts into practice wherever leaders and followers are working together. Hopefully, readers will agree that anyone can successfully lead like a servant–anyone who possesses a servant's heart.

Servant leadership
Reflecting

Just arriving at her desk following a 45-minute commute to work, Bridget looked over her to-do list for the day then pulled from her top drawer a few sheets of paper that were starting to yellow a bit from age. She had used these same sheets for the last several years on the job, and she was finally beginning to think about digitizing them for easier access. But, somehow, she felt comfortable still using them the same way she always has. Maybe she'll type them up next week.

Bridget read three random questions from the list, then sat quietly and thought about her honest answers.
- Am I clear about the values that guide my life and leadership?
- How effective are my relationships with constituents?
- How well do I handle disappointments, mistakes and failures?

After 5-10 minutes, she continued her day's work by addressing the first of her to-do items.

Servant leaders listen effectively to others, but they also make sure to listen to themselves. They habitually spend time alone, inviting silence so they may better sense what is in their own minds and hearts.

CHAPTER TWO

ATTITUDES

Our attitudes–our general outlooks on life, work, relationships and so on– largely determine the way we experience reality. An attitude is a mental state of readiness we learn and organize through our experiences. Commonly, attitudes are thought to be functions of our personalities, perceptions, feelings and motivations.

Personal Attitudes
low ⟵⟶ high
adaptability
confidence
flexibility
optimism
passion
pride
self-respect
satisfaction

Some common personal attitudes involve what we think about our own adaptability, confidence, flexibility, optimism, passion, pride, self-respect and satisfaction. Some relationship-based attitudes–outlooks we have about others–include acceptance, approval, devotion, disdain, dislike, intolerance, rejection, respect, scorn, scepticism and trustworthiness.

Attitudes are determinants of behaviour. That is, attitudes have a significant effect on the way we respond to people, objects and situations. Additional factors affect our behaviour, but attitudes play a key role in determining how we act.

How we perceive others and how they see us depends on attitudes. A generally positive attitude toward others (acceptance, approval) likely leads to friendly, supportive behaviours and positive outcomes in relationships. A negative attitude toward others (disdain, scepticism) typically leads to unhelpful behaviours and negative relationship outcomes. To be sure, attitudes drive behaviour. They are precursors, pre-determinants of behaviour. And they affect the outcomes of our relationships.

ATTITUDES ⟶ **BEHAVIOURS** ⟶ **OUTCOMES**
about self and others   toward others   of relationships

Attitudes provide an emotional basis for our interpersonal relationships and identification with others. Therefore, attitudes relate to our comfort and willingness to use specific leadership styles–such as autocratic, participative or servant leadership styles.

Leadership is about relationships, and you can choose whether or not to adopt certain relationship-oriented attitudes. To behave like a servant leader, you have to have the attitudes of a servant leader. The purpose of this chapter is to identify and discuss various attitudes that are linked closely to servant leadership behaviour in the literature. If you possess or can willingly adopt the attitudes discussed here, servant leadership may well be an effective leadership style for you.

Relationship Attitudes
low ⟵⟶ high
acceptance
approval
devotion
disdain
dislike
intolerance
rejection
respect
scorn
skepticism
trustworthiness

Think and say "We" not "I"

Servant leaders are other-centred. They place the needs, desires and contributions of others above their own. Therefore, they seldom say "I," but tend to use the inclusive "we" when referring to efforts they lead. "We envision our future." "We recognize and celebrate our common values." "We plan together." "We succeed." In communications the terms "we," "us," and "our" are used much more frequently than "I," "me," and "my." Servant leaders do not seek personal success in organizational efforts. They seek the common good achieved by collective efforts–and use speech that coincides with that attitude. Servant leaders are the ultimate team players. They naturally share the credit for successful organizational performance with their followers who contributed to it. While they are quick to point out the contributions of others, they do not seek attention for their own contributions. They share credit, emphasize the team over themselves, and define success collectively rather than individually.

When is it acceptable for a servant leader to say "I"? When things go wrong, when goals are not achieved, when failure is encountered, servant leaders shoulder the blame personally, shielding the group they lead from their responsibility for failure. This is not to say that servant leaders will not meet with followers privately to discuss each constituent's role in failure. They will hold people accountable, and they will discuss how better performance will be achieved in the future. However, in public servant leaders will say "That failure is my responsibility."

Servant Leader Tips – Think and say "We" not "I"
Use team-related terminology such as "we," "us" and "our"–not "I," "me" and "my"
Distribute credit for success to followers
Accept personal responsibility for failure

Value statements are meant to be practiced, not stored on a shelf

Cooperation, customer focus, growth, honesty, innovation, learning, productivity, quality, respect, service, teamwork. These are only a few of the values organizations tend to include as elements of their official values statements.

Expression of organizational values has become quite popular over the past few years. That's a very good thing. Businesses, not-for-profits, government agencies and the like have recognized the important role values play in their identity and operations. Values statements are expressions of what community members believe collectively. They are principles and standards that serve as common ground for all members. They are the truths that bind together otherwise diverse constituents, providing a common foundation for behaviour, decision-making and action-taking within the organization.

Organizational Values
cooperation
customer focus
fairness
growth
honesty
innovation
learning
productivity
profitability
quality
respect
service
teamwork
winning

Far too often, however, after initial development and publication, usually as part of an organization's strategic planning process, value statements are relegated to a dusty shelf never again to see the light of day. Therefore, they fail to fulfil their impactful promise. They guide no behaviour. They do not form members' common ground.

Servant leaders give life to their organization's values in many ways. They are used to define unity and community within promotional and public relations documents that link the organization to its environment. Values are applied internally to community-building (discussed later in this chapter) by forming the foundation of interviews with potential workers, hiring decisions ("getting the right people on the bus"), on-boarding programs, performance evaluation systems as well as recognition and reward schemes.

Sometimes the 4-6 values typically expressed in an organization's values statement are designated one per year for special attention. That is, one of several organizational values is identified annually for continuous emphasis in leaders' speeches, celebrations, letterheads and other forms of communication. Importantly, values are given life in the stories a servant leader tells about the organization's heroes–past and current members who have achieved success by living the organization's values. Through such stories all can learn how "we" think, act, decide, relate, serve and succeed.

Servant leaders know that values have a central place in the organization's vision. Why does a community envision a particular future? The answer has to be structured around the community's common beliefs. Values and vision unify communities of workers. But values are only pretty words unless leaders give them life through continuous use.

Servant Leader Tips – Value statements are meant to be practiced, not stored on a shelf
Create an organizational values statement, identifying 4-6 values that define your community
List values in order of priority for organization members to consider and apply
Provide a sentence or two description for each value; don't assume members will share the same interpretation of each value
Use organizational values regularly in promotional and public relations communications; link them to significant decisions and actions
Make organizational values part of your candidate interviews, hiring decisions and on-boarding programs for new hires as well as your systems for performance evaluation, recognition and rewards
Designate one organizational value each year for special attention; include it prominently in leaders' talks, written communications, organizational events, celebrations, and so on
Tell stories of organizational heroes (past and present workers) to demonstrate application of organizational values

Vision isn't everything, but it's the beginning of everything

The goal of servant leadership is to institutionalize the virtue of serving others first, not serving oneself. This can only be accomplished if the leader leads with a compelling vision, sets clear behavioural expectations and serves as an authentic practitioner of the values proclaimed.

First and foremost, servant leaders lead through their vision, their motivating description of what tomorrow will be like. Their vision is the mental picture of success they create for others. It expresses high ideals and values, giving focus to human energy. A servant leader's vision inspires both the leader and his or her followers to take action and to accomplish goals.

Visions incorporate hopes, dreams and aspirations. They are ambitious and optimistic. David McAllister-Wilson writes, "Vision isn't everything, but it's the beginning of everything" (2004, 56). Sometimes visions require leaps of faith. McAllister-Wilson describes visions as necessarily hyperbolic, unrealistic and irresponsible. That is, they are far from being safe and practical. They have a rainbow quality. Very often new leaders of mediocre, unsuccessful or failing organizations say, "There are so many problems. Where do I start?" The best approach is to start by developing a vision. A vision is a good story, an energizing future story. It is a call to action.

Where do visions come from? Often they emanate from followers themselves. Leaders know what inspires their constituents because they invest time listening to constituents' needs and desires. Leaders listen deeply with their ears, eyes and hearts–not just to followers' words but to their emotions. Servant leaders know how to enlist others in a common vision by appealing to shared aspirations that can be shaped into a unified purpose. Effective leaders apply what they hear from constituents to formulate an appealing vision that demonstrates how each individual's personal needs can be met while serving the common good of the organization and/or the constituents served by the organization. (See the Visioning skills section in Chapter 3 for discussion of relevant visioning methodologies.)

Sipe and Frick tell us that servant leaders see where to go in the future through their own foresight, stimulated by collecting information from their followers. Then they paint a compelling picture of the destination, the vision, and invite others to "Come, follow me." They suggest that a worthy vision doesn't need to be grandiose, but it must be grand. That is, it must appeal to workers at all levels of an organization. Followers must see it as a means of attaining their own personal satisfaction. A vision shows them they can be part of something they value that is bigger than themselves. Through visioning, servant leaders give voice to constituents' feelings. Workers at all levels of an organization have to see their stake in the organization's vision. They must recognize their own aspirations. A vision statement is not likely to excite followers unless they help create it and recognize their own aspirations within it.

"Growing return on sales to 8% per year" or "increasing market share to 15%" is not a vision. These may represent worthwhile organizational goals, but they don't motivate all followers to get out of bed in the morning and give their all for the cause. Neither does a generic call to achieve something like "be recognized for world class customer service."

An excellent vision will provide heroic context for even workers with the most mundane tasks. With an effective vision, everyone and everything counts. "Every activity is a small sparkle that contributes to the larger light the team is generating" (Sipe and Frick 2009, 120).

All followers at all hierarchical levels should see their stake in the enterprise's success and their contribution to its vision. Servant leaders' foresight is possible if and only if their organizations and their members have the vision to know who they are, whom they serve, how they serve and where they want to go in the future.

> As you sit down with colleagues to express or revise a vision, remember that this is not an exercise in semantics. It is the stuff of your very identity (Sipe and Frick 2009, 121).

Kouzes and Posner (2002, 143) discuss the vision as a shared sense of destiny:

> Teaching a vision–and confirming that the vision is shared–is a process of engaging constituents in conversations about their lives, about their hopes and dreams. Remember that leadership is a dialogue, not a monologue. Leadership isn't about imposing the leader's solo dream; it's about developing a shared sense of destiny. It's about enrolling others so that they can see how their own interests and aspirations are aligned with the vision and can thereby become mobilized to commit their individual energies to its realization. A vision is inclusive of constituents' aspirations; it's an ideal and unique image of the future for the common good.

Helpfully, Kouzes and Posner recommend Martin Luther King Jr.'s "I Have a Dream" speech as a model for people who are drafting a vision. The speech is about seven minutes long; about two typed pages or so. It is not just a sentence or a slogan (although millions of people inspired by Dr.

King's famous call to action remember it by its four-word title, which was repeated throughout the speech). A vision takes on many formats. It can be a 5-10 minute speech, a letter to constituents, a paragraph in an annual report, a 30-second elevator pitch, a slogan or a word. Passion matters, not length. As a truly effective vision statement, Dr. King's "I Have a Dream" speech is long enough to deliver vivid detail for people curious to know where a leader wants to be several years into the future–and how it feels to really be there. That's the power and emotional connection, the call to action a servant leader can deliver through a vision.

> **Vision formats**
>
> 5-10 minute speech
> Letter to constituents
> Paragraph
> 30-second elevator speech
> Slogan/bumper sticker
> Single word

Now, many visions are abbreviated into a slogan or a sentence or two so they can be shared quickly and, hopefully, remembered. That's the vision form with which most readers are likely to be familiar. A few examples of these types of well-constructed, broadly appealing vision statements are provided as examples. (It's up to the reader to judge whether or not these statements inspire.) However, it's important to realize that these represent only one form of a vision statement. Effective servant leaders have much more richly developed visions to deliver in a conversation, speech or document.

Servant leaders actively use a vision as a tool for communicating, unifying and motivating. The vision is not a static document or statement.

> Once the vision is in place, a Servant-Leader will refer to it frequently, using it to paint a compelling picture of what it means to work with *these* people for *these* ends. A Servant-Leader will constantly reinterpret the vision and not be afraid of refining it. This is all part of being a "visionary leader" (Sipe and Frick 2009, 121).

Inspirational leadership is not about selling a vision to others. Rather, it's about showing people how the vision can benefit them and how their personal needs can be satisfied. Servant leaders strive to sense the purpose in others. Followers don't really want to hear the leader's vision. They want to learn how their own aspirations will be met. They want to learn how their hopes and dreams will come to fruition. They want to be able to see themselves in the future picture being painted by the leader. The best leaders know that it's about inspiring a *shared* vision, not about selling their own personal views of the future.

Vision slogan examples

- Shaping the future by preserving our heritage, discovering new knowledge, and sharing our resources with the world (Smithsonian)
- To transform communities by inspiring people throughout the world to open their minds, accept and include people with intellectual disabilities and thereby anyone who is perceived as different (Special Olympics)
- To enrich people's lives with programmes and services that inform, educate and entertain (The BBC)
- To make people happy (Disney)
- Creating community through food (BiRite)
- Better health and active ageing for all Australians (Australian Department of Health)
- To be the number one advocate in the world for human worth in organizations (Ken Blanchard)
- A South Africa in which all our people have access to lifelong learning (South African Department of Education)
- Spreading the power of optimism (Life is Good)
- Capture and share the world's moments (Instagram)

Through careful listening and assimilation, leaders identify their followers' common themes then serve as the unifying force for their organization by expressing these themes as a vision for a better tomorrow. Consider a skilled craftsperson working with a fine piece of hardwood. The wood has a grain. It can be shaped successfully into some forms–and not into others. Groups of followers also have a "grain." They can be shaped into some futures–and not others. An effective servant leader reads the grain. Also, consider that people support what they help to create. (And they tend not to support what they don't help to create.) If constituents are convinced their leader has listened to their aspirations and included them in the vision, they are more likely to become motivated followers.

Of course, leaders must also be motivated personally by the vision. Therefore, they may infuse the "big picture" with their own personal desires to which they can commit and from which they can derive a personal sense of achievement. A vision, then, may meld the best of what constituents desire and what the servant leader personally wants to accomplish.

Consider this vivid image: as spokespersons for their organizations, leaders hold up a mirror and reflect back to their constituents what they most desire. Servant leaders can articulate what their group of followers are thinking and feeling. They know that the secret to winning the support of numerous constituents is to lead them (at least in part) where they already want to go. The servant leader assimilates the collective vision then empowers constituents to achieve it.

Visions can also serve as useful recruiting tools. A well-communicated vision can aid in attracting those who share the values and aspirations expressed in the vision. Attracted followers are strong "fits" for the community the servant leader is seeking to build and maintain. Conversely, those who do not share the vision's expressed values and aspirations will realize that this is not the purpose that will help them fulfil their personal passion–and in the long run potential members' decisions not to join a team can be just as valuable to effective community-building as decisions to join.

The first step of a servant leader's success journey involves expressing a vision that will unify, energize and attract followers to what everyone can recognize will be a better tomorrow. An effective servant leader realizes that "vision isn't everything, but it's the beginning of everything." Servant leadership starts by expressing how you and your followers will serve in a meaningful way.

Servant Leader Tips – Vision isn't everything, but it's the beginning of everything
Ask workers and stakeholders about their hopes and dreams; invest time in listening to the responses with your ears, eyes and heart; discover their emotions as well as their ideas
Assimilate major themes that appeal to common aspirations
Write an inspiring vision that is a call to action; create multiple formats
Include organizational values in your vision
See other visioning tips in the Skills section of this book

Everyone is good at something (and I am a talent scout helping people connect their talent to the organization's vision)

Often people do not see in themselves what someone else sees in them. Effective servant leaders share a common attitude that "everyone is good at something" (Ortberg 2004, 93). Imagine the positive environment that is created when leaders adopt this perspective. Upon encountering an employee or peer, servant leaders realize it is their responsibility to identify that person's special talents and help them realize how they can apply their gifts toward achievement of the organization's vision.

This is a powerful approach to human resource development. Followers' contributions are not limited by their formal organizational role or by their specific job description. They are enabled by a servant leader to use their special talent to take the organization toward its vision via new, perhaps unplanned, directions.

Servant leaders see themselves as talent scouts. They believe that everyone has a unique contribution to offer. Further, they believe it is their job to recognize it (even if the follower does not) and direct it toward vision attainment.

Servant Leader Tips – Everyone is good at something; I am a talent scout
See every personal encounter as an opportunity to recognize what special talent a person possesses
Accept the responsibility to link this talent to the organization's vision
Communicate this link to the person you encounter
Follow up to ensure people are applying their talents to accomplish the vision
Be a facilitator; remove obstacles that may prevent individuals from applying their special talents

I am committed to your success

Another attitude that reflects the servant leader's other-centred approach involves seeing the leader's role as facilitator, educator and coach.

The support of a servant leader can make a difference in the lives and careers of their followers. Servant leaders let followers know they will be working with them to help them grow. Leaders observe followers executing tasks, encouraging them and doing everything possible to develop them into high performers and future servant leaders. If they sense there is something they cannot develop personally, they will find others who can and bring their tutelage into play. Servant leaders will make sure followers' gifts are fanned into flames so that constituents are strengthened and serve others well.

Followers, in turn, come to believe in their leaders and trust their intentions to help them develop skills. Strong leaders stand apart because they assess the abilities of others and assist them in capturing the best of those abilities. Figuratively speaking, servant leaders can bring others to life. They can improve a follower's performance dramatically because the leader cares deeply for each constituent and has faith in his or her capabilities. Followers can respond positively to the leader's high standards and expectations because they possess the abilities and because they trust the support and encouragement the leader extends to them.

> "It takes a leader to raise up a leader."
>
> "It takes one to know one, show one, and grow one."

Of course, facilitating followers' talents has a payoff for the organization's long-term success as well. John Maxwell's Law of Reproduction states: "It takes a leader to raise up a leader." Focusing on the growth of others and helping them develop their skills is what helps develop the next generation of organizational leaders. "It takes one to know one, show one, and grow one" (Maxwell 1998, 141). According to Nancy Ortberg, some of the most powerful words a leader can offer to a follower are, "I am committed to your success" (2004, 95).

Take an example from the animal kingdom. As wild geese fly thousands of miles annually, they cheer each other on by honking encouragement to one another. Leaders who cheer those around them, offering well-directed praise for things done right, are leaders who will win the hearts of others and see great things accomplished by their team.

Servant leaders are motivated by the intention of serving others and are committed to develop their followers. When leaders work toward building character and competence among their followers, they add to their own credibility as well as the credibility of their team members. By directing followers' special talents toward accomplishing the organization's vision, servant leaders create a collaborative and effective team environment by utilizing everyone's strengths.

An important prerequisite to developing followers' talents is trust. The servant leadership style contributes to trust building with employees, customers and communities. Servant leaders learn to put into others the same trust they have in themselves. Then leaders can release followers to do their work. Trust is the foundational element of good leadership. Of course, trust has to be earned. Leaders have to establish trust with followers before they can do their best.

Leaders can earn trust by working hard to recognize each follower's special talent, helping them see how it can be applied toward the vision and committing to the success of each follower. When this is accomplished, the leader's credibility increases, each follower's contribution grows and the organization thrives.

Servant leaders take a trusting approach to managing the talented followers they have recruited for their community. They understand the vision communicates the desired future and that organizational values serve as behavioural guidelines (or constraints, if you like). As long as followers are working toward shared vision and applying organizational values, they are pursuing the desired ends through the expected means. Trust them to do the work. Let them go. Servant leaders set the stage for success, and they trust followers to do the right things. There is no need to look over their shoulders. (See the Skills chapter to explore other methods for developing trust.)

Servant Leader Tips – I am committed to your success
See yourself fulfilling a role in the lives of your followers; you are a facilitator, educator and coach
Create opportunities to encourage followers, develop followers through training and challenging experiences and bring others into their lives to do the same
On a regular basis walk the shop, find people doing things right and praise them
Demonstrate trust in your followers; use vision to communicate the desired future and values to establish behavioural guidelines; release followers to make it happen; don't look over their shoulders

It's useful to give my power away

Many people are motivated to attain positions of leadership because they seek the legitimate authority associated with the leader's position. They conclude that formal authority within their organization will allow them to issue commands, implement their ideas, allocate resources and rewards and, generally, make things happen. They like to get things done and they see "being the boss" as the means to be effective.

> **Power Bases**
>
> **Formal Power:**
> Legitimate — the power a person receives as a result of his or her position in the formal hierarchy of an organization
> Reward — compliance of others is achieved based on the ability to distribute rewards that others view as valuable
> Coercive — the power to influence others is dependent on fear of negative results from failing to comply
>
> **Personal Power:**
> Referent — ability of a leader to influence a follower because of the follower's admiration, respect, or identification with the leader
> Expert — influence is based on the leader's special skills or knowledge

Servant leaders, however, are motivated by their desire to serve others. They view leadership as the best way to achieve this service objective, and they recognize the paradox of power; they become more powerful when they give their power away. Servant leaders are probably least motivated by and least dependent upon the legitimate power base (having a formal leadership position, being "the boss"), but they frequently find themselves building a strong referent power base as they give away their power to constituents through delegation, empowerment and the practice of subsidiarity.

Do servant leaders give all their power away? Certainly not. The assumption that they relinquish all influence and assume the role of cheerleader is one basis for the frequently encountered misunderstanding that servant leadership is passive–or even "warm and fuzzy." Servant leaders are very strong, even autocratic, in certain aspects of running an organization. They are careful to control definition of mission, values, vision, standards (how the organization defines and measures excellence) and accountability (what consequences accrue when there are gaps between standards of excellence and actual performance). Servant leaders don't commission a poll, hold a meeting or take a vote among constituents to answer these questions. In fact, people look to the leader to establish such direction. However, upon developing direction through mission, values, vision, standards and accountability, servant leaders help followers succeed by turning the traditional organizational structure upside down. Leadership becomes responsive to those being led. Leaders facilitate the success of others who are closer to those whose needs are being served.

The upside down organizational structure looks something like this:

At the top: those who are served by the enterprise
(such as Customers/Clients/Students/Patients/Passengers and so on)

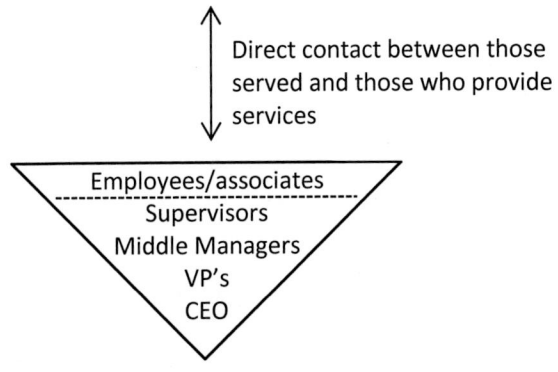

↑
| Direct contact between those
| served and those who provide
↓ services

```
\    Employees/associates    /
 \     Supervisors          /
  \   Middle Managers      /
   \     VP's             /
    \     CEO            /
     \                  /
      \                /
       \              /
        \            /
         \          /
          \        /
           \      /
            \    /
             \  /
              \/
```

For servant leaders giving away power contributes to their personal goal of facilitating others in growing to their maximum potential. Good leaders give away power by applying the organizing principle of subsidiarity. They push decision-making down. That is, they believe that matters ought to be decided and dispatched by the smallest, lowest or least centralized component authority and that higher level leaders should maintain a subsidiary function, performing only those tasks which cannot be performed effectively at the local level. Therefore, servant leaders tend to pass along as much decision-making authority and control as possible to the organizational level closest to those whose needs are being served. In other words, *at the operational level* the organizational pyramid is turned upside down.

Effective leaders strengthen others by creating a climate in which followers are engaged and feel in control of their own work. Constituents have latitude to make decisions based on vision and values. They work in an environment where they can develop their abilities to complete assignments and build self-confidence. They hold themselves accountable for results and feel ownership for their achievements.

Maxwell's Law of Empowerment states that only secure leaders give power to others. That is, leaders who give power to others make themselves indispensable by making themselves dispensable (at the operational level). By giving their followers power, leaders are empowering followers to reach their potential. When a leader can't or won't empower others, organizational barriers are created and workers cannot overcome them. If the barriers remain long enough, workers lose motivation, perform minimally or they move to another organization where they believe they can maximize their potential.

Giving away power may be challenging for many leaders, but a true servant doesn't always lead from the top. Leaders who give their power away do not blindly agree with the opinions and decisions of their followers. Rather, they accept the views of others and give them the ability to practice power. A servant leader applies Autry's Law of Acceptance which does not imply that the leader accepts everyone's ideas without critical analysis, discussion and judgment–only that the leader accepts ideas as valid for discussion and review, and that decision makers focus on the ideas themselves, not on the person who presented them. Giving followers the opportunity to express their ideas makes them feel like they are in control and have a say in decisions, bolstering job satisfaction as well as team and organizational success.

Servant leaders fulfil their roles as coaches and facilitators by moving from being in control to giving control away. Fulfilling the coach's role, servant leaders learn to trust each follower with the work that they are doing. Leaders are willing to delegate their authority while maintaining their organizational responsibility, standing on the side lines helping followers achieve their best results. Leaders place constituents at the centre of organizational operations, not themselves. Leaders use their power in service to others, not in service of themselves. Others may not do a job exactly the way the servant leader would do it. That doesn't make it wrong, just different. Results count. Don't judge approach and methods; measure performance.

Power holders will do well to learn to be servant leaders and not self-serving leaders. Humility is the key to a servant's heart and approach. Servant leaders don't think less of themselves, they just think of themselves less.

Servant Leader Tips – It's useful to give my power away
Fulfil the leader's direction-setting role; establish and communicate mission, values, vision, standards and accountability
Realize your role as facilitator, educator and coach
Push decision making down: let those closest to the customer make decisions and take action
Give budget authority to the lowest possible follower
Delegate meaningful tasks to others
Trust followers to accomplish mission and vision; set performance standards; hold people accountable for achieving vision and behaving within the guidelines of organizational values
Accept, even enjoy, the fact that other people will not accomplish tasks exactly the way you would
Empower followers to teach/train in their areas of expertise or on topics you want them to learn (people learn best what they have to teach to others)
Put followers on meeting agendas as discussion leaders; give them opportunities to lead

I don't have to be right all the time

Related closely to the practice of humility, servant leaders adopt the attitude that they need not be right all the time. They listen. They know and act on the concept that other people have good ideas, too. Their job is to surface the best ideas, not just their own. And they are comfortable crediting good ideas to others. In fact, they realize that is their job as a servant leader.

Further, servant leaders demonstrate their humility by admitting their mistakes. When appropriate, they admit errors. They know everyone is human and all of us make mistakes. In a work environment characterized by trust, leaders and followers admit their mistakes and work together to pursue continuous improvement.

Servant Leader Tips – I don't have to be right all the time
Listen to others' ideas; critique them on merit, not your opinion of the person offering them
Create opportunities for expression of ideas; hold brainstorming sessions for solving problems and developing opportunities
Admit your mistakes (you may even enhance your reputation for honesty)

Listening is hard work – and it's worth the effort

Servant leaders listen first. Robert Greenleaf (1970, 18) writes:

> Only a true natural servant automatically responds to any problem by listening *first*. When he is a leader, this disposition causes him to be *seen* as servant first.

Greenleaf goes on to suggest that the best test of whether we are really getting through to a communication partner is to first ask ourselves if we are really listening. Are we really listening to the one we want to communicate to? Also, he reminds us that we must not be afraid of a little silence because a relaxed approach to dialogue will involve welcoming some quiet, silent moments.

James Kouzes and Barry Posner, authors of the best-selling book *The Leadership Challenge*, advise leaders to "listen first–and often." Management guru Peter Drucker advised leaders to remember this good communication practice: when in a leadership position, "listen first and speak last." John Maxwell proposes this valuable lesson: "inexperienced leaders are quick to lead before they know anything about the people they intend to lead. But mature leaders listen, learn, and then lead." Also, Maxwell offers his Law of Addition. He observes that we add value to others when we know and relate to what others value. How do we know what others value? We listen to them.

Leadership and Listening
"Listen first–and often."
"Listen first, speak last."
"Inexperienced leaders are quick to lead before knowing anything about the people they intend to lead. But mature leaders listen, learn, and then lead."

By asking good questions servant leaders can identify their followers' dreams and aspirations. Listening allows the servant leader to sense the purpose in others, enhancing the leader's ability to incorporate their followers' hopes and dreams into a compelling vision that gives voice to followers' feelings. Kouzes and Posner (2002, 149-150) tell us, "Leaders find the common thread that weaves the fabric of human needs into a colourful tapestry. They develop a deep understanding of collective yearnings; they seek out the brewing consensus among those they would lead."

> **Walking the Shop**
>
> The Chief Administrator of a sizeable metropolitan hospital hired a management consultant to help assess the work-related attitudes of her large staff. Trying to demonstrate his willingness to get an early start during arrangements for an initial "get-to-know-you" meeting, the consultant asked the administrator when she started work. "Eight o'clock sharp," was her reply. On the meeting date the consultant appeared at the administrator's office promptly at 8:00. As it turned out, the administrator didn't arrive until 8:30. Not thinking much of the observed late arrival, the consultant proceeded as if nothing had happened. However, the same thing occurred for the pair's second and third scheduled meetings. Feeling more relaxed with their developing relationship, the consultant addressed the issue in this manner, "You previously mentioned that you started work at 8:00 so I have come to your office at that hour three times, yet you consistently arrive about 8:30. Should I assume you will be arriving late for our future meetings?"
>
> The administrator laughed and apologized for the misunderstanding. "I do start work at 8:00 sharp each day, but most mornings I do so by visiting different departments throughout the hospital. Typically, I bring doughnuts and spend a few minutes with the staff in each area before continuing to my office. Sorry that I have kept you waiting for our meetings." As the attitudinal research project progressed, the consultant realized that the administrator was quite well aware of the staff's attitudes, opinions and aspirations. She knew what they thought, what was very important to them and what was unimportant. In addition to knowing the names of many employees' spouses and children, she understood what staff members wanted to achieve professionally and personally through their employment in the medical field and in this particular hospital. She could predict with great accuracy how the staff would react to proposed work rule changes, introductions of new technology or any other management practice adjustments. The administrator didn't develop this knowledge through an attitude survey, but obtained it through her continuous casual conversations with staff as she walked the shop most mornings. The formal attitude survey was just corroboration for her.

Servant leaders are present. That is, they are available to their constituents. They "walk the shop," engaging in informal conversations in order to know their followers and be known by them. Servant leaders ask open-ended questions about both work-related and personal issues to draw out constituents' opinions and attitudes. They listen deeply with their ears, eyes and hearts. In so doing, they glean the emotional content of their follower's conversations so they can align the organization's vision with the professional and personal goals of constituents.

Of course, when the number of followers is too large to permit informal conversations with all, attitude and/or opinion surveys can be utilized as supplemental listening techniques. Surveys can help canvass large numbers of followers efficiently and effectively–and help the servant leader perceive changes in dreams, desires, attitudes and opinions over time.

Effective servant leaders are willing to adhere to the 2:1 ratio of questions to commands often suggested by trainers during listening skill development sessions. That is, when auditing their personal behaviours, it is apparent that servant leaders ask two questions for every direct order or instruction they deliver to followers.

Perhaps the most significant direct effects of listening involve: 1) building trust between the servant leader and followers and 2) increasing the self-esteem of followers. When a leader listens intently to followers' ideas, she demonstrates respect for their opinions, helping to develop a bond of trust. And trust is the cornerstone of the leader-follower relationship. Also, when a leader listens, followers conclude their ideas are important, helping to bolster their self-esteem and improve related outcomes such as job satisfaction, productivity and organizational commitment. Moreover, listening can inform servant leaders of their followers' experiences and lead to adapting such experiences to enhance organizational innovation.

Servant leaders maintain a strong commitment to listening. They share the understanding that listening is hard work which demands a considerable investment of their personal time and cognitive effort. Also, they share the attitude that the numerous positive outcomes of listening to one's constituents are worth every ounce of energy expended.

Servant Leader Tips – Listening is hard work – and it's worth the effort
When building a relationship or addressing an issue, problem or crisis, listen first
Welcome a little silence
Listen first–and often
Listen first, speak last
Listen, learn then lead
Sense the purpose in others

Seek out the brewing consensus in those you would lead
Be present to others; walk the shop
Ask open-ended questions
Adhere to the 2:1 ratio; ask two questions for every instruction or command you deliver
Demonstrate respect for others by listening
Build trust with others by listening
Enhance the self-esteem of others by listening
Listening is an expensive process; commit the time and energy necessary to be a good listener

Feedback is a gift

Another aspect of a servant leader's humility involves welcoming and accepting feedback. Since servant leaders recognise their purpose as serving others, what better way to improve their service than to receive from those served direct feedback regarding their performance and perceived effectiveness?

Feedback is a good thing if leaders adopt the attitude that others' opinions and perspectives provide an opportunity for personal improvement. Otherwise, feedback can be a threat.

A helpful method for telling the difference between servant leaders and self-serving leaders is to observe how they react to negative feedback. If leaders attempt to "kill the messenger," they are self-serving. Criticism ignites their deepest fears. When leadership flaws are pointed out, that may mean followers don't want them any longer. Since their position defines who they are, negative feedback is a serious personal threat. Since self-serving leaders are committed to maintaining both their position and their control, leaders may well dismiss the offered feedback and the bearers of this bad news.

However, servant leaders consider feedback a gift. Welcoming feedback is, of course, an important form of listening. Even negative feedback is received with appreciation. All feedback–positive and negative–should receive a reply similar to: "Thanks, I value all comments and suggestions I receive because I am always trying to improve. I am happy to consider your feedback along with all other comments I collect."

When things go poorly, servant leaders look in the mirror and ask, "What could I have done differently?" Ideas offered by those they serve are welcomed humbly because servant leaders have the attitude that feedback is a gift.

Sipe and Frick (2009, 65-66) adapt some ideas from Fred Nickols to offer very useful guidelines for servant leaders receiving feedback.

If you want to know how you are doing, you have to accept the responsibility of finding out. By inviting feedback you have a chance to measure how you are doing on progress toward attaining your goals. When receiving feedback, you should strive to be:

1. *Open*
   Listen without interruption, objections, or defensiveness.
2. *Responsive*
   Be willing to hear the speaker out without turning the table. Ask questions for clarification.
3. *Thoughtful*
   Seek to understand the effects and consequences of your behaviour.
4. *Calm*
   Be relaxed, breathe. Assume a comfortable body posture. Be aware of your own emotional reactions.
5. *Explicit*
   Make it clear what kind of feedback you are seeking, and why it is important to you. Offer a structure for the feedback–questions, rating scales, stories.
6. *Quiet*
   Refrain from making or preparing to make a response. Do not be distracted by the need to explain, defend or fix.
7. *Clear with your commitment*
   Describe how you have benefited from the feedback and what specific steps you will take toward improvement.
8. *Accepting*
   Open to assuming their good will.
9. *Clarifying*
   Make sure you are clear about what they are seeing, saying, and recommending.

Servant Leader Tips – Feedback is a gift
Regularly ask your constituents how they perceive your leadership abilities and practices
Apply helpful guidelines for receiving feedback: be open, responsive, thoughtful, calm, explicit, quiet, clear with your commitment, accepting and clarifying
Accept feedback–positive and negative–with a smile
Especially, resist the temptation to explain yourself or defend yourself
Say "thank you" when feedback is provided

I am a community builder

Servant leaders realize their success derives from the attitude that they are leading an organizational effort to develop a productive community. They strive to build a community centred on members' shared values and vision. And they employ collaborative decision-making and action-taking. Servant leaders know that leadership is a team sport, not a solo performance. It involves a relationship between those who seek to serve by leading others and those who make the conscious choice to follow. Organizations are built on trust, and trust develops from effective relationships between leaders and followers. Taking responsibility for relationships is more than a necessity, it is a duty.

To build community successfully it is imperative to select the right people. For servant leaders it's vital to know who to recruit, who to retain, who to develop and who to extricate from the ranks. Jim Collins explains that the "Good to Great" leaders in his research "… first got the right people on the bus, the wrong people off the bus and the right people in the right seats" (2001, 13). Strong communities are built around people who share the organization's values, are passionate about the vision and are motivated by it, and whose strengths match the organization's needs for achieving the vision–or at least they are ready, willing and able to be trained to develop such strengths.

Peter Drucker discusses the importance of looking for people's strengths. Developing the attitude to ask "What can a person do?" instead of "What can a person not do?" helps a leader see strengths clearly and determine whether or not those strengths can be directed productively toward the common vision.

Servant leaders stoke the fire of community through appeal to common vision. They help constituents see that their work is bigger than themselves. It is even bigger than the enterprise they work for. Their work is something ennobling. It serves vital needs, uplifts those served and even enriches society. This "bigger picture" approach lifts morale and increases motivation. The work is important, it matters to the servant leader–and that attitude is passed along to workers.

Organizational effectiveness depends on the strength of the community the leader builds, and the community's strength depends on choosing the right people. This is addressed by Maxwell's Law of the Inner Circle. The potential of the leader, as well as the potential of the entire organization, is determined by those closest to the leader. Building a community creates a cohesive network of personnel capable of achieving success in any situation. Maxwell explains that an effective leader brings into her inner circle people with five qualities:

1. potential value: those who raise up themselves
2. positive value: those who raise morale in the organization
3. personal value: those who raise up the leader
4. production value: those who raise others, and
5. proven value: those who raise up people who raise up other people.

A productive community is not a place free of conflict. Rather, servant leaders recognize that there should be a degree of conflict in a healthy community so that the best ideas emerge from honest discussions and analyses based upon high performance standards. A strong community is a place of conflict resolution, not conflict avoidance. Healthy conflict resolution is supported in an environment where people treat each other with respect, listen to each other, are comfortable being assertive in achieving high standards, are open to challenges, value diversity within the team and feel safe to be themselves. An organization's shared values either support such behaviour or they work against it.

Additionally, community building is supported by taking care to celebrate successes. This calls for leaders' involvement in hosting and/or addressing gatherings of constituents. Gatherings, of course, may include formal meetings, annual events, assemblies to mark milestone achievements, holiday celebrations and the like. Community may not be a characteristic of mediocre organizations, but it is the hallmark of great ones–ones with strong cultures. Servant leaders are aware that every gathering is an opportunity to renew organizational and employee commitment. They don't miss chances to ensure that followers know why they are gathered and how a particular celebration connects to values and vision. Through the inevitable daily encounter of problems and distractions, servant leaders keep constituents focused on these two key organizational guiding lights.

Servants walk the shop to provide listening opportunities, as discussed previously. However, walking the shop also contributes to community building. Leaders visit frequently the sites where work is being accomplished, where consumers' needs are being served. They make sure they observe their followers doing the right things so that, as leader, they can compliment followers on their successes, encouraging their hearts through verbal recognition. (You can't do this sitting behind your desk.) This helps develop community by affirming the type of work that supports the vision.

Also, servant leaders take care to recognize both individual contributions and team achievements through rewards, awards, gifts and "thanks-you's" of many types. Presenting a plaque, naming an employee-of-the-month and honouring a retiree are just a few of numerous opportunities to tell the stories of workers' successes and to reinforce the community's shared values and common vision.

Productive communities require building and tending. Servant leaders are aware of their vital role in bringing together the right people who are energized to achieve great things through shared values and vision. They know also that without a leader's continuous reinforcement, organizational values diffuse and visions blur. Therefore, servant leaders recognize the important role of gatherings and celebrations in maintaining community.

Servant Leader Tips – I am a community builder
Recognize that leadership is a team sport, not a solo act
Get the right people on the bus; staffing matters
Build community around common values and vision
Act on the conviction that strong communities are developed around people who share the organization's values, are passionate about its vision and who have the skills necessary to achieve the vision
Help followers see that their work is bigger than themselves
Encourage conflict resolution in communities by supporting values such as honesty, respect, openness and diversity
Celebrate the organization's values every chance you get
Create opportunities to celebrate successes with followers
Strong communities are no accident; they require building and tending and that's the servant leader's job

CHAPTER THREE

SKILLS

A skill is an ability to do something well stemming from one's knowledge, practice or aptitude. Typically, it's a proficiency acquired through deliberate, systematic and sustained effort. Leaders, of course, require a very large number of skills no matter what style(s) of leadership they may prefer. This chapter does not attempt to cover all leadership skills but only those particularly relevant to servant leaders.

Servant leaders are committed to serving others first. Among other things, this means servant leaders are "people-growing" and "community-building." Therefore, it is particularly important that servant leaders develop and apply the following skills:

- being acutely aware of their personal values and freely sharing those values with others
- listening
- communicating
    - asking questions
    - telling stories
    - being optimistic
    - saying "we"
    - stimulating informal conversations
- visioning
- managing time
- running a meeting, and
- forgiving.

While managing time and running a meeting are skills relevant to all leaders, there are sufficient special approaches for servant leaders that warrant inclusion here.

Just as all others acquire skills, servant leaders develop proficiencies through formal education, on-the-job training, life and work experiences and by modelling their behaviours after other leaders. As already discussed, Robert Greenleaf stated that a test of a servant leader is that those being served grow as persons, become healthier, wiser, freer, more autonomous, and more likely themselves to become servants. Modelling the skills discussed in this chapter for others is one way servant leaders make it more likely their followers will be capable of becoming effective servants.

Knowing and sharing personal values

Milton Rokeach, a renowned social psychologist, tells us values are enduring beliefs about the way things should be done (means) or about the results (ends) we desire. Values are underlying principles that guide our decisions and actions. They are unwavering core beliefs, the moral compass by which we live our lives. Other people assess our character and integrity by the values we demonstrate through the way we live and work, therefore our personal credibility emanates from our values.

Depending on the particular research you reference, there are between 150-250 words in the English language that represent values. Examples of personal values are: ambition, balance, bravery, careful, compassion, dignity, discipline, equality, family, freedom, fun, growth, hard work, health, honesty, humility, joy, justice, love, moderation, optimism, patience, power, respect, risk, satisfaction, security, spirituality, success, tolerance, toughness, trust, unity, wealth and wisdom.

One quick way to get in touch with our values is to consider which 4, 5 or 6 best represent guides to personal decisions like:

- Which friends should we choose?
- Which people should we trust?
- Which organizations should we join?
- Which job should we take?
- How should we invest our time and money?
- Which appeals for support should we respond to?

Answers to questions like these cause us to consider what is most important to us as well as to assign a priority order to the values we identify.

We develop our rules for living and relating during the value-forming stage in early life–usually from the age at which we become capable of judging right from wrong through early adulthood. Typically, personal values remain relatively fixed after that point. Some of the major influences on our values are parents and family members, teachers, clergy and coaches as well as the heroes with whom we identify and the peers we admire. Our values are also shaped by major environmental factors to which we are exposed during our value-forming years such as social trends, the economy, politics, technology, media, literature, and so on.

Personal values examples		
Accountability	Gratitude	Realistic
Achievement	Growth	Respect
Ambition	Happiness	Restraint
Balance	Hard work	Risk
Beauty	Health	Satisfaction
Bravery	Honesty	Security
Careful	Humility	Self-reliance
Charity	Joy	Spirituality
Compassion	Justice	Success
Dignity	Love	Thoughtful
Discipline	Loyalty	Tolerance
Empathy	Maturity	Toughness
Equality	Moderation	Trust
Fairness	Optimism	Understanding
Family	Order	Unity
Freedom	Patience	Wealth
Fun	Power	Wisdom

Developing an appreciation for our own personal values and understanding where they came from is essential for orienting our lives. They are like compass points. The clearer our values are to us, the easier it is to stay on our chosen path.

Values inform our decisions about what to do and not do, when to say yes and when to say no. To really understand our personal philosophy for living and working, to tap into *why* we make decisions and take actions, we need to be aware of our own value-forming influences. Our personal philosophy becomes clearer as we understand more about the values we chose early in life. Mature persons control their decisions and actions, and they are aware of the sources of their "internal controls." They don't take their values for granted. As they grow older they evaluate their values regularly for relevance to current decisions and actions.

To be a credible leader you have to comprehend fully your deeply held beliefs. You have to be aware of your values and where they came from (your influences), and you have to be capable of communicating those values to followers.

> Who are you? This is the first question your constituents want you to answer. Finding that answer is where every leadership journey begins (Kouzes and Posner 2012, 43).

Consider an announcement in your organization that a new leader of your work group has been named. Let's assume this leader comes from another area of the organization in another geographic region. No one in your group has ever met this individual. When the announcement comes out what questions naturally pop into your mind and the minds of your co-workers? It's not hard to imagine because many of us have had this experience. "Who is this new leader?" "What will he or she expect from us?" "How will things be different compared to work under past leaders and how will things be the same?" Essentially, you are asking, "What will this new leader want?" "What does this person believe?" "What means and ends will she or he prefer?" Even if you don't phrase the question exactly this way, in psychological and behavioural terms you are asking, "What are this new leader's values?"

One good way for the new leader to handle an introduction to constituents is to communicate their personal values. He or she can talk about what they demand of themselves every day in terms of output and what principles guide their work each day. Are they honesty, humility, wealth, service to others, family, profitability, productivity, loyalty, growth or something else? The leader can relate stories that provide examples of how their own personal challenges were handled successfully in the past. Alternatively, tales of past personal failures–and important lessons learned from them–can be shared. Through such stories followers can begin to develop understanding, relationship and trust.

No appreciation of leadership is complete without study of James Kouzes and Barry Posner's research published in numerous editions of *The Leadership Challenge*. It is very helpful to attend to their First Law of Leadership: "If you don't believe in the messenger, you won't believe the message" and their corollary to the first law: "You can't believe in the messenger if you don't know what the messenger believes."

> The first step a leader must take along the path to becoming an exemplary leader is inward. It's a step toward discovering personal values and beliefs. Leaders must find their voice. They must discover a set of principles that

guide decisions and actions. They must find a way to express a leadership philosophy in their own words and not in someone else's ... Leaders stand up for their beliefs. They practice what they preach. They show others by their actions that they live by the values they profess. They also ensure that others adhere to the values that have been agreed on. It is consistency between words and actions that build credibility (Kouzes and Posner 2012, 42).

To be an effective servant leader be transparent about your values. Let people know what you believe is right and wrong, good and bad, fair and unfair. Tell stories about your value-forming and value-applying experiences. Speak out on matters of values and conscience. People expect that of their leaders. And be as passionate about behaviour as you are about results. Ensure that your behaviour is consistent with your personal values and the values of your organization. Insist the behaviour of others is congruent with organizational values as well.

Sipe and Frick remind us that leaders like to be recognized for their character and integrity. This is another way of describing their operating values, the values that others see them putting into action. Leaders who are seen as persons of character are more likely to generate loyalty, creativity and productivity among followers.

In *The Leadership Challenge* James Kouzes and Barry Posner offer several highly useful exercises for getting in touch with your personal values. They are used as the bases for the few exercises presented in this section. Complete one or more to get in touch with your personal values.

Servant Leader Tips
Personal Values: Write Your Credo

Imagine your employer gives you the opportunity to take a six-month sabbatical with all expenses paid. But there is a stipulation that you may not take any work along with you. And you will not be permitted to communicate to anyone at your work site while you are away.

Before you leave your followers need to know the principles and beliefs that you feel should guide their decisions and actions in your absence. In other words, they need to know the *values* that should steer their decision making and action taking.

You may only write a one-page Credo Memo to communicate with them. Take out a piece of paper and write that memo.

| **Servant Leader Tips** |
| **Personal Values: Write a Tribute to Yourself** |
| What is your ideal image of yourself? How would you most like to be seen and remembered by others?

Imagine that tonight you will be honoured as the Leader of the Year in your organization. Hundreds of people will gather to pay tribute to you. Presentations will be made praising you.

What words or phrases would you most like to hear others use to describe your performance and character? How would you like to be described? What portrayals would make you feel proud? |

| **Servant Leader Tips** |
| **Personal Values: Record Lessons from Leaders You Admire** |
| You can get in touch with your values by listening to the voices of your mentors and role models.

Which historical leaders do you most admire? Why? What values did they espouse or practice? How do these values show up in your own actions?

Make a list of the individuals who have served as your leadership role models throughout your life. What values did they espouse or practice? How do these values show up in your own actions? |

Listening

One of the typical servant leader attitudes identified in an earlier chapter directly addresses listening. If you possess the attitude that "listening is hard work–and it is worth the effort," then you have one of the pre-determinants to act like a servant leader. Listening with sensitivity and openness also demonstrates a servant leader's attitudes that everyone is good at something, I don't have to be right all the time, feedback is a gift and I'm a community builder. Additionally, listening effectively can help a servant leader identify common purpose and vision among constituents. Clearly, receptive listening is a foundational skill for practicing servant leadership.

 Robert Greenleaf opined that listening is the premier skill of a servant leader. The best way to connect to another person in empathy is to listen with full presence and attention. In their excellent book *Seven Pillars of*

Servant Leadership James Sipe and Don Frick relate the story of Greenleaf deciding to teach a listening course to AT&T managers. Greenleaf called it "Talking With People" because he knew from experience that most bosses were not very interested in learning how to listen. Instead, bosses wanted to know how to get their own ideas across in ways that would oblige others to listen to them and do what they said.

Being an astute student of human nature, Greenleaf did not reject this attitude. He basically said, "OK, we can go from there and see what develops." He was well aware that people assume they are good listeners because they hear. But hearing is just picking up the sounds a communication partner offers. Many poor listeners are distracted from their challenging task because they are simply waiting for the speaker to finish. When it is their turn to speak, they can start getting their own points across and "win" the discussion. They are passive listeners–and hard-working speakers. However, passive listeners are poor listeners. They hear with their auditory system, but they often don't appreciate the entire message being sent.

Empathetic listening is the practice of extending yourself to and for other people by seeing and feeling a situation as your communication partner sees and feels it. As an empathetic listener, you are capable of appreciating a situation from the speaker's perspective. You may not agree with the speaker, but you can understand what he believes and how he feels about it. Servant leaders perform best when they develop empathy with a speaker, when as receiver they are able to place themselves in the sender's position.

Deep, reflective listening is a particularly vital servant leadership skill because it is a way of giving attention to others, a way of recognizing their importance. When leaders recognize the importance of each constituent and are willing to work hard to understand them, they demonstrate characteristics often attributed to servant leaders, kindness and respect. That is why good listening helps to build trust in relationships. Additionally, the self-esteem of communication partners can be enhanced because they recognize that a leader respects them and thinks they are important.

Of course, listening is an expensive proposition. It has a high cost in terms of cognitive effort and time. In these days when multi-tasking appears as a required skill on many job descriptions, people who seek to serve others really have to commit to listening. They realize that when they listen to another person speak, they are engaged in an active search for meaning. It is a demanding cognitive activity. They are thinking. Intellectual effort is required. And, of course, listening requires considerable time. An effective leader must commit to being available to others on a regular basis in formal settings, such as meetings, in informal formats, such as walking the shop (being in the workers' home territory) or being in "third places" (neutral sites).

James Hunter relates a very good piece of advice about the value of listening. He confesses that he used to be unhappy about attending social functions and tedious gatherings such as cocktail parties. But a friend offered some good advice that helped turn around his situation. And it is effective in workplaces as well as at cocktail parties. The magical advice is simply this: forget about being interesting; work on being interested.

If you desire to be a servant leader, learn and practice the skills of active listening. Active listeners are engaged in the communication process and make sense out of everything that is being communicated, such as body language, gestures, facial expressions, tones of voice and emotions.

According to Stephen Robbins, active listeners develop and practice these skills:

Servant Leader Tips – Active Listening

Make eye contact. People judge whether or not we are engaged in listening by looking at our eyes. Making eye contact with a speaker focuses our attention, reduces potential distractions and encourages the speaker.

Use affirmative head nods and appropriate facial expressions. Even when you are listening, you can be engaged in two-way communication. Use nonverbal techniques to provide feedback to the speaker. Demonstrate you are interested in what is being said. Head nods and affirming expressions communicate that you get the point so the speaker can understand the message is received and move on to the next point or stop talking. Head shakes or quizzical looks can demonstrate the opposite, signalling to the speaker that a different method of making the point may be needed.

Avoid distracting actions or gestures. This is the opposite of showing interest through eye contact, head nods and facial expressions. Try never to appear distracted by checking your watch, shuffling through a stack of papers or playing with a pencil. These are signals that you are not committed to paying full attention.

Ask questions. At appropriate times (without interrupting the speaker) ask brief questions to request clarification, ensure understanding and assure the speaker you are listening.

Paraphrase. In your own words restate what you understand the speaker has said for the purpose of verifying the accuracy of the communication. Use phrases such as "What I hear you saying is ..." or "Do you mean ...?"

Reserve judgment; avoid interrupting the speaker. Before you ask questions or try to respond, allow the speaker to complete his or her thoughts. Don't anticipate where the speaker is going. Suspend your judgment until the speaker has the opportunity to complete the message. The goal is to receive the entire communication; don't distort the message through premature judgments or interpretations.

Don't overtalk. Talking may be more enjoyable for you and silence may be a bit uncomfortable, but it's impossible to talk and listen at the same time. Communication is a shared experience. Do your share of talking, but don't overtalk. Be sure to do your share (or even more than your share) of listening.

Here is another helpful and highly descriptive approach to sharpening listening skills. Sipe and Frick offer "The ABC's of Communication:

- Act interested
- Be encouraging
- Clarify."

Servant Leader Tips – ABC's of Communication

Act interested. When someone wants to talk to you, stop what you are doing and pay attention even if you are rushed, overwhelmed or do not like what you are hearing. Display a "posture of involvement": turn and face the other person squarely, lean slightly forward, maintaining a comfortable distance. Look directly at the speaker's face, making appropriate eye contact and adopting a pleasant or neutral facial expression. Use your body language to let the speaker know that you are interested in her and in what she is saying. Relax and continue to listen.

> **Be encouraging.** Effective listening requires overcoming one's natural tendency to analyse or judge what the speaker is saying. Keep listening, for now. Avoid the temptation to evaluate the other person's statements from your own point of view. Do not interrupt or hurry up. Instead, offer the speaker words of encouragement. "I see ... that's interesting ... then what? ... you don't say!" Be positive, invite the speaker to express what is in the heart and on the mind. Communication experts call this "facilitative responding."
>
> **Clarify.** In order to help the speaker feel truly listened to and fully understood, periodically summarize what you've heard and, in your own words, reflect back to him your understanding of his point of view. The speaker can then determine if you have received the message as he intended. And, if you're off message, he has an opportunity to set you straight (2009, 60-61).

The authors explain that some people may worry about the insincerity (manipulation?) of the "acting interested" directive. However, they claim, that concern neglects the power of the "as if" philosophy.

> When we act *as if* we are interested, soon we *will be* interested. When we begin making eye contact and acting *as if* we are present to another, soon we *will be* present (Sipe and Frick 2009, 60).

Two final and related thoughts on the skill of listening involve the importance of silence in communication and the practice of personal reflection.

Servant leaders recognize the value of silence. In communications they listen for it and interpret it. Silence is not "nothing" as many assume. Failing to attend to a silent portion of a communication can result in missing an important part of a message. Perceptive servant leaders look for gaps, pauses and hesitations because they may signal the need to choose different terminology, identify better examples, reflect rather than speak or analyse rather than decide. Greenleaf wrote:

> One must not be afraid of a little silence. Some find silence awkward and oppressive, but a relaxed approach to dialogue will include the welcoming of some silence. It is often a devastating question to ask oneself–but it is sometimes important to ask it–"In saying what I have in mind will I really improve on the silence?" (1977, 31).

Servant leaders practice the skill of periodic withdrawal and its associated self-reflection. That is, they take care to listen to themselves. They plan regularly to spend time alone, inviting silence so they can better sense what is in their own minds and hearts. This practice is vital to long-term success. Leaders need to get in touch with their own inner voice and recognize when it is necessary and appropriate to change themselves, their team and/or their organizations. Self-reflection is so important that it has been identified as a separate servant leader behaviour that will be addressed later in this book.

Communicating

People connect with and influence others through communication. Therefore, it is a foundational skill for *all* leaders, no matter which particular leadership style they may prefer. For servant leaders communication is particularly important for conveying their personal values as well as the organization's values, building relationships, supporting collaboration, sharing information, encouraging new ideas and promoting internal and external communication. A few specific communication skills are especially important for achieving these ends and will be addressed in this section. They are: asking questions, telling stories, being optimistic, saying "we," and stimulating informal conversation. Building these skills will help any individual excel at the servant leader style.

Asking questions

Asking questions helps a servant leader listen deeply, build trust with followers, coach others, challenge the status quo, learn about and convey values, tap into followers' mind-sets and clarify feedback when it is offered.

Servant leaders can listen effectively if they put themselves in position to converse with followers and co-workers (for example, by walking the shop) and by asking good questions. As discussed elsewhere in this book, good leaders observe the 2:1 ratio rule: they ask two questions for every instruction or command they issue. Therefore, they spend much more time listening than speaking. One of the strongest needs people possess is the need to be heard. If leaders develop the skill of asking open-ended questions, they will be on the path to feeding this need, honouring the people with whom they work and building trusting relationships.

Open-ended questions are simply questions that cannot be answered with a yes or a no. Leaders may be well aware of the negative side of asking questions that are not open-ended.

Boss: "Did you get the memo I sent last week about the new project?"
Worker: "Yeah."
Boss: "Do you have any questions about the client's expectations?"
Worker: "No."

The boss may think there is opportunity for conversation by approaching this worker, but the form of questioning leaves too much room for very succinct interactions that contribute little to communication.

Open-ended questions begin with words or phrases like what, why, how, where, what do you think about, tell me about, and so on. Examples are shown in the accompanying insert.

Open-ended question examples

What do you like about working here?
What do you like least about working here?
How does your work add value for those we serve?
What do you need from me to improve your job performance?
How can we improve the unit/department?
What do you think about our new procedures/equipment?
What's the best option if we change current practice?
What frustrates you about your job?
How can I better support you so you can do your best?
What accomplishments at work are you most proud of?
If you could make one change in your job, what would it be?
What keeps you from falling asleep at night?
What do you think competitors do better than us?
What's the most important thing you are dealing with right now?
Tell me about your career goals.
Tell me about your personal goals.
Tell me about your family situation.
How do you think I could improve as a leader?
What questions do you have for me?

Leaders need to pay attention to the questions they ask followers. Open-ended questions will provide more opportunity for deep listening. While developing this skill, here is a quick little technique that might help. If you find yourself asking a closed-ended question, you can always open it up at the end. For example, if you start by asking, "Do you have any questions about the client's expectations?" you can follow it up with, "If so, please tell me what you think we should expect at our first meeting."

Questions asked by a leader are powerful in focusing followers' attention.

> When leaders ask questions, they send constituents on mental journeys–quests–in search of answers. The questions that a leader asks send messages about the focus of the organization, and they're indicators of what is of most concern to the leader. They're one more measure of how serious you are about your espoused beliefs. Questions direct attention to the values that should be attended to and how much energy should be devoted to them (Kouzes and Posner 2012, 81-82).

Good questions help people escape the boundaries of their own personal paradigm by broadening perspective. It is one thing to ask an employee, "What new initiatives do you think we should pursue next year?" and another to ask "What new initiatives do you think we should pursue next year if money was no object?"

Also, good questions require followers to take responsibility for their own viewpoints. Therefore, questions help develop people. They help people think and problem solve more effectively. Be sure to recognize, however, that asking good questions creates a responsibility to listen carefully to constituents' responses. In carrying out this responsibility, good things happen. A leader demonstrates respect for followers' opinions and ideas as well as wins support for implementation of suggestions–because, after all, ideas come from the people who will have to implement them. It's not as if the leader is selling her own ideas.

Effective leaders consider the questions they ask in meetings, phone calls, face-to-face interactions, interviews, performance appraisals and so on. They determine how their questions help clarify and strengthen commitment to shared values. Servant leaders attend to how their questions help focus constituents' attention to customer service, loyalty, honesty, quality, safety, innovation, growth, or other values espoused by their organization.

Servant leaders support others through coaching; that is, through teaching and training, asking probing questions and offering constructive feedback. Whenever possible, they let constituents figure things out themselves. Kouzes and Posner tell us:

> Coaching stretches people to grow and develop their capabilities, and it provides them with opportunities to both hone and enhance their skills in challenging assignments. Good coaches ask good questions. Frances Hasselbein, former CEO of the Girl Scouts of the U.S.A., and founding president of the Leader to Leader Institute, says her personal motto is, "Ask, don't tell." She learned it from Peter Drucker, who said, "The leader of the future asks; the leader of the past tells" (2012, 266).

Servant leaders ask a follower how they see a problem and what solutions they believe would be effective. The follower's first response is met with additional questions, such as "What consequences might your solution have for each stakeholder?" or "How does your idea fit in with our vision and values?" Leaders avoid giving their own answers. Through questions, leaders train followers to analyse and decide within the context of the way their enterprise does business. Each conversation is a training session in the development of a new generation of organizational leaders.

Asking questions offers many benefits, including giving others the room to think and to frame issues from their personal perspective. Also, asking questions demonstrates an underlying trust in others' abilities.

When receiving feedback from followers (remember: feedback is a gift!) servant leaders demonstrate respect for the feedback provider and interest in self-improvement by asking detailed questions and requesting specific examples. Through their questions leaders ensure they understand both the content and context of the feedback offered.

Recall the first day you spent on a new job. Very likely you were introduced to co-workers as the "new person" in the office, factory, hospital or what have you. Along with the introduction you received an imaginary shiny, golden halo which represented a "pass" for a few weeks, maybe even a couple of months. The halo entitled you to ask "dumb" questions about "what we do," "why do we do it," "where does that go from here," and so forth. Everyone understood that asking simple questions was part of your learning experience. Your questions were welcomed and expected. The more you asked, the more involved in your work you seemed to be.

But, if you were in a typical work environment, soon your halo lost its shine and simple questions that called into question the operational status quo started to be treated as inappropriate. In other words, your co-workers started to assume you should "know better" by now. Their verbal responses or body language may have communicated this message to you and caused a bit of personal embarrassment. So you stopped asking.

Well, remember how much you learned during your "halo days." Asking simple questions about "the way we do things around here" as well as the reasons behind them can help "challenge the process." As Kouzes and Posner say:

> ... the work of leaders is change. Leaders don't have to change history, but they do have to change "business as usual." To them, the status quo is unacceptable. Leaders *challenge the process*. They search for opportunities, and they experiment and take risks (2004, 22).

The authors go on to propose that some standard practices, policies, and procedures are necessary to desired outcomes such as productivity and quality assurance. However, many are simply matters of tradition. Workers come to accept familiar methods ("the way we've always done it around here") as the best methods because they are never questioned.

A servant leader helps set the stage for innovation by asking consistently, "How useful is our standard operating procedure in helping us be the best we can be?" And the leader encourages others to ask the same type of questions. Through supporting the practice of questioning the way things are done rather than honouring the status quo, leaders help establish a culture of continuous improvement and innovation.

Give yourself (and others) permission to ask simple questions as a way of challenging the status quo. Give permission to others as well. Don't inhibit others' questioning by treating them as if they've made a dumb query. Thank them for asking it. Realize it is part of the job and a fruitful way to identify opportunities for improvement.

Set a standard for yourself and stick to it: "I will ask at least two simple questions of myself or others every day." Be someone who challenges the status quo, who welcomes and supports innovation.

Moving the broom

While having lunch with a corporate recruiter named Charles, a business school dean decided to pick the recruiter's brain by asking what he looked for when deciding which of the school's graduates he wanted to hire. Upon hearing the dean's question, Charles said, "Oh, that's easy, during the interview I look for people who I can be sure will move the broom."

Puzzled by Charles' response, the dean said, "OK, you have intrigued me. What do you mean you hire people who will move the broom?"

Charles explained, "One Saturday morning a few years ago I was sweeping our kitchen floor and my phone rang. I was expecting an important call so I hurriedly picked up the phone and just propped up the broom against the kitchen door, unthinkingly blocking the doorway. As I spoke to the caller over the next 20 minutes my teenage son walked into the kitchen three times retrieving various items for his breakfast, each time carefully stepping over the broom that blocked his path. When my phone call ended, having observed my son's careful steps over the broom with hands filled with orange juice glasses, a cereal bowl, etc., I asked him, 'Why didn't you just move the broom?' With a look that indicated he was surprised by the question, he replied, 'The broom was already in the doorway when I got there. I just assumed it was for a good reason and I wasn't supposed to touch it.'"

Looking the dean straight in the eye and with a wry smile, Charles said, "When I interview young people at your school I assess whether or not they would move the broom. My company can only succeed if we improve. We want workers who ask questions and take initiative to change things for the better."

Telling stories

One very interesting, perhaps surprising, element of servant leaders' communication skills involves storytelling. Warren Bennis, a pioneer of leadership studies, wrote, "One aspect of leadership that is routinely overlooked is the extent to which it is a performance art."

Howard Gardner, distinguished Harvard educator and author of the book *Leading Minds,* instructs that as early as age five children understand the world through dramatic stories. These stories feature heroes with whom they can identify and represent life's dramas that reflect the world around them. Of course, as people mature, their worldviews become more complex, but adults never lose their interest in or sensitivity to these fundamental narratives: a setting, an antagonist, the hero's role.

A veteran college management professor relates his experience regarding the power of storytelling and its relationship to memory. Over his thirty year career he would deliver to each class of third- and fourth-year students a semester's worth of lectures, academic theories, facts, figures, charts and formulae. Trying his best to keep student interest keen and eyes wide open he would sprinkle into his presentations illustrative stories of the scientists who developed the theories as well as the successes and failures of the practitioners who applied the ideas in the real world. On every final exam his students wrote, the professor noticed the best remembered material, by far, involved the stories. Theories and factual information took a back seat to the stories which students could recount in close detail–names, dates, places–and, most importantly, lessons learned. People remember stories. They are powerful learning tools.

Stories exist in all organizations. They are a vital part of defining what the organization is and what membership means. Cultural lessons can be learned by listening to and appreciating the organizational stories related by its representatives, especially its leaders.

Typical uses of stories within organizations include: communicating the values of the enterprise to new members, passing along the culture and traditions, identifying and memorializing successful contributors (heroes), recruiting and hiring employees who "fit" and even selling the organization's products and services.

Stories assist servant leaders in fulfilling their responsibilities to help followers determine their personal, social and moral identities. Servant leaders collect stories that demonstrate values. Such tales are used to teach and strengthen the organization's shared values, highlighting how past and current personnel have lived the espoused principles. Servant leaders relate their own values, assumed to be congruent with the organization's beliefs, to followers through their personal stories for the purpose of revealing how they prefer to act and make decisions. Importantly, this helps to build trust between themselves and their constituents.

Noel Tichy, noted management consultant, educator and author of *The Leadership Engine*, describes the leader's roles as setting the organization's direction and providing guiding principles by teaching, learning, generating ideas, promoting values, creating energy and displaying edge. Energy relates to motivating, rallying to a purpose, calling to action and creating positive emotional energy in others. Edge refers to making hard decisions, showing the courage of one's convictions.

According to Tichy, storytelling helps leaders fulfil their necessary roles by appealing to followers not just rationally but also emotionally. Stories speak to both parts of the mind: reason and emotion. Well-crafted and delivered stories reach inside people and pull them along with the storyteller. They simulate actual experience and give people a compelling way of learning.

To craft effective stories Tichy suggests leaders keep in mind three vital story components: 1) ideas (such as the enterprise's strengths, weaknesses, opportunities and challenges as well as environmental and/or competitive changes that mandate some type of transformation); 2) values (behavioural guidelines for members); and 3) emotional energy and edge (fear, anxiety, hope, excitement, the elation of success–elements of motivating, calling to a specific action as well as doing the right and hard thing, exhibiting courage). When creating a story, leaders may find it helpful to jot down words, phrases, images or concepts that cover each of these elements. Then proceed to craft a story that integrates the "ingredients" in an appealing and entertaining manner with one or more action-taking heroes.

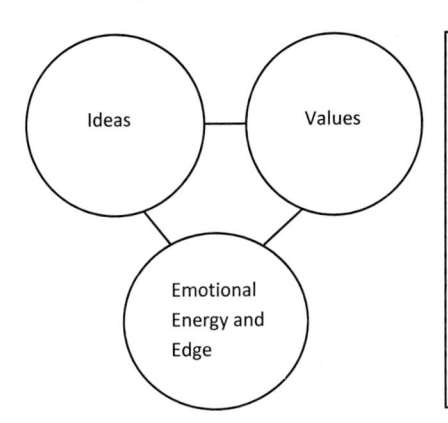

Ideas — Values

Emotional Energy and Edge

| **A leader's teachable point of view** |
| Noel M. Tichy |
| *The Leadership Engine*, 1997 |

Start by getting a basic sense of the plot, where you want to go and how you will get there. For leaders this is the ideas, values, emotional energy and edge they bring to their organization. Sketch your teachable point of view before constructing your story.

Stories are formidable tools for engaging people emotionally as well as intellectually and for leading them into the future. By crafting and delivering stories that feature members of the organization as the heroes in an unfolding drama, constituents can develop understanding of how they must behave and what they must accomplish to help create that future. These stories are what Gardner called "identity stories." They are narratives that help people think about and feel who they are, where they come from, and where they are headed. Gardner calls these identity stories "the single most powerful weapon in the leader's arsenal." One of the most powerful things leaders can do through stories is to give people a clear picture of what their lives will be like as the future unfolds.

Organizational culture is passed along from one generation of workers to another by stories. Through stories leaders create organizational role models to whom everyone can relate. Behaviour is taken from the abstract and put in a real context. Values become more than simple rules–stories make values come alive. Stories quickly translate information about how people are actually supposed to act and make decisions. Leaders identify organizational heroes and tell their stories. Anthropologists have a saying: whoever tells the stories defines the culture. If you want to shape a servant-led culture, begin by telling stories of serving. Stories inform, entertain and inspire. They are effective means for teaching people what is important and what's not, what works and what doesn't, what *is* and what *could be*. Through stories leaders pass on lessons about shared values and establish the means by which people can work together.

Stories communicate standards for behaviour such as teamwork, customer service, performance, quality assurance, risk-taking, dealing with failure, and on and on. Within an organization's culture are employees rewarded or reprimanded for speaking up? A story can deliver the lesson.

One often-employed type of story involves a lower level worker who takes initiative. One form of the tale involves a low level designer who recognizes an error in the VP of Engineering's specifications just before plans are due to a client. The designer takes initiative to correct the simple mistake without obtaining specific approval. Usually, the story contains a plausible reason for not obtaining approval, such as lack of time or inability to contact the executive while travelling (in "older technology" versions of the story, of course). This tale has two potential endings. Either the designer is recognized for using personal initiative, praised and rewarded or is chided for changing a superior's work without authorization and reprimanded, perhaps even fired. The story's ending relates how an organization's members are expected to use (or abandon) their personal initiative. What is the culture here: are you expected to apply your initiative or are you expected to do only as you are told?

Stories put a human face on success and failure. They serve as a kind of mental map that delivers lessons about behavioural expectations in much more palatable ways than an HR manual or a corporate policy statement. In an administrative climate frequently permeated with wordy reports, graphs and charts, storytelling is a soft way of teaching lessons about hard things.

Tichy tells us that leadership is about change–taking people from where they and the organization are now to where they need to be. He says the best way to get people to venture into unknown territory is to employ stories to make the terrain familiar and desirable. Leaders take workers to the future first in their imaginations. They fashion and deliver future stories to help followers break away from the accustomed, comfortable present and venture intrepidly ahead to create their and their organization's improved future. Through stories not only do leaders describe future conditions in terms that are personal and compelling but also they help others understand why and what they must do to attain that future.

Howard Gardner defines "stories" in very broad terms. They include actual and fictionalized accounts that serve as organizational symbols. Screenwriter, director and lecturer Robert McKee claims interestingly that good storytellers and good leaders share certain traits. Both are highly self-aware and both are sceptics. As sceptics they realize that to some degree all people and organizations wear masks. McKee says that compelling stories are found behind those masks. A good story takes an audience beyond what can be seen at the surface and increases their understanding of events and behaviours.

To be effective storytellers leaders must struggle with their own identities and their own desires for the future. What type of leader am I? What do I want my legacy to be? What values do I want to ensure are embodied in my organization? Also, searching for relevant stories forces leaders to pay close attention to their constituents; they must notice what people are doing right and decide what behaviours they want to hold out as heroic examples. Critical incidents in leaders' personal lives or in the lives of their organizations are dramatic sources of moral lessons about what is or is not important, what members do or do not believe and how constituents do or do not act. Leaders tell dynamic stories that put followers in the roles of protagonists and then engage them to act out those stories with a stream of examples and anecdotes.

Stories can be thought of as celebrations. They celebrate their message of values, identities, cultures, expectations, heroes and potential futures.

What specific kinds of stories should leaders tell? Noel Tichy offers very helpful advice on this topic by proposing three categories of stories:

> Over the years, I have noted that there are three basic types of stories that leaders use to engage and energize others. The first of these are "who I am" stories ... Leaders use these stories to describe to themselves and others their fundamental views about the world and to explain how they developed those views. These stories serve as vehicles to both communicate the leader's views and build understanding between the leader and his or her would-be followers.
>
> The second type of story is the "who we are" story. These stories are similar to the leader's "who I am" story, except instead of being about the personal experiences and frame of mind of the leader, they are about the joint experiences and attitudes of the people within the organization and their shared beliefs ...
>
> Lots of leaders have "who I am" stories, and even more organizations have "who we are" stories. Both are essential to communicating ideas and values, and they help create the energy necessary for organizations to succeed ... But there is a third kind of story that in my experience is uniquely found among winning leaders and in winning organizations. These are what I call "future stories." Tied together, these three stories are what I call a leader's storyline (1997, 173-174).

Future stories can be called visions–stories that have not yet come true.

Tichy goes on to say that there is a classic pattern for leaders' future stories. Three essential elements are covered: the case for change, where we are going and how we will get there. Leaders' stories create scenarios for success. They build the case for organizational change as well as describe a winning future.

Servant leaders' stories should be dynamic and motivating. To achieve these characteristics stories can cast followers as protagonists who make change happen and guide participants to identify their own roles in success. Leaders put stories in the frame of their audience. They talk about where they are going in the context of what it will take from followers to get there and what the payoff will be when they arrive.

Of course, leaders need to appreciate what constitutes good stories and then develop skills that will produce them.

In an effective story leaders' words are often used not for their literal meanings but as symbols of the organization's characteristics such as values, beliefs and culture. Symbolic language such as metaphors and analogies is used to enable constituents to picture the lessons offered. For example, leaders have long applied metaphors that relate organizational activities to sports competitions (running a marathon or a sprint, getting a slam dunk, putting on a full court press, dropping the ball, building bench strength and so on). Common leadership metaphors refer to enterprises on journeys led by early pioneers or trailblazers or being captained by a steady hand. Organizations are compared to ships, machines, movies or the natural environment. Further, within stories time can be money, knowledge can be power and information can be either flowing water or food for nourishment.

Lead by storytelling: three kinds of stories
Noel M. Tichy
The Leadership Engine, 1997

Servant leaders are teachers and facilitators. They must adopt a teachable point of view in order to express themselves clearly and instruct others. Also, a leader needs a dynamic story about where the organization is headed. These stories excite people about the future and spur them to act.

1. **"Who I am" stories**
   - relates what makes you tick, what kind of person you are; shares your personal values with others

2. **"Who we are" stories**
   - provides a sense of identity for the group, either through common mission or common experience

3. **"Future" stories (Vision)**
   - provides a description of why the group must change, where they are going and how they will get there

---

A servant leader's ability to enlist others in a common vision will be enhanced by learning to use figures of speech. If you want people to act like a community, tell community stories and use community language. Storytelling offers a framework for relating to the message. Something that people encounter in their own lives can bridge to the main point.

Kouzes and Posner ask "What makes for a good storyteller?" and provide some very instructive guidelines. They advise leaders to tell personal stories. Tell stories the leader knows a great deal about, or give examples that both the leader and audience can relate to on a personal basis. For example, many people relate easily to children and pets, making them favourite subjects for stories that touch heart strings.

Be vivid; it helps people remember. For vividness, a story should be about a real person the leader and audience know. It should have a strong sense of time and place, so provide specifics and include details about when and where the action occurred. Also, to make a story vivid, include colourful and animated language.

Whenever possible, leaders should speak from a first-person perspective. So the leader should place herself or himself in the story. If the leader is not a major character, at least play a bit part or be a direct observer of the action.

As the leader relates the story allow emotions to surface. This brings excitement to the voice and increases natural use of physical gestures. Be sure body language matches the point of the story. If the storyteller is excited about an activity or future possibility, striding quickly, waving arms or pointing forward and upward, toward the future, will help convey the excitement.

Smiles are always important body language. If the story is about something happy or funny, be the first to smile. Others will follow. It's natural for them. If the story addresses a deeply concerning topic, use slower speech, wear concern as a facial expression and allow guarded posture to match the tone.

A leader may start a story by sharing a heroic deed. It captures audience attention.

Make sure the story has a clever title that will capture people's attention and help them catalogue it in their memories.

Ensure the story has a theme, and repeat the theme throughout the tale. Keep it short; don't include excessive details, too many incidences or a large number of characters. Use the characters' specific names. Finally, end the story with a conclusion that demonstrates concretely the intended lesson or message to be learned (that is, the moral of the story).

In terms of storytelling Tichy offers the following imperatives: be sure to understand your audience–that is, know who they are and what must change within them to achieve future success; appreciate the nature of your audience–think about their changeable and non-changeable features; and be sure to embody in your own life the principal theme(s) of your story.

After fulfilling the aforementioned imperatives, apply these guidelines to create an effective story: speak to valued aspects of the past and honour timeless traditions; deal with new and complicating future trends such as the impact of technology on your organization, the evolving nature of the workforce, and so on; define a successful future in which the organization and its people are victorious; and appeal to examples of courage, morals and ethical codes.

Some of the best stories portray the future as an unfolding drama. Again, servant leaders tell stories that engage followers emotionally as well as rationally, and their stories weave together ideas, values and modes of behaviour.

Importantly, leaders should never take for granted the "performance art" nature of their storytelling. Recognize that there is good reason that new theatrical productions are usually played before small road audiences where the plots, dialogue, props, staging and so on can be honed prior to opening on Broadway. For the same reason it's better to test each element of an intended important story before using it with its primary audience. Don't hesitate to use smaller groups for trial runs with different heroes, metaphors, settings, body language and the like. Many memorable stories were begun this way.

Servant leaders make a habit of putting stories on the agendas of meetings. Either the leader assumes a teaching point of view and relates a story at the beginning or end of each meeting or on a rotating schedule attendees are given the responsibility to tell a meaningful story that instructs, inspires or envisions. Over time an inventory of useful stories is created and storytelling becomes a natural element of the group's culture.

Remember that effective stories are public forms of communication, and they are the means by which lessons are passed from generation to generation and culture to culture. They take on a life of their own because they are meant to be repeated and reach an ever-growing audience. Smart leaders find many ways to perpetuate their important stories, such as relating them in public ceremonies, publishing them in organizational newsletters or annual reports or even broadcasting them over internal networks. Recognizing that stories teach important lessons and have a natural place in a variety of organizational celebrations, some forward-looking HR groups adopt a strategy of soliciting organizational stories from their employee ranks, recording and cataloguing them to capture the culture of their enterprise.

Servant Leader Tips – Telling stories
Servant leaders have a responsibility to educate their followers; remember that leadership is part performance art; people remember stories; they are powerful teaching and learning tools
Use stories to help define what your organization is and what membership means, pass along culture and traditions, identify and memorialize heroes as well as recruit and hire candidates who "fit"
Collect stories that demonstrate desired values; use them often
When developing an original story, remember to integrate ideas, values and emotional energy and edge
Use stories to communicate what type of leader you are, what legacy you desire and what values you want to embody within your enterprise
Tell stories at organizational celebrations you host or participate in
Master three kinds of stories: "Who I am" stories, "Who we are" stories and "Future/Vision" stories (where we are going)
When teaching through storytelling, include vivid language and recognizable characters and places so people can picture them in their minds; include a hero the audience knows or cares about; tell stories in first-person perspective; allow your emotions to surface; have a clever, memorable title; keep it short; repeat a recognizable theme; lead to a clear message or moral
Put stories on meeting agendas (first or last); encourage followers to develop leadership skills by becoming good storytellers themselves

Being optimistic

Optimism is feeling or showing hope for the future. Kouzes and Posner provide helpful and inspiring views on the value of hope in our personal lives as well as in our leadership roles:

> Hope is an attitude in action. It enables people to mobilize their healing and their achieving powers. It helps them to transcend the difficulties of today and envision the potentialities of tomorrow. Hope enables people to find the will and the way to aspire to greatness. Hope is testimony to the power of the human spirit. Leadership is often a struggle, and the only way to thrive is to keep hope alive (2004, 126).

The authors go on to say that leaders keep hope alive by demonstrating the courage of their convictions, by painting positive images of the future, by taking charge of change, by trusting the abilities of others and by recognizing the dedication of others as they accomplish extraordinary things.

Optimism, sometimes appropriately referred to as the "hidden asset," is an emotional competency that can help increase productivity, boost morale and overcome conflict. For some fortunate people being optimistic comes naturally. Happily, even for those who are not optimistic by nature, viewing things with optimism is a skill that can be both learned and practiced.

Optimism can produce many positive personal outcomes. Through countless studies psychologists tell us that those who learn to be positive about life and living are far more likely to achieve success than those who view current situations and events through a lens of pessimism. People with a hopeful outlook develop healthier relationships, enjoy improved mental as well as physical health and even live longer. Further, through optimism people experience positive emotions and good things happen– their minds stretch, their worldviews expand and they open to new possibilities. Optimism contributes to curiosity about how things work and what is going on in the environment. Optimists see more options and become more creative and innovative.

Those applying the pessimistic outlook commonly approach changes to the status quo with familiar responses such as, "It won't work" and "We've tried that before." These are the types of people who like to play the role of devil's advocate. But optimists tend to be open to new ideas, see new possibilities, are willing to take some risks and even encourage others in risk-taking.

Optimists accentuate the positive and display a steely determination to master their destiny. When facing new challenges, they determine factors they can control and those they cannot. Then they ascertain at least a few ways they can positively affect the outcome and take a few steps to get things moving in the desired direction. They create some forward momentum.

In *The Power of Optimism* author Alan Loy McGinnis tells us that in tough times optimists embrace partial solutions. They stay free from the tyranny of perfectionism and from the often-encountered paralysis by analysis. Instead they are open to taking small steps toward success. Importantly, they place what Kouzes and Posner call a *learning frame* around their leadership experiences. They refuse to focus on the negative. Instead they consider the lessons they have learned and the forward progress they have achieved. Negativity does not stifle their performance. Outside influences that affected less-than-desired results are recognized and outcomes are reframed in terms of lessons learned.

Pessimists view adversity as unchangeable, pervasive and personal. However, optimistic persons view adversity as temporary, specific and external. Facing setbacks, optimists will persevere. They have the capacity to bend without breaking. Even in very tough times they have the capacity to spring back.

Optimists employ their imagination to rehearse success. They play positive mental videos of preferred outcomes just like professional athletes do. Like basketball legend Michael Jordan, they never play a game they haven't visualized first.

Also, optimists demonstrate a capacity for "stretching." They believe their personal best has not yet been achieved. Their future performance will be better than today's.

Consider these communication skills for optimistic individuals. Avoid statements like "We can *try* to ..." or "We *hope* that ..." "Try" and "hope" are wishy-washy terms. They don't express high expectations for results, just that some effort will be expended or that there will be a chance for success. Substitute more definite words such as *will* and *are*. That is, "We will ..." and "We are ..." Also, avoid the phrase "Yes, but ..." when responding to communication partners' suggestions. "But" turns off many people. They stop listening when they hear it. They assume you will be disagreeing with them or that you will be explaining (yet again) how your idea is superior. A simple switch to "Yes, and ..." can make a positive difference in your discussions. Your partners will assume you agree and will be adding to the ideas on the table.

Audit your recent conversations. Just think about the people to whom you spoke recently and think about your contributions to the dialogues. Count how many times you talked about problems or obstacles to success and how many times you talked about solutions. It's natural to mention both, but optimists speak about solutions far more often than problems or obstacles.

During exchanges with followers and colleagues, take advantage of every opportunity to express your personal confidence in them and their abilities. Get used to using words and phrases like "I trust your judgment," "I'm sure you have the skills," "I know you will do well" and so on. When people fail or make mistakes, help to build their confidence by expressing support: "I'm sure you will do better next time."

While we are on the topic of practices for optimistic individuals, consider where, how and with whom you spend your time. Avoid professional complainers. All organizations contain some. Seek the company of positive people and groups. It's easy to tell the difference, and your personal optimism will get a big boost once you abandon the complainers in the break room.

When and where possible, stick to your strengths. Focus your activities on what you do well. It's fine to spend some time improving your weaknesses, but be sure to dedicate most of your time and effort to achieving success by applying your abilities. You will feed your sense of accomplishment and build your optimism.

On a daily basis spend at least a little time on your emotional and spiritual well-being. Read a few great quotations or stories about great innovators and innovations. Perhaps read about successful people in your field. Their stories can inspire and motivate. Join the World Future Society and read their materials about positive projections for the world we will live in. In other words, adopt personal practices that let other people and ideas bolster your optimism.

Be spontaneous on occasion. Spontaneity helps many develop their optimism muscle. Forget your planned activity and take a walk or play a game. This can be effective at either home or at work. Doing something unexpected can get you out of your comfort zone and help you think differently and feel better. Exercising a little impulsiveness and personal freedom every once in a while will feed your hope.

Servant Leader Tips – Being an optimistic individual
Use positive, decisive words: "will" and "are"–not "try" and "hope"
Say "yes, and …" not "yes, but …"
Talk about solutions; recognize problems and obstacles but don't dwell on them
Tell people you have confidence and faith in them
Avoid negative environments; seek the company of positive people in your personal life and organization; steer clear of complainers
Celebrate your strengths; play out your abilities; spend less time correcting your weaknesses; focus on what you do well
Attend to your emotional and spiritual well-being; read material that inspires you daily, such as quotations, biographies of successful people in your field, stories about innovations, projections of the positive future
Stay free from the tyranny of perfectionism; manage or ignore what you cannot change; identify what you can change and find ways to do something about it; create forward momentum
Look for positives in negative situations; reframe; shift your perspective
Cultivate spontaneity; put aside your plans on occasion and develop your optimism muscle; take a walk, play a game, do something unexpected; get out of your comfort zone

Leadership expert Warren Bennis tells us that optimism is one of the key characteristics followers need to see in their leaders in order to achieve positive results. He wrote that optimistic leaders have a sixth sense for possibilities that realists cannot or will not see. Bennis claimed that every exemplary leader he met possessed what seemed to be an unwarranted degree of optimism that helped generate the energy and commitment necessary to produce results. Such leaders have a transforming effect on their constituents. They demonstrate the gift of convincing others that they are capable of achieving performance levels beyond those previously thought possible. In other words, these leaders can truly take people to places they've never been before.

Being optimistic does not imply leaders fail to recognize reality, hardships or struggles that are attached to a desire to make good things happen. Instead, the more leaders comprehend the reality of their challenges, the more prepared they are for adversity.

Servant leaders are well aware that negativity is contagious and can quickly pervade a team. It can stifle group performance. Optimism is essential, especially in difficult times. It doesn't mean leaders stick their heads in the sand and ignore challenges or limitations. But it does mean the leader approaches challenge and unpleasantness in a productive manner.

Constituents expect leaders to be forward-looking. According to Kouzes and Posner, it is the characteristic that most differentiates leaders from individual contributors. Followers want leaders to have and convey a sense of direction, to articulate where their organization is going. Getting the team focused on exciting and ennobling possibilities that the future holds is the leader's special role. If the leader doesn't talk about the future, who else will?

> Developing the capacity to envision the future requires you to spend more time in the future–meaning more time reflecting on the future, more time reading about the future, and more time talking to others about the future. It's not an easy assignment, but it is an absolutely necessary one. It also requires you to reflect back on your past to discover the themes that really engage you and excite you. And it means thinking about the kind of legacy you want to leave and the contributions you want to make.
>
> None of this can be done by a pessimist. You must remain optimistic and hopeful about what is yet to come. You must truly believe that the future will be brighter and be confident that we'll all get there together. A positive difference can only be made by a positive leader (Kouzes and Posner 2010, 58-59).

Servant leaders can engage in numerous activities to support an optimistic work environment. For example, Ken Blanchard encourages leaders to accentuate the positive by catching people doing things right. Make it a habit to show workers you care by walking the shop and noticing the things they are doing right. Talk to them about their productive activities, encourage them to continue, thank them for their contributions to success. Don't wait for good things to be brought to your attention. It doesn't happen often enough. Consider it part of your job to find them.

Be sure to speak positively about your organization and its personnel. Avoid the trap of criticizing the enterprise or the mistakes people make. Negative people find other negative people and commiserate with each other on their common ground of complaining and blaming. Organizations are comprised of human beings and all humans make mistakes. Identifying them is never a challenge. Be exceptional, not common. Talk about positive things.

Set the stage for positivity. Enthusiasm is contagious. Show your enthusiasm by smiling (the world's least expensive advertising that good things are happening), using gestures that communicate inclusiveness and progress (enthusiastic handshakes, outstretched arms), walk with purpose (quickly, resolutely), speak with some excitement in your voice, look people directly in the eye and in meetings sit on the edge of your seat (don't lean backwards or "recline" passively in your chair, even when listening).

Be very well-versed in your organization's vision. Make sure it is a statement that is exciting and ennobling to others. Know the good your organization will accomplish and deliver for others–and why it is important. Use the vision's key words and phrases every chance you get. Speak hopefully about the future and encourage others to do the same.

Be aware that the leader sets the stage for the organization's culture. Make sure it is a culture of optimism. Set high expectations for results and by your speech and behaviour make it clear that you expect people to succeed. Encourage others. Ask them what you can do to support their success–and do it.

When something new or different (even off-the-wall) is introduced in meetings, take on the role of supporter–at least until the idea has a fair chance to be discussed. By providing vocal support for new ideas a culture of openness and innovation will be reinforced. Don't let the devil's advocate role dominate your group's meetings and discussions.

If these types of activities are unfamiliar at first or if they make you the least bit uncomfortable for any reason, practice them within small groups of trusted friends or colleagues. Develop complete assurance with these skills before rolling them out to the larger population. Your behaviours should be perceived as natural and sincere. Sometimes a little practice helps you get there.

Let's recognize, of course, that sometimes leaders and organizations encounter very difficult times. While optimism for the future is always appropriate, there will be times of hardship and loss. Sacrifice will be necessary. In such times servant leaders follow this rule: *suffer first*. Exemplary leaders should never permit anyone to suffer more than they do. Be the first to accept some hardship yourself. Your pain-sharing will inspire others by demonstrating your passion for the organizational cause. As servant leader, don't forget: suffer first.

Servant Leader Tips – Being an optimistic leader
Make it a habit to catch people doing things right; remember that leaders travel; get out from behind your desk; pay attention to people and what they are doing; notice what they are doing right and talk to them about it
Speak positively about others and your organization; don't join the pessimists at the watercooler discussing how bad things are and how poorly people perform
Enthusiasm and emotions are contagious; let yours show; smile, use gestures, move your body, speak clearly and quickly, make eye contact, sit on the edge of your seat
Have an ennobling vision of your organization's future and keep articulating it; remind people what you are building and why it matters
Nurture a culture of optimism; expect people to succeed and tell them about your expectations; encourage them
Provide vocal support for new ideas introduced at meetings; keep ideas alive until they can be fully vetted; avoid playing the devil's advocate
If you are uncomfortable doing any of these things, start with trusted friends and colleagues; develop these skills, then extend them to others
And don't forget: in times of hardship be first to suffer; never ask others to sacrifice more than you; set the example by sharing the pain

Saying "we"

Think and say "we," not "I" has already been identified as a key attitude of servant leaders. In this communications skills section, therefore, it is sufficient to mention that saying "we" is a natural result of the servant leader's attitude that the leader does not accomplish anything significant alone. Once the conviction that leadership is a team effort becomes part of a leader's thinking, it is only natural that it comes through in verbal or written expressions.

Inclusive language reinforces the perception among followers that a leader is collaborative, not exploitive. When the leader articulates what is planned or what has been achieved, it is essential to refer to *our* values, vision, goals, accomplishments and success.

Peter Drucker offers the following explanation for the necessity of leaders thinking and saying "we" rather than "I":

> Effective executives know that they have ultimate responsibility, which can be neither shared nor delegated. But they have authority only because they have the trust of the organization. This means that they think of the needs and the opportunities of the organization before they think of their own needs and opportunities (2004, 63).

Similarly, John Maxwell contends that leaders earn respect by making sound decisions, admitting their mistakes, and, importantly, by putting what is best for their followers and their organizations ahead of their own personal agendas.

Language flows from attitude. Saying "we" is a strong indicator that leaders put the needs of followers and their organization ahead of their own.

Applying Sipe and Frick's seven pillars of servant leadership, by the simple act of saying "we" a leader can be perceived as providing some evidence that he or she is a person of character, puts people first, is a compassionate collaborator and leads with moral authority. That's a lot of positive impact for the application of an elementary communication habit!

Also, the "I"–"we" communication convention can be applied as an effective differentiator when interviewing candidates for a leadership position. Ask interviewees to describe a successful leadership experience from their past and just listen to the manner in which they describe their success. Do they attribute their accomplishment to themselves personally or to their team? Their language will give away their mind-set. If hired, are they likely to be a servant leader who says "we" or a self-serving leader who tends to say "I"?

Saying "we"	
Sipe and Frick's Servant Leadership Pillar	Leadership Trait/Competency
Person of character	- demonstrates humility
Puts people first	- displays a servant's heart - shows care and concern
Compassionate collaborator	- builds teams and communities
Leads with moral authority	- shares power and control

Stimulating informal conversations

Servant leaders are not only dedicated to communication between themselves and others but also among all others in the workplace. To achieve this objective leaders know it is necessary to create environments that support informal interactions because communication does not always just happen on its own. Environments nurture conversations.

A large, suburban university was in the early stages of a strategic planning process, and the planners established an objective of creating a more engaged student body. It seemed that for many years faculty and administrators had observed and regretted that students didn't talk among themselves sufficiently and certainly didn't talk to them enough to engender good relationships. This behaviour was evidenced in numerous ways–the most obvious was the number of students sitting alone in their cars in the parking lots between classes. The assumption was that some sort of training intervention was needed to change student behaviour. Therefore, a "more engaged student body" objective was established in the plan.

During the research stage of planning one small committee undertook a very simple investigation. They counted the number of chairs in the university's common spaces–cafeterias, libraries, student lounges, waiting areas near faculty and administrators' offices and the like. Results were telling. There were far fewer chairs than students. It seemed the university heads had long assumed there was sufficient on-campus seating because the classrooms contained so many chairs. But that is not where students interact informally. That's not where they talked to each other about non-academic matters of interest. Part of the strategic plan, then, became establishment of spaces for informal interactions between the students themselves and between students and their faculty and administrators. In a very short period of time student engagement improved noticeably. The problem wasn't the students. It was the environment.

What has been a strategic success secret for Starbucks? As often discussed, early leader Howard Schultz recognized the human need for third places (besides home and work). People need a place to gather for a short time and talk. Happily for the company it turns out that you can sell them some coffee while they visit with each other. Of course, Schultz was not necessarily a human behaviour expert; all he had to do was visit Europe, especially Italy, and observe the effect of third places on human interaction.

Kouzes and Posner observe:

> What do Main Street, the English pub, the French café, the Italian tavern, the Japanese teahouse, the American coffeehouse, the German beer garden, and some bookstores and hair salons all have in common? They are what sociologist Ray Oldenburg calls "third places" or "great good places." These are neutral ground–places that include diverse people, where conversation is the main function and playfulness is the norm. They're not the big entertainment centers and malls that make the masses anonymous; they're places that enable small groups of regulars to gather in a home-away-from-home environment. They provide us all with a way of interacting with others informally without regard to status or role. There we have casual conversations, catch up on community news, relax, and make and meet friends. *They serve a vital role in creating bonds of community trust* (italics added) (2002, 275).

Organizations benefit from creating neutral spaces where workers can converse without regard to rank or role. Informal conversations help improve relationships among workers and between leaders and workers. Also, communication among work groups improves as informal interactions lead to more information exchange. People work more effectively when they have opportunities to socialize, discuss opportunities and solve problems informally.

While many organizations have implemented the architecture-affects-behaviour concept by incorporating shared and flexible work layouts, open spaces in offices, workers' lounges, recreation and gaming areas as well as other interaction-stimulating design approaches, it remains incumbent on leaders to ensure that many opportunities for informal communication are utilized–including those of much smaller scale that affect leaders and their followers. Some potential applications are: creating inviting common spaces with tea and coffee, refrigerators and other shared resources which can be accessed by members of different work groups, placing small arrangements of comfortable seating in neutral areas to make cosy corners instead of empty spaces outside elevators or stairwells, providing flexible dividers to break up large conference rooms into much smaller, more personal spaces and so forth.

Once neutral third places are created, servant leaders ensure they are utilized to enhance communication. In such spaces they hold organizational celebrations or brief stand-up meetings to start the work day, provide occasional free lunches or snacks on a "pop-up" basis, schedule community updates following important meetings, and on and on. The point is to get together diverse sets of workers so that both personal and organizational communication can flow. People need human moments, face-to-face conversations in their lives–even, and perhaps especially, at work.

Servant Leader Tips – Stimulating informal conversations
Ensure third places are designed into work areas (such as open office spaces, workers' lounges, gaming areas) or create them where possible (like common spaces with shared resources, cosy seating areas, dividers in large conference rooms)
Hold organizational celebrations in neutral spaces
Hold brief, stand-up meetings in neutral spaces
Provide free lunches or snacks on a "pop-up" basis
Hold updates for the community of workers after important events or meetings

Visioning

"Vision isn't everything, but it's the beginning of everything." That's the quote from David McAllister-Wilson that led to identifying this specific attitude as one of several that are vital for practicing servant leadership. The attitude that visioning is necessary as well as the nature of visions themselves is discussed in another section of this book. However, to enable leaders to envision the future in a manner that expresses high ideals and values, incorporates followers' as well as the leader's hopes and aspirations and serves as a call to action for working together to create a better tomorrow, many skills are necessary. Some of the most important are addressed in this section.

To succeed at visioning leaders should have the following in their arsenal of skills:

- how to get in touch with their own values (already discussed)
- how to gather sufficient input about followers' aspirations from casual conversations and planned encounters
- how to ask questions and listen effectively (already discussed in general, but specific visioning questions will be presented here)
- how to stimulate creative thinking to collect useful information about followers' aspirations
- how to identify themes or categories of aspirations for inclusion in visions
- how to construct a good vision message
- how to refine the early versions of a vision, and
- how to present a vision to followers.

Before discussing these specific skills, let's review briefly what a vision statement is and what role it plays in unifying and motivating followers.

A vision is a mental picture of what tomorrow could be like. Conception precedes perception. As described by Sipe and Frick, a great vision paints a picture of a brighter future that connects us to our deepest identity. It lures us forward to action with its compelling power. A vision appeals to what Abraham Lincoln called "our higher angels" by inviting us into a great and worthy shared experience.

According to Kouzes and Posner, finding *one's own* vision for the future is an intuitive, emotional process. It involves self-exploration and self-creation. When leaders first assume their responsibilities, they often lack a clear vision; they may have at best a general theme or two about what they would like to accomplish. Typically, new leaders are aware of their personal concerns, desires, dreams, postulations and contentions. Then leaders start on the visioning journey by discovering their personal themes. Perhaps they involve human development, new venture creation, discovering knowledge or opening minds, preserving heritage, transforming communities, enriching lives, sharing resources or what have you. Very likely, a new leader's themes are connected to their past successful experiences and their personal values. As already discussed, leaders need to have the skills to know themselves well and to be in touch with their personal values. This is base ground for a leader's vision. Developing a clear picture of one's own desired future and one's contributions to others' futures may take quite a long time and involve many varied experiences. Personal visions flow from the inside out. For most leaders developing one's own personal vision requires patience and insightful self-reflection.

But becoming aware of one's own personal desired future is not sufficient for organizational visioning. Servant leaders must inspire a *common* vision. To accomplish this leaders strive to enlist others by revealing and appealing to shared aspirations. Servant leaders get in touch with constituent's motivators by listening. They ask relevant questions, accumulate responses and identify shared themes among followers.

Kouzes and Posner's commitments for exemplary leaders include the necessities to "envision the future by imagining exciting and ennobling possibilities" and to "enlist others in a common vision by appealing to shared aspirations." To learn what inspires and motivates followers, servant leaders continuously engage them whenever and wherever possible. Leaders walk the shop at random times and in random places. They get to know what makes followers tick through frequent casual conversation. Also, leaders arrive at meetings a bit early and have conversations with other participants–or they stay a few minutes after the meeting concludes. They attend organizational celebrations and events, taking advantage of the opportunities presented to talk to individuals or small groups who are also attending. They sit with different workers in the cafeteria at lunch time or during coffee breaks. They may hold monthly lunches or weekly coffees to conduct exchanges about the enterprise and its future with randomly selected parties. Servant leaders are always on the lookout for chances to have informal exchanges with a very wide variety of followers.

Aside from chance encounters, leaders who want to unify and motivate through visioning prudently strategize which individuals and groups they want to enlist in their vision. Who, especially, do leaders need or want to follow them? Whose support should be cultivated? If future support is needed from certain followers, their aspirations for tomorrow should be understood and included in the vision.

Pragmatic leaders reflect on whose inclusion is necessary and make a list. They set up meetings to engage in dialogue starting with a set of planned questions. Time is scheduled, questions asked, responses recorded. Input for a future vision may be solicited from key executives, members of the organization's central office or people at remote sites. The list of constituents to be engaged could include potential followers from internal functions or departments, members of labour organizations or different groups of employees, such as those with long-tenure, the newly hired, members of certain generational groups, and so on. Support may also be necessary from external stakeholders like client groups, lenders, suppliers, government agencies and the like so plans should be made to collect input about future aspirations from such groups.

The point is that servant leaders recognize how vital it is to collect information about future hopes and dreams and incorporate it into a vision that will inspire many, and they don't leave collecting information to chance meetings alone. They purposely identify whose support they seek and arrange conversations with those individuals and groups.

Questions for visioning

- In your own words, how do you describe our organization? Who are we?
- Whom do we serve?
  (Alternatively: Who benefits from our organization's work? Who else could benefit?)
- How do we serve them?
- How will we serve them better in the future?
- What truly inspires you about who we are and what we do?
- What excites you about your own job?
- What inspires you in your personal life? Could our organization play a part in that activity?
- Assume it is a few years from now and our organization has become a truly exciting, inspiring place to work.
    - What are people doing?
    - What are people saying?
    - How are people feeling?
    - What positive things are occurring?
    - How is the common good being served?

What questions do leaders ask to assess personal and organizational dreams that should be included in an encompassing and energizing vision? Fundamentally, leaders want to start by tapping into followers' understanding of who the organization is, who is served by the organization and how that service is created and delivered. Also, leaders want to know what inspires people. That inspiration could be generated by the work the organization already does or could do in the future. Alternatively, inspiration could be generated from the personal activities people choose to pursue on their own time. The idea is to tap into inspiration. What inspires and excites the people leaders want to attract as followers? Get people to express it. Develop an understanding for excitement triggers.

Leaders ask people to assume it is a few years in the future and that their organization is already an inspiring place to work. What are people doing, saying and feeling? What positive things are going on? What is inspiring about the work and workplace? What contributions are being made to the common good?

Some people have the ability to think about the future without much support. Usually, it is because they often consider their own future and their family's future. However, some people have considerable difficulty thinking about how things could be different in future times. It's just not the way they usually think. They are past and present focused. So leaders know it is helpful to apply different creative thinking practices that can stimulate others in thinking about the future, that is, to help put them in a visioning frame of mind.

There are numerous helpful resources on creative thinking methods. A few useful (and fun) techniques are outlined below. These specific techniques are taken from Roger von Oech's insightful and entertaining book *A Whack on the Side of the Head: How You Can Be More Creative*.

First, ensure followers that there is no single right answer to questions about the future. Therefore, it is best to generate many possibilities without assessing their usefulness or validity. Just get them down on paper. It is helpful to picture each of us with an artist (a creator) and a judge (an evaluator) inside her or his brain. There is an important role for each. Engage the artist first. Give the judge some time off. Think about future possibilities for the enterprise and express as many as possible. Don't worry whether or not they are practical. Don't consider adequate resources; accept them as limitless. Don't consider practicality; anything is possible. Just make a long list of inspiring things that could be done. To focus thinking a time limit of ten minutes might be set.

If additional stimulation is needed, leaders might try asking questions that throw people off guard to change their thinking habits: questions like "What are three things this organization is most mediocre at?" or "How could we ruin the organization's future?"

Metaphor usage is another approach to helping people think creatively about the enterprise. Metaphors are mental maps that make the unfamiliar (the future organization) more familiar. For example, leaders may ask people to consider how tomorrow's organization will be like a museum or a school playground at recess or perhaps like a debating society, an amusement park, an upscale restaurant, a revolutionary army, a church service, a new language to be learned, a tree to be planted, a blended family, a garden in springtime, a newly discovered territory to be colonized, a house to be remodelled, laundry to be washed, or a stand-up comedy routine to be delivered. When a variety of metaphors is presented as a potential aid, people may more readily think about their organization in very different ways–and concoct futures they had never conceived.

The future is not always about constructing something new. It might be about destructing some things that exist, such as current organizational rules. Frequently, thinking and behaviour are constrained by attention paid to rules that are simply taken for granted. Creative thinking can be stimulated by bringing rules to the surface and thinking what the organization will be like if the rules are purposely broken. Leaders may invite workers to spend a few minutes considering the formal or unwritten rules they observe when dealing with fellow employees, managers, customers, suppliers, regulators, paperwork, etc. Alternatively, they may consider rules for the ways products or services are used by customers. Then challenge followers to identify one rule they want to alter in their vision. How could the organization's future be more exciting and inspiring if that rule were broken? A visioning session like this can be run under the title "Sacred cows make great steaks."

People can think about the organization's future more creatively if they let others do it for them. That is, they can imagine how others well-known to them would do things differently. What if Spiderman was running the enterprise? What would be different and more inspiring in the future? What if Mother Teresa or Albert Einstein headed the organization? Or a 10-year-old school child or the follower's mother? What would they do differently to make things more exciting? This "wearing another hat" exercise can stimulate new ways of considering the future if followers are stuck in their own notions about what could possibly be more exciting and inspiring in their enterprise.

A combination of the "rule-breaking" and "wear another hat" techniques can be applied in meetings with familiar groups, such as a leader's own staff. A leader may say, "Today we are going to break the rule that everyone sits in their normal seat" and require each group member to sit in another member's regular chair. Then during the visioning meeting each person has to think about the future as if they were the person who normally sits in that seat.

Although there are many creative thinking approaches leaders could adopt to help put followers in a visioning frame of mind, the last to be described here involves sending people on a visioning quest. This involves giving a follower half a day off from their normal duties to visit another organization that is well recognized for being an exciting place to work. To apply this method a follower identifies an organization that has a reputation for being an inspiring place and spends considerable time observing or talking to employees about what they do and how they do it. Often this means the follower will assume the role of customer or donor so some real funds may have to be allocated for this approach to make a purchase or a donation. The follower's task is to return the next day with at least three ideas for adapting the target's inspiration methods to their own organization. Much of the power of this technique is found in changing the follower's environment (get out of their organization and into another) so that they think differently. As von Oech might say, this is a real whack on the side of the follower's head because sending the follower somewhere else during working hours makes this a real leadership commitment and creates a real follower responsibility to think differently about how to increase excitement and inspiration back "home."

Creative thinking supports for visioning

- No single right answer
  - be an artist; give the judge time off
  - throw people off guard with a question
- Use a metaphor
- Break a rule; sacred cows make great steaks
- Wear another hat; think like someone else
- Send a follower on a visioning quest

As discussed previously, the purpose for collecting visioning input from constituents is to recognize common themes among many followers and to include those themes in the leader's vision. Followers' ideas will likely be focused on the specific activities in which they engage on a daily basis, their own organizational touch points. Necessarily, visioning themes will be higher level, more general and encompassing; themes such as community, justice, optimism, learning, advocacy, enabling, innovation, family and sustainability. Upon hearing a leader's vision message, followers will be able to make the connection between the organization's aims and what they personally desire.

Once a large number of ideas about future excitement and inspiration have been collected and recorded, it is the leader's task to recognize the themes. Leaders can assimilate many ideas into a few common themes by grouping the ideas into general categories. Simple tasks such as sorting index cards into like piles or cutting-and-pasting key words into columns is all that is needed. When the sorting is complete, read the contents of each pile or column. What title embraces all these inputs? The leader's insight is the valuable asset here. Through the multi-step visioning process and many listening sessions, servants typically have strong inferences about what touches their followers' hearts and motivates their actions.

In Martin Luther King's "I Have a Dream" speech, Dr. King included themes of equality, freedom, justice and brotherhood–all of which his followers recognized and could apply to their own specific experiences. Also, his famous speech was meant to touch the hearts and minds of a wide audience so he included encompassing values like family, church and country. To mention just a few other techniques Dr. King employed, he used vivid word pictures and strong images so that people could visualize what he was talking about, and he shifted from using "I" to "we" about halfway through the speech as he called upon others to join him in enacting a better future. The speech was honest in recognizing the major problems that existed at the time and the challenges that lay ahead. There were no promises that change would be easy. There was recognition that sacrifices would have to be made. However, the speech's overall tone was hopeful and promising because he described what the better tomorrow would look like as he issued his call to action.

Sample vision themes			
access	empowerment	innovation	participation
advocacy	family	inspiration	stewardship
community	flexibility	justice	support
connection	growth	opportunity	transformation

When identifying and titling vision themes servant leaders ensure their vision nomenclature connects with the organization's mission and values. Together the leader's message of mission, values and vision tells an integrated organizational story: purpose, beliefs, future directions.

Here the reader is again reminded that the leader's vision is not simply a slogan, sentence or paragraph. It is a compelling message that inspires. It's meant to be remembered and retold. In its full form it is suitable for telling at organizational celebrations and events. It fits perfectly as a kick-off for a planning effort. Developing such a message is not an easy task since every value, theme, metaphor, phrase and word is critical. Servant leaders dedicate much time and effort to drafting, refining and practicing their vision message. They search for powerful, action-oriented verbiage. They inject meaningful metaphors and word pictures that help their audience see the future they are describing. Also, they may use evocative quotations significant to followers and themselves.

In preparation to compose a vision, servant leaders can organize on a sheet or screen key words or phrases that express:

- the organization's mission
- the organization's values
- what they are personally passionate about regarding their organization's future
- the themes that inspire their followers
- what is recognized as serving the common good
- metaphors relevant to the challenges and successes ahead, and
- visual images that can appeal to followers and help them visualize the better tomorrow.

Then leaders begin composing in four to eight paragraphs vision elements that express their personal hope, confidence and connection to the future, the enduring character of the organization (past, present, future), relevant current conditions or situations and an inspiring description of the improved future. Basically, the "what," "why," "who" and "where" questions are answered regarding the need for planned change, and the better tomorrow is painted in inspiring terms. The "how" is not addressed. Specific goals and strategies come later in the process. Followers called to action by the vision will be partners in conceiving how to bring the leader's vision to fruition.

Once a leader's vision is written, the other shorter vision formats can be developed rather easily through creative editing. With the appropriate perspectives of different audiences in mind, the vision can be reduced to a paragraph for the annual report, an HR recruiting talk, a thirty second elevator pitch for potential donors, a new employee orientation welcome, a website slogan or whatever servant leaders may need as they fulfil their various communication responsibilities across their organization.

As discussed previously in the storytelling skill section, many leaders take their vision speech "off-Broadway" to hone it. That is, they develop their best draft then deliver the message in whole or in parts to various individuals or small audiences who can critique each element and offer suggestions for improvements. Staff, colleagues, friends, remote branch offices and so on may well serve as supportive and helpful sounding boards. Professional speech writers and coaches are frequently consulted. Only after they are confident of every element will a servant leader begin to deliver the vision message to followers.

Appropriate body language for delivering a vision speech may differ somewhat from typical public speaking. Commonly, speakers are advised to make eye contact with audiences, maintain a stable posture and stationary position and limit gestures to emphasize only the main points one is making. Visioning calls for something different. Since the nature of the vision involves futurism and inspiration, speakers may sometimes find it more fitting to look above and beyond the audience–straight on and over their heads–as if looking into the future. Also, visions communicate excitement (even risk) so speakers may move in ways that demonstrate enthusiasm and eagerness; striding about a stage, standing on the edge of a platform or, if seated in a meeting, sitting on the edge of their chair. There should be excitement in their voice, of course. Therefore, the pace of speech quickens and vocal tones elevate. Hands can be used to point straight ahead into the future. Arms can be outstretched with palms open and extended to embrace the audience, calling them together to join the speaker in the vision effort.

Managing time

Practice of highly-developed time management skills is recognized by numerous researchers and writers as common to excellent leaders. Managing the limited resource of time plays a central role in focusing action and helping leaders achieve goals. Leadership expert John Adair tells us time management is not simply about being organised or efficient, or completing certain tasks. Rather, it is about managing time with a focus on achievement. Time management should be goal driven and results-oriented. Also, it's important to recognize that time management skills play a pivotal role in one's personal as well as professional life.

Some of the benefits of good time management include:

- tasks completed and goals attained on schedule and with high quality
- perceived by others as being organised, disciplined, productive and punctual
- less personal exposure to stress and anxiety
- increased self-confidence and sense of achievement
- strong focus on tasks (less distracted), and
- more time freed up for family, friends and recreation.

Research has demonstrated that there is a strong link between time management and stress management. Most people experience stress when they feel as though they lack control over the events in their lives. They may perceive they are being overwhelmed with demands due to lack of time and/or abilities to meet those demands. Effective time management can enhance a leader's sense of control and bolster confidence that demands can be satisfied; therefore fewer of the deleterious effects of stress are experienced on body, mind, emotions and behaviour.

Effects of stress	
Body	**Mind**
headaches	worrying
fatigue	indecision
breathlessness	hasty decisions
twitches	impaired judgment
skin irritations	negativity
Emotions	**Behavior**
irritability	restlessness
depression	insomnia
apathy	loss of appetite
alienation	accident prone
loss of confidence	drinking/smoking more

Peter Drucker tells us, "Effective leaders know where their time goes." For leaders looking to increase their personal effectiveness Drucker suggests "know thyself, know thy time" by keeping a log of personal activities and the time consumed in each. His experiences indicated that upon examining one's own time logs, leaders should "… try to identify and eliminate the things that need not be done at all." Many of such activities cling to us as bad habits left over from previous experiences and responsibilities. Also, Drucker suggests leaders ask themselves, "Which of the activities on my time log could be done by somebody else just as well, if not better?"

Insightfully, James Kouzes and Barry Posner remind leaders, "How you spend your time is the single clearest indicator, especially to other people, about what's important to you." They go on to ask, "Is there a connection for you between how you allocate your time and what you consider to be priorities and key values?" There should be.

Followers take important cues from what leaders do. And they don't just notice the big, obvious examples–for instance, what actions leaders take during a crisis. Each day numerous little opportunities for behaviour modelling occur, and they help followers learn what leaders think is important. When do leaders arrive and leave? What events do they attend? How much of their day is spent working alone or with others? Who are the "others"–customers, bosses, subordinates, peers? How much time does a leader spend in training or investigating new, innovative tools and techniques? As Kouzes and Posner state, followers assess how serious their leaders are about the organization's key values by watching how much time is spent on them.

Dennis Slevin, management professor, consultant, and practicing manager, advises that busy leaders can save four hours per week (ten percent of a typical forty hour schedule) if they adopt some of the time management skills he includes in his book, *The Whole Manager*. His appealing framework will be adopted for this time management skills discussion. As the reader proceeds through the following approaches to managing time, keep an open mind and try to select a few favourites to apply to your own specific leadership situations. It may be motivating to realize that saving four hours per week could represent one week of vacation every ten weeks, five extra weeks of productivity each year or seventeen more hours per month to spend with family and friends.

Slevin's framework divides time management skills into two categories: *doing less* and *working faster*. Leaders can spend less of their own time on activities by delegating some tasks to qualified others, getting help through their own personal networks, saying "No" when appropriate and keeping other people's monkeys off their back. Leaders can work faster and get more mileage from their existing work hours by knowing their best time of day, setting priorities, filtering out interruptions, developing a system to manage the flow of messages and paper, using technology, keeping a calendar and "to-do" list and finally, setting aside time to reflect.

Readers are encouraged to identify one or two of these numerous techniques that seem most promising for their particular situations. Put it/them to use and monitor results. If time is saved, adopt the approach permanently. Make it part of your regular leadership routine. If significant time is not saved, go back and choose another time management practice and see if results are more satisfactory. There is little to lose and much to gain.

Based upon the "Two Ways to Save Time" framework
Dennis P. Slevin
The Whole Manager, 1989

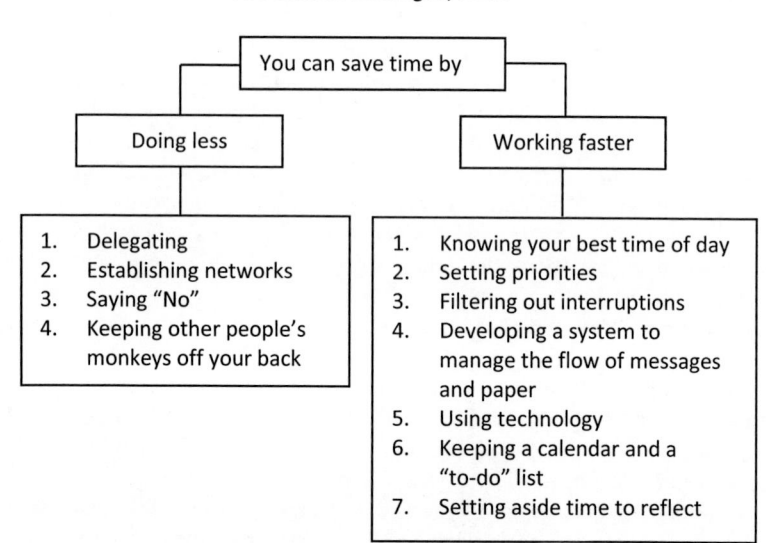

```
                    You can save time by
                    /                  \
              Doing less            Working faster
```

Doing less	Working faster
1. Delegating 2. Establishing networks 3. Saying "No" 4. Keeping other people's monkeys off your back	1. Knowing your best time of day 2. Setting priorities 3. Filtering out interruptions 4. Developing a system to manage the flow of messages and paper 5. Using technology 6. Keeping a calendar and a "to-do" list 7. Setting aside time to reflect

Delegating

The most effective way for leaders to do less personally and still ensure that all necessary organizational tasks are completed is to delegate. Of course, it is necessary to remember that leaders can only delegate authority to others for task accomplishment. A leader's *responsibility* for performance is constant. It cannot be delegated away. Delegation implies the leader's ongoing interest in and oversight of the delegated activity.

Delegation involves:

- allocation of duties or tasks a leader desires someone else to do
- delegation of authority, empowering someone else to act for the leader
- assignment of responsibility, assigning the equivalent obligation to perform effectively, and
- creation of accountability, making the person answerable for carrying out the task and achieving expected results.

Many leaders fail to delegate as effectively as they could. Consider this example. A hospital administrator realized that he spent about a day each month compiling the "Monthly Operations Report" required by his superior. Yet, while analysing the previous six month's reports, it was evident that each report was pretty much the same. The few differences involved some specific performance statistics relevant to that month (which were available from anyone in the department) and a number of "special issues" that required expressing his opinions on matters of immediate importance each month. The department head realized that all the routine report elements could be compiled by an assistant for his review and approval. He retained the task of writing the "special issues." The result: half a day's time saved each month.

Delegation is probably the single most effective step toward improved time management for busy leaders, and it can be an effective method for empowering others in the organization. Besides saving some of the leader's time, delegation can offer other significant benefits. The quality of decisions may be enhanced because the leader pushes decision-making down the hierarchy to subordinates who are closer to the customer or user. Followers can experience higher levels of motivation and job satisfaction because they are given opportunities to address important issues under the guidance and oversight of their leader. Handling meaningful tasks can stimulate followers' personal development and growth since they will be called upon to apply higher-level and/or a greater variety of skills.

Delegating tasks to others increases involvement in decisions. Therefore, employee commitment is enhanced and worker "buy-in" to new ways of operating increases. Of course, delegation of meaningful tasks from leaders to followers can improve personal relationships as well through trust-building between the parties and enhancing followers' self-confidence. Since servant leaders are particularly concerned about empowering constituents, supporting followers' growth and development and building strong relationships, delegation offers numerous payoffs besides saving the leader's personal time.

Many leaders hesitate to delegate because they are concerned that tasks will not be accomplished effectively by other people. In such instances the leader retains responsibility for failure or under-performance. Therefore, leaders may desire to exercise a degree of necessary caution in choosing which tasks to delegate and which followers to involve. Certainly, leaders' attitudes concerning risk-taking and dealing with failure enter the delegation equation. However, effective servant leaders see themselves as teachers and facilitators, and they take a "learning" approach to failures.

Thus, delegating meaningful tasks to others can be quite natural for servant leaders.

Delegation

"Push down" decision-making; empower others; let others be comfortable doing things "in your place"

Why delegate?
- Frees up your time
- Improves decision-making by getting closer to the problem
- Stimulates personal growth and development
- "Buy-in" enhances implementation
- Improves relationships by demonstrating trust and confidence

Delegation involves:
- Allocating duties to qualified others
- Empowering others to act for you (sharing authority)
- Assigning and sharing responsibility to perform
- Assigning accountability to perform

Once a decision to delegate is made, it is helpful to view the process in two communication steps. First, leaders should explain *what results* are expected. It is not necessary to explain how to do the task, unless the followers are being asked to tackle tasks well beyond their ability or experience. Let workers apply their own analyses and approaches to tasks. It's part of the empowerment element of delegation. Depending on specific circumstances, leaders may also communicate deadlines for task completion. Once tasks are delegated, servant leaders should remain available to facilitate as they fulfil their responsibility for oversight, support and teaching.

Second, leaders should communicate clearly *how much authority* is being delegated to carry out the assignment. This is a step often overlooked by leaders, and it is a major cause of failed delegation attempts. If followers do not know how far they may proceed on their own in decision-making and action-taking, they may fail in the leader's eyes by not demonstrating expected initiative or by going too far and exceeding the authority the leader intended to delegate.

One way leaders may communicate the level of authority being delegated is to clarify which of three alternatives is in force. Leaders may intend for followers to: 1) take action on their own, and notify the leader routinely (for example, during weekly staff meetings); 2) take action on their own, but notify the leader immediately when action is taken (this may be best when the importance of a task is high or involves key stakeholders); and 3) recommend only, take no action without approval (this may be best when the importance of a task is extremely high).

Delegation as a communication task

1. Communicate *objectives*.
   Focus on results; tell people <u>what</u> you want done
   (if necessary, <u>how</u> to accomplish it)
2. Communicate *authority* for decision-making.
   Tell people how far they can go in making decisions:
   - Take action—notify me routinely (weekly, …)
   - Take action—notify me at once
   - Recommend—take no action without my approval

Servant leaders save personal time and empower followers by delegating meaningful tasks to others. To delegate well remember that it is a two-step communication process. Leaders should tell followers what results are expected (not how to do the task) and how much authority is being delegated by the leader. Followers will be most comfortable assuming responsibility if the leader follows these effective delegation guidelines.

Establishing networks

It's well-established in the literature that effective leaders employ a widespread network to accomplish their work. Networks of help and support are so essential to leaders' success that "establish a network" is identified in this book as one of the necessary servant leader behaviours, so more on this topic is included in a later chapter. It is sufficient here to state that networks may consist of hundreds of members and they are built gradually over time.

A leader's job is not as simple as arriving at the workplace each day and dealing directly with each task, simple or complex, that comes across the desk. Effective servant leaders make it their business to know a lot of experienced people and experts in their specific fields, and they establish relationships with them to construct a mutually-supporting network of assistance. When a unique issue is encountered, leaders have opportunities to contact members of their network with the specific type of experience or expertise necessary to address it. Expert support is used to handle the task as well and as expeditiously as possible. Then the leader moves on to other tasks.

Leader = Centre of help and communication network

- Law
- Accounting and Taxation
- Government
- Education
- Banking/Lending
- Human Resources → **Leader** ← Supply of Goods/Services
- Information Tech.
- Purchasing
- Operations
- Real Estate
- Transportation/Delivery

Remember the three magic words: "I need help."

Of course, support received from other experienced people comes with a responsibility to provide support for network members when the leader's expertise is valuable to others. That's the "cost" of networking. In most cases, it is far outweighed by the benefits. Also, providing advice to others can be a professional gratification for many leaders, and it is a small price to pay for available expertise.

Leaders who care about managing their own time effectively develop and apply the skills of network building. They meet new people at every opportunity, exchange contact information and record each new acquaintance's area(s) of expertise. They don't leave such meetings to chance, however. They adopt strategies of joining a variety of professional associations both within and outside their areas of training and experience so that meeting different people becomes a common event. Further, they join new groups on a periodic basis, rotating memberships in and out of different associations over the long term. Leaders know that at some future point the person they are adding to their network today may be the best individual to advise them on an issue that cannot even be imagined at present. Servant leaders know that it's the quality of work that matters, not the idea that they handle their problems by themselves.

Saying "No"

Another way leaders manage time by doing less is learning to say "No" at appropriate times. This is an important time management skill requiring personal discipline and a strong appreciation of priorities. Effective leaders say "No" respectfully, quickly and cleanly. No doubt is left in the minds of constituents. Responses such as "I'll think about it" and "I'll get back to you on that" simply raise false hopes, draw out decisions and waste everyone's time.

As usual, Drucker gets right to the point: "... learn to say 'No' if an activity contributes little to one's own work organization, to oneself, or to the organization for which it is performed." One practical test is to ask oneself upon fielding a request, "How much difference will my 'Yes' response make next week, next month, next year, or even next decade?" If the short- and long-term impact of "Yes" is low, it's an easy decision to say "No."

One reason some people fail to say "No" is the fear that feelings may be hurt and relationships affected negatively. If that is the case, a good way to say "No" is to turn the request into a self-perceived compliment and thank the requestor for honouring you with their invitation–for example, "I am honoured that you consider me capable of helping you in your important work, but, no, that is not something I can commit to at the present time."

Generally, many people find it difficult to say "No" to others' requests or to opportunities, especially interesting ones, they have the chance to accept. Refusal may go against the grain of a generous person, such as a servant leader, who believes it is right to support others' efforts. Perhaps refusal seems particularly costly on a personal level because it might be an opportunity that is unlikely to occur again. However, "No" is an appropriate response for activities that have little association with current organizational or personal priorities so that more time can be spent on tasks that support such priorities.

Also, it is appropriate to say "No" to tasks that *others can do better or faster than you* (see the previous section on network-building). Often capable leaders know network members with specific expertise who can provide higher quality help than they. In such cases, the leader serves everyone well by making the necessary contacts and introductions, then returning to concentrate on priorities.

When saying "Yes" or "No," leaders need to be aware of their personal priorities as well as the priorities of their organization. More on this topic is discussed in the *Setting priorities* section. Here it is sufficient to mention that leaders must be aware of mission, values, vision and goals that frequently emanate from an effective planning process.

The habit of saying "No" to low-priority tasks and to tasks for which others are better suited will allow leaders the free time to say "Yes" to tasks that are more impactful for their organizations, more helpful to others in need, emerge unexpectedly, or are more personally exciting or satisfying to the leader.

Saying "No"

- Know your priorities.
  Apply your sense of mission, values, vision and goals.
  Attend to what is most important first.
- Use your network for referrals.
  Say "No" if you do not possess the necessary knowledge or skill to help. Say "I'm not the best person to help, but I know who is." Give a referral– and follow up to ensure a connection has been made.
- Learn to say "No" if an activity contributes little to your work organization, to you, or to any organization for which it is performed.
- Don't say "I'll think about it" or "I'll get back to you." They are time wasters.

Keeping other people's monkeys off your back

An interesting aspect of the saying "No" approach involves the classic concept of monkeys introduced long ago (the 1970's) by William Onken, Jr. and Donald Wass. This is a visualization technique to help leaders deter followers from delegating their work up to the boss.

A monkey is a task. Once a task has been assigned or assumed, envision it as a monkey sitting on the back of the worker responsible for its care and feeding until the task is completed.

Consider the following situation: an assistant enters a leader's office shortly before quitting time and announces, "Boss, we've got a problem. You asked me to set up a meeting tomorrow afternoon with members of the Quality Committee. I've contacted three of the six members, and they can attend, but I can't reach the others no matter what I try. I've been working on it all day." The assistant pauses, standing before the leader, obviously expecting some sort of response. The ball is clearly in the leader's court. "OK," the leader says, "leave their names and contact information on my desk. I'll try to get through to them this evening."

The assistant carried the "arrange a meeting" monkey before entering the office. Now who has it? Intentionally (or perhaps not), the job was delegated upward to the leader. The assistant will go home to enjoy a stress-free evening while the leader has more work to do. Perhaps the leader wants to be seen as a problem-solver, or wishes to avoid conflict with the assistant or desires to be perceived by followers as a "kind and friendly" person. We don't know for sure. One thing we do know: this leader is not a good time manager. If there are five more direct reports in the office and each one executes a monkey leap each day, the leader's work will never be done.

Have faith in your organization's structure. Act as if you believe that effective outcomes will be achieved if everyone carries out their own job responsibilities. (If that is not the case, change the structure.) In this situation a simple, respectful response such as, "Thanks for the update. Let me know when you have finalized the meeting arrangements," would prevent the monkey leap and let the assistant know their responsibility is still active. After one or two such experiences constituents learn to stop trying the monkey leap gambit.

The moral of this simple story is straightforward: keep other people's monkeys off your back. Any jobs given to others should remain with them until they are completed. Some people are highly skilled at getting their monkeys to jump onto others' backs. Some even make a career of it. (Perhaps you know one or two.) So the next time constituents enter your office, or you encounter them in the hallway, use the monkey visualization trick. As your interaction begins, picture them with their monkeys on their backs. When they turn to leave, make sure every one of their monkeys is still on their shoulders.

Keep other people's monkeys off your back

Don't let followers delegate up to you. Visualize their tasks as monkeys on their backs. When your interactions with followers are complete, make sure all the monkeys they carried at the beginning of your conversation are still on their backs (not on yours).

- Have confidence in the organizational structure. High quality results will be achieved if everyone does their job. Respectfully let others know it is their responsibility to do the work assigned to them—and to do it well.
- Buy some plastic moneys through the restaurant and bar industry supply chain (they are often used as adornments for cocktails). Here's what you can do with your plastic monkeys:
    - Place one next to the clock you view most often (on the desk or wall). Let it remind you about the "visualize monkeys on others' backs" technique.
    - Put in on your desk or bookshelf. Let others ask you why you have a plastic monkey. Then tell the story—show them you are not an "easy mark" for upward delegation.
    - Keep a few in your pocket. When necessary, hand one to an "offending" follower and say, "That's not my monkey!"

Some *working faster* time management techniques are now considered.

Knowing your best time of day

What kind of person are you: an early bird, an afternoon dynamo, a night owl? Leaders, like all others, are subject to rhythms of the mind and body. Some people experience peak energy, alertness, concentration and productivity when they first wake up. Others are slower starters but peak in late morning or early afternoon. Still others reach maximum effectiveness after the sun sets.

Typically, we find that our bodies run on a 24-hour internal clock. We sleep, wake up and experience alertness peaks and valleys around the same times each day. The specific times can be different for everyone, but the cycle is pretty much universal. That 24-hour cycle is called a "circadian day." Blocks of peak productivity time are known as "ultradian cycles," and the way we cycle in and out of them is called our "ultradian rhythm." The beginning of each ultradian cycle is when our brain is most energetic and focused. Energy slowly depletes, and at the end of each ultradian cycle, we can keep working, but we simply won't be as effective. Like our bodies, brains need some rest and relaxation, too.

The important thing to remember in terms of managing your work day is that you have a few peak hours when you can do your best thinking, strategizing, creative problem-solving and decision-making. Therefore, be jealous of your best time of day. Plan to perform your most challenging or most important tasks during that block of time. You can perform tasks during other periods, of course, but you won't be as productive with the minutes you dedicate to your work.

A very successful business manager recognized her best time of day was early morning. That's when her mind was clear and focus was sharp. On occasional mornings she started her work day at home where she had maximum control over her early hours, travelling to the office in mid-morning. On a typical day, however, she arrived at work and followed her habit of "retreating" into her office for an hour or two to tackle the most demanding creative or analytical tasks on that day's to-do list. As much as practicable she kept her door closed to indicate a preference to work without interruptions. After 90 minutes or so, she usually felt she had gotten her day off to a strong start, and the door was opened. Now her time was available to all. During the "off peak" hours of the day she spent a great deal of time in meetings (scheduled after 10:00 whenever possible), walking the shop and listening to others. Over time her co-workers recognized her preferred method of working so they adjusted their interactions to accommodate her time management habits. The system worked for her and her colleagues.

Of course, no one has full control over their schedule each day because the boss may call a meeting at any time or a follower may require timely guidance and support. However, good time managers protect their peak productivity hours as much as they can and schedule their most demanding tasks for that block of time.

Setting priorities

Very simply, it's a leader's responsibility to set priorities. Once established, priorities should be kept in the forefront of thinking and used as guidelines for how to spend one's time. Use this simple rule: schedule your priorities. Many unsuccessful leaders are hard-working and passionate, but they fail to get the *right things* done in the available time because their priorities are unclear or inconsistent.

Where do priorities come from? Effective leaders engage in planning, and planning involves understanding one's mission, values, vision and goals. That is, good leaders develop a clear awareness of purpose, core beliefs and a preferred future as well as the undertakings necessary for attaining that future. Bringing to fruition the preferred future in step-by-step fashion requires building the right relationships, attaining the necessary resources and accomplishing the essential tasks. These, and only these, relationships, resources and tasks constitute a leader's priorities. Everything else must be lower in importance. They may be nice, they may be fulfilling, but they are not necessary.

For servant leaders, this type of planning, prioritizing and time management is relevant to both their organizations and their personal lives. Since significant overlap should exist between organizational and personal missions and values, there should be overlap among preferred futures and priorities.

Priorities imply making choices. What determines choices? A leader's plan. If a leader has no plan, priorities will be unclear and decisions and actions will be inconsistent. And the way leaders spend their precious time will be haphazard.

Of course, plans and priorities are not constant because the environments in which organizations and individuals operate are subject to continuous change. Reflection, periodic evaluation and adjustment, is necessary to keep plans and priorities up-to-date through mid-course corrections. Reflection is important servant leader behaviour, and effective leaders build adequate reflection time into their schedules.

Planning = Priorities

Know well your organizational and personal mission, values, vision and goals.

Annually
With your mission, values and vision in mind, set goals for the year.
Attend to the following categories:
- routine goals that must be accomplished
- problem-solving goals to improve performance
- innovation goals that will make a difference, and
- personal development and life goals.

Monthly or Quarterly
Evaluate progress toward annual goals.
Revise goals and priorities as necessary.

Weekly
Identify specific goals to accomplish this week.

Daily
Create a "to-do" list.

	Build Relationships	Attain Resources	Accomplish Tasks
Annually			
Monthly or Quarterly			
Weekly			
Daily (to-do list)			

Too often leaders' behaviours are driven by things that are defined as urgent or important by others. Examine an unsuccessful leader's calendar. You will likely find it filled with events, meetings and other activities that others impose upon him or her–not filled with the leader's priorities.

What is time management about for leaders? It's about achievement, being goal driven, getting results in the time available. How many leaders say, "If I only had more time, I could accomplish everything I want." Leaders have as much time, no more or less, than everyone else. If they spend their time working their plan, they will get results and be successful. If they spend their time doing what others want, they will be very busy, and their plan will suffer the consequences. The key to leaders' effective time management is to schedule their priorities, not to accommodate what others want to put on their schedule. Successful leaders manage time from the driver's seat, not the passenger's.

Examine the "Planning = Priorities" figure for a simple, but useful, overview of a leader's priority-setting task.

Filtering out interruptions

One of the most significant time management challenges facing servant leaders involves potential interruptions of their daily work activities. While servant leaders desire to spend time listening and communicating, they also want to dedicate sufficient time to focusing on necessary tasks. Every time a leader begins an activity, is interrupted, then returns to the activity, valuable set-up time is lost.

Telephone calls and texts may be the most severe interruption threats. When a phone rings or a text is received, it might be an urgent message about a work emergency, a routine check-in or a simple social call. Due to the unknown and random nature of messages, phone calls and texts are extremely powerful. They can subdivide long periods of a leader's productive time into small, far less efficient intervals.

Therefore, leaders should establish guidelines to protect themselves as much as possible from unwanted or unnecessary interruptions while leaving themselves accessible to others who need to get in touch. If an assistant is available to the leader, make sure calls and texts are screened for importance. Guidelines can be set up to identify whose calls or texts or the types of calls or texts that should demand immediate attention. Others can wait until a more convenient time for a return message. Some leaders have good results by setting up a few regular periods throughout the typical work day when all calls and texts are reviewed and returned. Communications flow without long absences, but concentration on work activities is not compromised. The point is: make sure the leader controls calls and texts, not vice versa.

A second common source of interruptions is people. Constituents may drop by to engage in both work-related discussions and casual conversations. Again, if an assistant is available to screen "drop-byes," guidelines can be established for certain people or certain times of the day when the leader's "open door" policy is in effect and times when work activities will be protected from interruption. If there is no assistant for screening visits, some leaders have enjoyed success by making known the general time of day they prefer to concentrate of their major tasks and the times when visits of all types are more welcome. Simply, they are direct with others about trying to protect their "best time of day."

Sometimes the mere physical arrangement of an office space can solve the dilemma of too many drop-byes. For example, turning a desk away from the entry door and toward the wall or window may help decrease the number of interruptions caused by simple eye contact with passers-by that could result in several unintended casual conversations throughout the course of a work day.

Filtering out interruptions

Most common interruptions are:
- telephone calls, texts, emails
- people dropping by

If you have an assistant, establish guidelines:
- when, for whom, and for what you accept interruptions

Schedule specific periods of your day for calls, texts, emails. Do not attend to them as they occur.

Arrange your work space to minimize unintended eye contact and resulting interruptions.

Developing a system to manage the flow of digital messages and paper

Effective servant leaders are great communicators. The more they communicate, the more and better they can serve others. That means they are exposed to ever-increasing messages that are not only verbal but messages that take on digital and paper forms as well. Leaders manage their time effectively when they manage their digital messages and paperwork efficiently.

Keep message management as simple and direct as possible and strive to comply with this objective: *handle each message only once.*

Adopt the attitude that there are three kinds of electronic or paper-based messages: A) Important, B) Worthwhile and C) Junk.

**Developing a system to manage the flow
of digital messages and paper**

Goal: Handle each message or piece of paper *only once*.

A. Important   Take action
- *Immediately* take appropriate and complete action and dispense with the message or paper.
- If action cannot be completed at the present time, put in a *pending* file. Establish a date when you want to see it again and put it on your schedule.

B. Worthwhile   Read
- *Distribute* if it is significant to others. Be considerate; they get enough junk.
- *File/Save* only if you need to see it again.
- *Delete/Toss* after you have gained all its information.

C. Junk   Delete or Toss

Important texts, emails and paper should be acted upon at once. If possible, take all required action to complete the necessary task(s), then dispense of the text, email or paperwork. That is, delete it or throw it away. Don't accumulate message into files, lists or piles. If it's not possible to complete the important task(s) communicated by the message, take action as far as possible, then store the text, email or paper in a pending file. Update your calendar so that the task appears again on the date when you can reasonably expect to take the job to completion. Upon completing the task, dispose of the important message.

Worthwhile messages should be read then one of three alternatives should be taken. *Distribute* it to others (but only if it is significant to others; be considerate, they get enough junk). *File* it (but only if you need to see it again). *Toss* or *delete* it (when you have gained all its information).

Junk is junk. Recognize it and get rid of it. Don't fall into the trap of hanging on to it because you might need it again someday. Junk is what delete keys and waste baskets are for.

Be confident that uncluttered minds are the result of uncluttered desks and files. The cleaner and neater your desk appears and the fewer overflowing files you have, the more stress-free you will feel and the more organized you will appear to others.

Picture what a servant leader's desk should look like–ideally. To pay maximum attention and respect to a communication partner sitting across the desk, the servant leader should dedicate full attention to the conversation. There should be no piles of unfinished tasks distracting either party. The leader should find it natural to maintain eye contact with the visitor and not be distracted by materials on the desk. The guest should not be under the impression that the leader can't wait for the end of the conversation so he/she can get back to "more important" tasks.

Remember the ultimate aim of a time-conscious and stress-conscious leader is to handle each message only once. You are going to have to spend the same amount of time completing tasks whether you have looked at messages five times previously or not, so you might as well deal with them the first time you see them.

Again, if a leader has an assistant available, they can be trained to review incoming texts, emails and paperwork and sort messages into categories A, B or C as the leader would do. Even more time saved!

Using technology

It's well recognized that leaders can enhance their time management skills and personal productivity with the support of a variety of technology-based tools. Devices, systems and applications are available to support a leader's needs to: organize time, information, ideas and images; share information and calendars; connect to and interact with others; remain aware of changing internal and environmental conditions; expand creative thinking capability; focus on thoughts and tasks; and even optimize personal breaks.

Depending on leaders' specific responsibilities, tasks and preferred work styles, useful tools may include personal organizers and schedulers, voice recognition systems, tools for messaging, meetings and group decision support and on and on. Capabilities are expanding at an amazing pace as specific applications are being developed for traditional time management techniques as well as for professional specialities and conventional functional areas.

Detailed discussion of technology-based time management and productivity tools is far beyond the scope of this book. However, it is reasonable to suggest that it's a wise investment of leaders' time to monitor available tools and periodically update their personal devices and applications.

Keeping a calendar and to-do list

On a monthly, weekly and daily basis leaders need to be acutely aware of how they will be using their time. Effective leaders have a mental image (or an easily referenced digital image) of the total picture of their time and expectations, as well as a moment-by-moment awareness of what they should be doing.

A daily "to-do" list helps a leader manage both time and stress. At the end of each workday consider all the tasks that must be accomplished tomorrow. Don't make it a long list. Include only the five or ten things that must be done, and, once accomplished, will make it a successful day. Referring to one's work-related and personal priorities helps with this type of task identification. Write down the list of things that must be done tomorrow and store it in a place or on a device where it will be accessed easily first thing at work (not at home) in the morning.

Then, importantly, forget the list. Forget work. Focus on the vital non-work parts of your life that help you maintain a healthy balance of mind, body and soul. The list will wait for you, and you will pick up right where you need to. If you don't already do this, try it. Your mind will rest easier and you may well sleep better knowing that you will not forget anything important the next day.

When work resumes the following day, focus on the list. Accomplish every one of those tasks–or take them as far as you can before you "hit a wall." Say "No" to people who try to knock you off your productivity track. You can always go back and say "Yes" to them after your list of tasks is completed. It's okay to focus on your work first. You will be a more effective, responsible and productive leader.

Do the math here. If you complete five to ten tasks each day, how many is that per week, per month, per year? It's enough accomplishments to convince everyone, including yourself, that you are a highly productive leader.

Keeping a calendar and "to-do" list

- Have a graphic calendar and mental picture of your time and how you will use it–monthly, weekly, daily.
- Maintain continuous access to your calendar.
- Last task of each work day:
  Prepare a "to-do" list for the next day. Include 5-10 tasks you must accomplish. Keep the list where you will access it first thing tomorrow. Resist other tasks until all "to-do" tasks are completed or accomplished as far as possible.

Setting aside time to reflect

Greenleaf tells us that servant leaders withdraw regularly to renew themselves through contemplation and reflection. This is such a vital characteristic of servant leaders that it has been identified in this book as a servant leader behaviour, and it will be discussed in more detail in the next chapter.

Here it is sufficient to say that leaders will find it helpful to set aside a few minutes each day or at least a couple of times a week to sit down peacefully and reflect on the time management question, "Am I getting the important things done?" Depending on the answer, leaders can determine whether or not they should re-focus priorities and tasks–even adopt different time management techniques.

There is constant pressure to spend precious time on lower-priority issues and jobs. Resist it. And remember, being busy isn't necessarily being productive. A leader's responsibility is to achieve, that is, to accomplish the right things, not just things. And a leader's responsibility is to reflect as well as act.

Additional time management techniques

In addition to the time management techniques included in the Slevin framework, two "bonus" and potentially helpful concepts are offered here.

First, consider the "dreaded task." If we have worked long enough, we have all encountered (or, more appropriately, tried to resist) the dreaded task. It's the assignment you always put off for another day. For example, the boss gives you a task, so you recognize it is your responsibility, but you just don't want to do it. Perhaps it involves a person, a topic or a chore you just don't like. You hope the boss forgets about it, or somebody else does it, or the need just fades away and everybody forgets about it. Basically, it's the equivalent of the math homework you never wanted to do at school so you told the teacher your dog ate it. So you keep material related to the task in your desk's "bottom drawer" or in your computer in whatever digital equivalent you have for a bottom drawer. And it sits there neglected. If the boss remembers and calls you out on it someday, you will make up a quick excuse and finally dust it off–or you will try to get out of it again.

What to do about the dreaded task? Here is a suggestion that might be palatable: apply the 10-minute rule. Resolve to work on a dreaded task 10 minutes each day. Sometimes just overcoming the mental hurdle of getting started can set you on the path to task accomplishment. Ten minutes isn't too big a commitment to look it over and consider a plan for doing it. Who knows? You may find the job much easier than you thought at first. Don't feel guilty. Just know you are in good company. We all have dreaded tasks in our bottom desk drawers.

The final time management approach to be addressed is more philosophical than the others, but it is probably the most significant. It aims at ensuring that you are living a values-centred life.

When giving advice to children, students, younger colleagues, and so on, we most likely tell others to do this. From time to time it's good to check that we are following our own advice.

Think about what is important to you. Is it family, health, job, spirituality, leisure, wealth, or other things? Use your answers to create a personal mission statement. Answer the questions: What is my mission in life? What do I hope to be, to do? What values form the foundation of my mission? Actually write it down: commit!

Then get behind your mission statement. Decide how you will act on your values and beliefs, how your behaviours will reflect your values. That is, really understand your personal priorities.

Next, put it on your schedule. Be sure you spend appropriate time doing the things that are important to you. Don't procrastinate. Put the things most important to you on your monthly and weekly schedules and on your daily to-do lists.

Lastly, go gently on yourself in putting your personal mission statement into practice. Personal change can be stressful. Don't berate yourself for setbacks in the ways you use your time resource. Slowly the new, better way will become for you the natural way. Do one thing at a time with all your energy, attention and heart. Don't try to accomplish too much personal happiness at once. You will get there. And give yourself credit for what you do.

Running a meeting

This section presents some practical skills for running effective meetings and for making them instruments of community-building. Of course, one of the common attitudes identified in this book involves servant leaders seeing themselves as community-builders. Meetings can be important expressions of this attitude.

There are numerous types of meetings in organizations. One simple typology suggests six common meeting types: status update, information sharing, decision making, problem solving, innovation and team building. Another wide-ranging categorization suggests sixteen kinds of meetings: team cadence, progress updates, one-on-ones, action review, governance cadence, idea generation, planning, workshops, problem solving, decision making, information gathering, introductions, issue resolution, community of practice, training and broadcast. Leaders may find different organizing approaches and processes appropriate depending on the particular meeting's intentions, formats and participation profiles.

The purpose here is to discuss fundamental skills for running meetings and to suggest how servant leaders may take a somewhat unique approach to a meeting's organization and process for the purpose of enhancing community. This general discussion can be considered applicable to most organizational meetings, especially those of the status update, information sharing, decision-making and problem solving types. Commonly, these include staff, team or project meetings held on a regular basis to align group members via updates on progress, challenges and next steps as well as special meetings called to address specific problems or issues. Such meetings may take the form of one-time committee or task force meetings. Typical group activities in all meetings discussed here involve information exchange, problem solving, decision making and coordination of task assignments.

Well-planned and executed meetings can engage organization members in dialogue, create an environment of shared responsibility, be instruments for gathering and dispensing valuable information, enable effective decision-making, and help support a culture of transparency and accountability. Unfortunately, research indicates that workers believe many meetings are poorly planned, unfocused, last too long and waste far too much of the participants' time.

From an organizational and servant leadership standpoint, meetings are opportunities to come together and be heard, to speak with and listen to others and to organize and energize a community. Meetings demonstrate well the lesson that in some cases process can be more important and contribute more to organizational well-being than content. They are central to achieving mission and advancing vision, but they must be constructive and productive, effective and efficient. Otherwise, meetings have the potential to create the negative impressions described above. For example, readers may recognize this typical statement, "We just spent two hours in a meeting and didn't accomplish a thing."

In serving their overall purpose of community-building, meetings can be instruments of servant leader listening. Commonly, constituents welcome meetings that offer an open environment, presence and full attention of the leader and other participants, empathy, issue orientation, openness and non-judgmental orientation.

Some helpful ground rules servant leaders can provide to attendees for meeting participation include:

- show up on time and come prepared
- stay mentally and physically engaged (don't attend to non-meeting business during the meeting)
- all participants are expected to contribute to meeting goals by sharing ideas, asking questions and contributing to discussions
- let everyone participate
- seek first to understand, then to be understood (listen and think before speaking)
- stay on point and on time (keep comments short and to the point and don't waste everyone's time by repeating what others have said)
- attack the problem, not the person (respectfully challenge ideas, not people)
- come to decisions and identify action items, and
- record outcomes and follow up.

Meetings as instruments of listening

Open environment
Remove distractions; arrange furnishings to facilitate conversation and interaction (such as circular, square or U-shaped table formations).

Presence/attention
Demonstrate through attention, eye contact and nonverbal behaviours that members respect others and want to hear their ideas and opinions. Establish a rule: During the meeting do not attend to non-meeting business (no phones, etc.).

Empathy
Try to put yourself in the other person's place and experience so that you can appreciate their opinions.

Issue orientation
Don't judge people on their presentation styles or emotional expressions, but rather on their observations on issues.

Openness
Be patient when listening to others. Keep an open mind. Don't assume you know what another will say. Do not interrupt. Let others complete their thoughts.

Non-judgmental orientation
Ask questions for clarification. Don't argue the legitimacy of another's opinion. Honest and constructive discussions are necessary to achieve the best results.

The most important part of a meeting takes place before the meeting–in the preparation stage. Preparation involves:

- considering the leader's objective and deciding that a meeting is the best forum for accomplishing that objective
- selecting participants
- choosing an appropriate location and environment, and
- establishing an agenda.

During the meeting the leader is challenged to manage the process and fulfil a servant leader's responsibilities.

After the meeting, minutes must be produced and distributed to participants and other appropriate individuals and/or offices. Finally, for a period of time post-meeting the leader must engage in follow-up communication to ensure agreed upon tasks are completed and due dates respected.

This should sound like a lot of effort–because it is. One primary lesson about running meetings is that it requires a lot of organization, time, skill and effort to do it well. Therefore, don't have too many of them. Holding fewer and better meetings will be good for almost all organizations as well as their leaders and workers.

In discussing skills for running meetings, focus will be on seven steps that contribute to effective meetings: clearly communicate objectives; select participants; select location and set-up style; develop and distribute an agenda; exercise leadership and manage group process; generate and distribute minutes; and follow-up. In some steps, as appropriate, discussion will be dedicated to making meetings particular instruments of the servant leadership style.

Seven steps for effective meetings

1. Clearly communicate objectives
2. Select participants
3. Select location and set-up style
4. Develop and distribute an agenda
5. Exercise leadership and manage group process
6. Generate and distribute minutes
7. Follow-up

Clearly communicate objectives

Have you ever arrived at a meeting a few minutes early, looked at your fellow attendees who also arrived a bit early, then asked, "Does anyone know what we are doing here?" It's all too common an experience. Sometimes people appear for a meeting, but they don't know why they have been invited. It's hard to imagine they will be well-prepared to be active participants.

Leaders who call a meeting should first consider its purpose. In a very few words and simple language articulate the reason the meeting is necessary and what result or work product will be produced from the convening. This will help identify the topics to be covered and suggest the best group process and approach. Of course, the purpose should be achievable within the scheduled meeting time. After due consideration, leaders should not hesitate to decide that a meeting either isn't necessary or isn't a sufficient approach to accomplish the intended purpose. There may be better methods for attaining desired results.

Some typical purposes of meetings are: inform the participants, coordinate a team's activities, identify a problem, brainstorm a solution to a problem, plan for the future or review past actions.

Whenever appropriate, no matter what the specific objective of a meeting might be, servant leaders like to set the stage for conversation by encouraging a few minutes of community-building before they get down to official business. For example, if "family" or "work-life balance" is an organizational value, a leader may informally ask attendees to share upcoming vacation plans or if they have any family outings planned for the weekend. If "service" is an organizational value, a leader may tell a story of an organizational hero who excelled at providing service related to the topic of the meeting–or arrange in advance for another participant to tell such a story.

Since sharing a communal meal can be a hallmark of community-building, some sort of food service appropriate to the time of day may be included on the agenda either before, during or following the meeting. Especially if participants are not well known to each other, sharing food before or during a meeting will help them get to know each other on a social basis. This, in turn, may facilitate meeting-focused conversation.

Select participants

Carefully consider who has to be in attendance to accomplish the meeting's purpose. A general rule for effective group size is five to eleven, although there are certainly times when smaller or larger groups may be needed. If a group is too small, leaders may not be able to gather adequate information or expertise to achieve the meeting's purpose. If a group is too large, there may be insufficient time for each member to interact with others or have enough opportunity to contribute to discussions. Leaders may identify participants based on their information or expertise, authority and the need for coordination.

Consider who possesses information the group may need during discussions or who has specific expertise to offer advice to the group during decision-making or action planning.

Reflect on the authority of each participant. Be sure to invite organization members who have the authority to commit to decisions or future actions that may be the focus of the meeting.

If coordinated activity among different organizational groups may be an issue, be sure to invite members of all groups that will have to work together to achieve the meeting's goal.

Select location and set-up style

There is a message in where the leader decides to hold a meeting. If the leader wishes to project authority of position, have participants come to the leader's office or conference area. That is, hold the meeting on "home turf" where the leader may feel most comfortable and attendees will be "visitors."

If the leader desires to project a cooperative attitude, go to participants' offices/areas where they will feel comfortable or go to neutral organizational sites where all will be on equal terms.

To achieve concentration on topic, consider going offsite. Take participants away to a local hotel's conference area or a similar remote location so that attendees will not be interrupted or distracted by normal operational questions or issues.

Also, the set-up of the room affects the quality of the group's process. Remove potential distractions in the meeting area, and be careful to arrange seating in a manner that matches the leader's objective. If the purpose of the gathering is to deliver information, a classroom setting can be effective. The leader will stand in front of the group with all chairs facing forward. Attention is focused on the speaker only, and interaction is discouraged. If discussion and interaction among participants is desired, arrange tables and chairs in a circular, square or U-shaped configuration. In this case there will be no "head" of the discussion. These arrangements imply equality of status and are more supportive of face-to-face conversation. Servant leaders tend to favour circular, square or U-shaped set-ups to represent equal status among attendees and to stimulate discussion.

In the situation where a typical oval-shaped or rectangular conference table is the setting, servant leaders tend to stay away from the head of the table. Commonly, they occupy a random seat and invite another participant to sit at the head seat. This removes the potential stigma of a random participant assuming the head seat. The leader's message is "we are all equal participants in the discussion."

To ensure adequate preparation, one or two people should arrive at the meeting site early to inspect the facility arrangements and make adjustments, if necessary. That is, don't allow participants to arrive at a meeting that is not 100% ready to go. Purposeful preparation witnesses to the leader's recognition of the importance of the meeting and respect for the time and comfort of attendees.

Develop and distribute an agenda

An agenda should indicate the name of the team/group, meeting date, location, start time, end time, topics and discussion leaders.

Agenda sample

Name of the meeting/group
Date, location, start time, end time

Objective

Topic	Discussion Leader
Story	Terry
	(theme = meeting's objective)
A	Maria
B	Carlo
C	Dr. Z

Golden Rule: Stick to the agenda

The leader should decide what topics must be covered to achieve the meeting's purpose and in what sequence they will be discussed. Carefully consider timing: establish how long the meeting will last and how much time will be allocated to each topic. Allow adequate time to accomplish the meeting's objective, but keep the meeting as short as possible. Generally, meetings should be no more than an hour, although some topics may require up the ninety minutes. Avoid meetings of longer durations. It's better to have two short meetings than a single long one.

Then decide who will serve as discussion leader for each topic. Clearly indicate on the agenda the discussion topics, their sequence and the identity of each assigned discussion leader. If necessary, indicate how much time will be allocated to each topic.

Servant leaders like to put other people on the agenda. They do not dominate meetings. They provide others with opportunities to demonstrate their knowledge and abilities, develop leadership skills and even learn by teaching (there is no better means of learning than being assigned to instruct others on a topic). In other words, servant leaders typically use meetings to shine the spotlight on others, not themselves.

After all this planning has been accomplished, be sure to apply the Golden Rule of meetings: *Stick to the Agenda*.

While others serve as discussion leaders, one of the major roles assumed by the leader involves the control function. The leader should recognize when discussions go off topic and remind participants of the Golden Rule. Meetings will end on time only if the designated topics, and no others, are addressed.

Determine the manner in which the meeting will be announced to invitees (letter, memo, phone, email, etc.). Be sure the announcement includes the meeting's purpose, date, starting and ending times, location, preparatory materials or advance work needed and a deadline for confirming attendance. The agenda should be forwarded at least a few days in advance, preferably a week. Give people time to prepare–and expect them to arrive on time and prepared.

When appropriate, servant leaders put story-telling on the agenda. Meaningful stories of organizational heroes help strengthen the culture so leaders encourage the practice of beginning or ending meetings with an assigned story offered by a designated discussant.

Exercise leadership and manage group process

Even though others may serve as discussion heads, leaders maintain the responsibility to manage group process. They should keep the participants focused on the task and attend to members' interactions and needs.

Start on time and welcome participants. It is a good idea to thank those who have prepared the meeting as well as express appreciation that attendees have dedicated time and effort to prepare for their active involvement. That is, acknowledge that meetings are hard work.

The leader should orient the group by repeating the purpose of the gathering. Set the behavioural stage by clarifying expectations. Make clear for all whether the task is information-sharing, coordinating, brainstorming, advising, decision-making or something else. The leader assumes responsibility for moving through the agenda with full participation and achieving the stated purpose, but without dominating or controlling. Effective servant leaders see their jobs as maximizing the talent in the room, minimizing eccentricities, encouraging consensus and managing potential conflict.

If necessary, clarify the importance of confidentiality. Should or should not participants repeat information discussed and decisions made or disclose to others the identities of specific discussants and their opinions? In other words, set all necessary ground rules attendees are expected to observe around the confidentiality issue.

Throughout the meeting the leader should introduce each discussion leader and remain proactive in maintaining an open environment for discussion.

When complex issues are addressed, it is helpful to get many ideas on the table without ownership of or commitment to any. Creativity is encouraged when participants understand that the goal is to explore all possibilities without championing or rejecting any particular one as discussion begins. Once all ideas have been brought forward and recorded, the group will turn to its task of evaluating the effectiveness of ideas.

Leaders often employ visual aids and/or ongoing written reporting on newsprint, a white board, etc. to keep the group focused–or encourage discussion leaders to use the same.

On occasion extreme participant behaviour may be encountered in meetings. On one hand a member or two may remain "strong and silent," not revealing themselves or their opinions and thus making no contribution to the discussion. At the other extreme, one or two members may seek to dominate or take the discussion off course. In such situations leaders must intervene with discipline and respect by gently correcting the individual(s) and offering advice to the group as well. Some sample leader responses are included here under the title "Aids to participation."

The more loquacious group members may need restraining while the timid may require encouragement. The extroverts might need some mild discipline, while the introverts may need some extra time. Clearly, it is necessary for the leader to bring good judgment and strong process skills to meetings.

> **Aids to participation**
>
> **Discouraging the loquacious**
> - "We will limit each participant to a brief comment and allow each person to speak before anyone speaks a second time."
> - "Once an idea has been presented, it should not be repeated or expanded upon until we have all our ideas on the table."
>
> **Encouraging the quiet/hesitant**
> - "We'd like to hear from those who haven't had a chance to speak yet."
> - "(Name), we haven't heard your opinion yet. This would be a good time to let us know what you think."
> - "Has everyone had an opportunity to offer their thoughts?"
>
> **Discouraging sidetrackers**
> - "Let's hold that idea for later in our discussion if there is time."
> - "Let's remember our purpose and limit our discussion to that."
> - "Could we please return to our meeting goals and see if this line of thought will help us achieve our goals?"
> - "Let's back up and review our goals for this meeting."

Groups can become unbalanced, even uncomfortable, when one member's role is inflated by speaking or "winning" too often. Servant leaders are aware that consensus is the goal: meetings should not result in winners and losers. In seeking consensus on preferences or in actual decision-making, it is good practice to ensure that every participant has a chance to express themselves to the group.

Before closing, the leader should take heed of Peter Drucker's advice, "Listen first, speak last." It is the leader's responsibility as well as an effective management control technique to summarize the information, discussion and decisions that took place at the meeting so that all have a common understanding of what the group has done and what next steps are expected. Be clear about what was discussed and agreed to, what is next, who is responsible for actions and what due dates are recognized.

Be sure to end on time. Demonstrate respect for attendees' other responsibilities and their need to manage their time well.

Generate and distribute minutes

Make sure the meeting's activities are recorded. Prior to convening assign a reporter to take notes or tape the interactions so that minutes can be developed at a later time. (Don't begin the meeting by asking for a volunteer to take notes. Attendance at future meetings will be minimal, or, at least, you will notice people arriving purposely late.)

Minutes serve as records for historical documentation as well as guidance for follow-up action. Minutes should direct follow-up activities much like the agenda directs the actual meeting. A typical format includes the general information of group name (if any), meeting date, start and end time and location. Participants should be identified (present, absent, excused), and a summation of major topics and discussions should follow. Generally, only high-level summarizations should be included. Attributing specific ideas or opinions to individuals is typically avoided. Provide a short, crisp synopsis of issues discussed, each organized under a topic. The agenda's topics are usually convenient guides to organizing minutes. New recommendations for consideration or action should be noted. For historical purposes, it is helpful to include the rationale for the group's recommendations or proposed actions.

There should be a section where next steps are delineated. Include actions to be taken, responsible parties and due dates.

If a next meeting is scheduled for the group, date, time and location should be noted in the minutes.

Follow up

The work associated with a meeting is not complete just because the meeting has ended. The leader must follow up over the next several days, perhaps weeks, with all participants who left the meeting with assignments. Keep open lines of communication with participants. Ensure that action steps agreed to at the meeting are completed and due dates are maintained.

Good meetings don't just happen. They are orchestrated. Effective meeting leaders fulfil the roles of planner, conductor, facilitator, integrator and evaluator. A demanding list of the traits of a skilled meeting leader includes:

- tact
- calmness
- respect

- knowledge of meeting purpose and expectations
- authoritative but not authoritarian
- capable of eliciting participation, relating ideas, tracking common threads of discussion and pointing out areas of agreement and disagreement
- objective and even-handed in treating people, ideas and proposals
- proficient in phrasing questions and issues so discussion is generated (avoiding simple "Yes" and "No" responses)
- capable of summarizing meeting progress and suggesting future activity of the group, and
- flexible in responding to a range of personality types and various group sizes.

Forgiving

With great insight James Hunter (2004, 100-101) writes:

> People often remark that they believe forgiveness to be a strange character skill to have on a leadership list, yet I remain convinced it is one of the most important. Why? Because when you are a leader, people are going to make mistakes. A lot of them. Your boss, your peers, your subordinates, your spouse, your kids, your teammates are going to screw up, make mistakes, and let you down. People will hurt you, sometimes deeply. Many will not make the efforts you believe they should or care as deeply as you do. Some will fail to respond to all the effort you have put in. A few will try to take advantage of you.
>
> Which is why it is essential for the leader to develop the skill (habit) of accepting limitations in others and the capacity to tolerate imperfection. The leader must develop the skill of letting go of the resentment that often lingers when people hurt us or let us down. After all, anyone could lead perfect people, if only there were any.

Most text books on leadership and management avoid the concept of forgiveness. Just check the index. There are words like reprimand, punishment, coercive power, positive and negative reinforcement, conflict, relationship conflict, conflict management, stressors, stress management, workplace misbehaviour and workplace spirituality. But rarely is there mention of the act of forgiving those who have wronged us or wronged the organization–whether it is for the sake of personal healing, preserving relationships, improving future effectiveness and productivity or for managing stress related to the challenges of leadership. Forgiving can contribute to all of these positive outcomes.

Perhaps forgiveness is not a popular workplace topic because it carries with it a sense of letting people get away with something–either they failed to produce an outcome that is part of their job responsibility, or they behaved in a manner that hurt us or others in a serious way. But, as Hunter assures us, forgiving is not the same as being passive about poor performance nor is it about letting people step all over us. Forgiving is not about letting people get away with their bad behaviour or pretending it is acceptable. Servant leaders hold people accountable for their actions. If their actions deserve consequences, those consequences should be delivered by the leader through legitimate authority. That's honesty. That's acting with integrity. Forgiveness has more to do with what happens after the action-accountability-consequence sequence has occurred.

Forgiving involves going to people and communicating assertively with them about the way their actions (or lack of actions) have affected us and/or others, dealing with the organizational and personal (perhaps emotional) results, then *letting things go without lingering resentment or vengefulness*.

Psychologists suggest that forgiveness be viewed as something for you, not a gift to someone else. It is not letting someone else off the hook for the wrong that they committed. In his Nine Steps to Forgiveness program, Fred Luskin emphasizes that forgiveness is best seen as something that will bring you peace and closure–and reduce your resentment. Forgiveness is more a strategic repair for us personally and for our relationships.

At one time or another all leaders find themselves in very negative situations that call for forgiving others. Followers may ignore their job responsibilities and boost their own egos by bragging to peers about putting one over on their leader. Co-workers might refuse to cooperate on a project to assert what they believe to be their greater power within the organization. Bosses may cause personal embarrassment by making statements to others about a leader's perceived character imperfections or limited abilities. These situations and countless others may cause emotional pain and risk initiating long-term resentment between a leader and others in the workplace.

Experts who study forgiveness make clear that when you forgive someone such as a follower, co-worker or boss, you do not gloss over or deny the seriousness of an offense against you or the organization. Forgiveness does not mean condoning or excusing offenses. Rather, forgiveness brings peace of mind to the leader and frees her or him from the effects of corrosive anger. Some debate exists over the nature of true forgiveness: does it or does it not require positive feelings toward the offender? But experts agree that it at least involves letting go of deeply held negative feelings. In that way, forgiving empowers us to recognize the pain we suffered without letting that pain define us, enabling us to heal and move on with our work and our relationships.

Yes, forgiveness is good for relationships. When we feel wronged, we may hold a grudge which makes us less likely as servant leaders to sacrifice for or support others. In turn this undermines feelings of trust and commitment. Forgiving can stop this downward spiral and help to repair relationships.

How do we develop the skill of forgiving? Certainly, we need to be honest with ourselves regarding our own feelings. This requires being in touch with our own values and emotions. We need to communicate our feelings to those we believe offended us through their behaviour or performance. Ruminating on negative feelings is both unhealthy and unproductive. Since the organization also possesses values that define boundaries of acceptable behaviour, leaders must bring those into consideration as well. Also, leaders need to measure performance so that accountability is brought into relationships in an equitable manner. Of course, we need to share performance standards with all so that expectations are clear. And we need to empathize with others, especially those we consider offenders, so that we are capable of assessing the distress or remorse offenders may feel as well as the effects such emotions may have on them.

Servant Leader Tips – Forgiving
Be honest with yourself: recognize the emotional element of your relationships with others; be aware how others' behaviour and performance affect you personally
Admit that emotions have a place in human interactions–even at work; be willing to express your emotions to others; they deserve to know how you feel about their behaviour or performance
Hold people accountable for their behaviour; know the organization's values and insist others' actions are guided by them as your actions are guided by them
Hold people accountable for their performance; set high standards and measure results; ensure others know the standards
Cultivate empathy; when you have been hurt, you'll be more likely to forgive—and less likely to retaliate—if you can appreciate the distress or remorse felt by the person who hurt you

Humorously, Hunter describes the "biggest jerk I know," the person who commits ridiculous blunders, who causes personal hurt and business losses. Of course, he goes on to identify that person as himself. Aren't we all guilty of underperforming at one time or another as well as causing ourselves embarrassment, even shame, through personal behaviour? Yet, we find ways to look beyond our own poor performance. We are able to separate ourselves from our bad behaviour, forgive the person (not the behaviour) and move on. "Forgiveness is an attribute of love. So the question now becomes, are we willing to love others as we love ourselves?" (Hunter 2004, 104)

In considering our own need to develop and practice the skill of forgiving, it's good to remember what Hunter says: anyone could lead perfect people, if only there were any.

CHAPTER FOUR

BEHAVIOURS

Behaviours are applications of servant leaders' adopted attitudes and developed skills. Attitudes are mental states of readiness leaders learn and organize through their experiences, and skills are abilities to do something well stemming from leaders' knowledge, practice or aptitude. But neither attitudes nor skills create real value for leaders or their organizations until they are put to use through behaviours.

Like all of us, leaders develop habits, acquired behaviour patterns followed until they become almost involuntary. As Stephen Covey suggests, habits exist at the intersection of knowledge, skill and desire. Over time these customary practices evolve into parts of a leader's routines and are recognized by others as part of a leader's character. Servant leaders practice certain behaviours that become integral elements of their personal leadership style.

Leaders who serve do special things for their organizations. They set the stage for other people to succeed. Because high numbers of workers realise success, organizations achieve great things. This chapter is about the behaviours servant leaders use to set the stage for others. It's about the way servant leaders act to establish and maintain a supportive, facilitative work environment or organizational climate.

Different terms and approaches are used to describe the work environment servant leaders create.

- John Maxwell says leaders empower people in the workplace. He discusses his Law of Empowerment where leaders themselves have a strong sense of self-worth, and where they believe not only in themselves but also in their mission and their people. To Maxwell *empowering* followers means leaders help others reach their potential by being on their side, encouraging them, giving them power and helping them to succeed.
- James Kouzes and Barry Posner write about *enabling others to act* through fostering collaboration by building trust and facilitating relationships. And they say leaders also enable others to act through

strengthening others by increasing self-determination and developing competence.
- Nancy Ortberg says servant leaders *release others to do their work* by trusting them as they trust themselves to accomplish outstanding results.
- James Hunter describes the servant environment as one in which mission-driven leaders and workers *simultaneously accomplish goals and build relationships*–where excellence is demanded, people are held accountable for performance and community is built.
- Ken Blanchard describes a climate where people willingly, even enthusiastically, contribute their hearts, minds, creativity, excellence and other resources toward mutually beneficial goals. That is, it's an environment where workers *commit to the mission and to becoming the best they are capable of becoming.*
- James Autry says servant leadership is concerned with creating a place in which *people can do good work, find meaning in their work and bring their spirits to work.*

Many leaders notice that some organizations seem to have climates which produce high employee motivation and initiative as well as outstanding outcomes. Naturally, they want their organization to have the same type of environment. They ask their peers or, perhaps, consultants or academics what they can do to offer the same type of work conditions. Typically hoping for a short prescription for success, they are disappointed. Instead, what their investigations help them realize is that they want the benefits of servant leadership. But they find out adopting servant leadership can be a long, challenging change process that begins with leaders adopting new attitudes, developing new skills and practicing new behaviours.

As discussed above, servant leaders create a climate where workers act on their own initiative, are empowered, enabled to act, released to do their work, simultaneously accomplish goals and build relationships, commit to mission and to becoming the best they are capable of becoming and/or do good work, find meaning in their work and bring their spirits to work. Use whatever terms are meaningful to you. This climate is created because servant leaders use the behaviours described here.

First, leaders are proactive and they set the stage for their workers to be proactive. This occurs because everyone understands in what direction the organization wants to move, and everyone is aware of the values they are expected to exemplify as they work. Therefore, all know what they are expected to achieve and how they are expected to behave.

Second, as discussed by Kouzes and Posner, leaders establish their credibility by being recognized by followers as honest, forward-looking, competent and inspiring. So followers have confidence in their leaders, and they are motived to act.

Next, servant leaders establish environments where people trust each other. Trust enables followers to talk about their values and feelings as well as show concern for each other. They are comfortable discussing the uncertain future and sharing information, opinions, feedback, goals and results. They admit mistakes and concede weaknesses that can be strengthened through self-improvement. Trusting leaders and co-workers acknowledge others' contributions, listen to each other and are willing to be influenced by others. So teamwork improves.

Finally, people feel confident they can do good work because they are connected through their own networks to all the resources they need. Leaders have their own productive and mutually supportive relationships, and they assist followers in establishing their own. Because workers operate within this environment, they use their initiative, are comfortable being accountable for their results and achieve great things without much direct intervention by the servant leader.

This empowering climate cannot be prescribed in a few bullet points by consultants or well-meaning peers. It is highly complex to those unfamiliar with servant leadership. Even some servant leaders are challenged to describe exactly what they do in their organizations. Typically, they just point to their workers and say something like, "It's nothing special I do, it's all about them. They accomplish great things." Yes, but the servant leaders set the stage.

Now that we have discussed servant leader attitudes and skills in earlier chapters, we are ready to discuss the behaviours servant leaders bring to their environments to encourage initiative, empower others, enable them to act, release them to do their work, and so on. We approach this task by examining how servant leaders are proactive and encourage followers to be proactive. Then we see how leaders establish their credibility with followers and build a climate where mutually trusting relationships flourish. Next we see how servant leaders build their own networks for support and communication, and how they support followers in building their own networks. Once these building blocks are in place, we examine in more detail how others describe this work environment that empowers others to act. Finally in this chapter, we turn our attention to a few other behaviours that tend to distinguish servant leaders from others.

Specifically, these include how servant leaders view and embrace change, engage in planning based on a shared vision and how they practice reflection on a regular basis.

Being proactive

In his powerful book *The 7 Habits of Highly Effective People* Stephen Covey identifies "Be Proactive" as habit number one. He writes that effective people use their strong self-awareness to be proactive and take responsibility for their choices. That is, in order to be effective one must be proactive. Proactive people know they choose their behaviour. They believe they are products of their decisions, not circumstances. They don't blame things on others or on conditions they cannot control. Proactive people take responsibility for their lives and choices. Reactive people take a passive stance. They believe that the world is happening to them. When things aren't right, they tend to blame their behaviour on external sources or the environment.

"Try to be more proactive." Have you ever heard those words in a performance review session or from a parent, coach or mentor? It's good advice for those who need it because people tend to be more successful when they are bold, driven and energetic rather than passive. Also, teams and organizations perform at higher levels when members are motivated and when individuals take charge and champion new initiatives. Proactive people make things happen. Research shows they are more likely to achieve positive results and encourage a joyful workplace. Proactive people create or control situations more effectively than those who wait to respond to events.

However, a problem may have arisen when you decided to take the suggestion to behave more proactively. You may have had no idea how to start. Proactivity can depend on two factors, individual behavioural characteristics and the environment in which one operates. It's the effects of the environment that interest us in this discussion because the proposition here involves servant leaders and how they create a workplace environment that supports their entire set of followers in being proactive. Yes, servant leaders set the stage for everyone to develop action plans and produce meaningful results.

To examine the relationship between servant leadership and followers' proactive behaviour, management expert Peter Drucker's ideas related to effective executive action will be examined. In his 2004 classic *Harvard Business Review* article, "What Makes an Effective Executive," Drucker poses two questions that executives must answer before they can be confident enough to develop action plans on their own. He writes:

> An effective executive does not need to be a leader in the sense that the term is now most commonly used. Harry Truman did not have one ounce of charisma, for example, yet he was among the most effective chief executives in U.S. history. Similarly, some of the best business and non-profit CEOs I've worked with over a 65-year consulting career were not stereotypical leaders. They were all over the map in terms of their personalities, attitudes, values, strengths, and weaknesses. They ranged from extroverted to nearly reclusive, from easygoing to controlling, from generous to parsimonious.
>
> What made them all effective is that they followed the same eight practices:
> - *They asked, "What needs to be done?"*
> - *They asked, "What is right for the enterprise?"*
> - *They developed action plans.* (italics of bullets added)
> - They took responsibility for decisions.
> - They took responsibility for communicating.
> - They were focused on opportunities rather than problems.
> - They ran productive meetings.
> - They thought and said "we" rather than "I" (Drucker 2004, 59).

Drucker goes on to tell us that the effective executives he writes about are doers; they execute. Their or others' knowledge and expertise are useless until translated into deeds. Prior to springing into action, executives must plan their course by thinking about results desired, likely constraints, potential future revisions, check-in points and the implications for how they will spend their time.

Drilling a bit deeper into Drucker's framework, he suggests effective executives' action plans should address the following questions:

- What contributions should the enterprise expect from me over the next 18 months to two years?
- What results will I commit to, with what deadlines?

Then, considering restraints on action, executives ask:

- Is this course of action ethical? Is it legal?
- Is this course of action acceptable within the organization; is it compatible with the mission, values and policies of the organization?

By asking "What needs to be done?" Drucker explains the executives he is discussing are able to focus their activities on issues of strategic importance to the organization's work. Their actions will be well directed, substantive and meaningful, contributing directly to organizational success.

By asking "What is right for the enterprise?" executives ensure their action plans take into consideration the short- and long-term expectations of all stakeholders in a balanced way, and their action plans will be developed to align with the organization's mission, values and policies. This alignment is vital so that their action plans will conform fully to these important organizational boundaries or constraints. Drucker concludes that collecting information through these two questions increases an executive's (read "individual's") confidence that initiatives will be welcome within their organization; that is, the "fit" will be right because meaningful results will be achieved and behavioural boundaries will be respected.

Also, Drucker instructs that an action plan should include checkpoints at which results will be compared to expectations. This allows executives to adjust their action plans to achieve desired results. Since an organization, its needs and its expected results evolve continually with economic, market and behavioural changes, it is important to assess intermittently answers to the above questions to ensure that a developed action plan meets organizational needs.

Notice that nowhere does Drucker suggest that effective executives (or others) sit and wait to be told what their assignment is or how to accomplish their tasks. Obviously, there is no room for waiting in today's dynamic marketplaces and demanding work environments.

Proactive behaviour means people take action. They get things done–accomplish tasks, advance the organization toward its goals–without being told what to do by anyone. Being proactive involves knowing what needs to be done for the organization's benefit (not one's own benefit), planning a course of action and achieving desired results through, as Drucker describes, effective decision-making, communication, focus on opportunities instead of problems and meetings. Typically, to engage in proactive behaviour, people ask Drucker's two questions to acquire the necessary knowledge, develop an action plan and forge ahead.

Now let's look at this approach from a servant leadership perspective. Servant leaders apply visioning skills to paint a picture of the organization's brighter future and help unify the enterprise by ensuring all constituents share that vision. Therefore, all followers are aware of the results desired within the organization. The ends are clear; accomplish the leader-articulated shared vision. Workers know it is their responsibility to create the means. Their action plans are meant to take the enterprise from where it is today to vision realisation. They don't need to ask the question, "What needs to be done?" The servant leader's vision provides the answer. And, since all followers share the vision, each individual's action plans should be expected to aim in the same direction. Conflicts caused by not "rowing in the same direction" are minimized.

Addressing boundaries or constraints to which action plans must conform, servant leaders build community around mission and shared values as well as vision. Behavioural values are well recognized (and, expectedly, lived) by constituents. Therefore, there is little need for followers to ask, "What is right for the enterprise?" They already know. If their proactive behaviours respect organizational values, their actions will be welcome. No need to wonder what activities are acceptable.

Aware of the organization's needs and what is right for the enterprise, all constituents of a servant led operation have the conditions of proactive behaviour. Everyone is prepared to take action. Facilitated by their servant leader, workers can be comfortable devising action plans to achieve the vision while respecting the organization's values. Leaders provide the direction and constraints through their practice of the servant leadership style. There is no need for wondering what to achieve or being intimidated by lack of boundary awareness. Followers are ready to act on their own.

For the servant led organization, proactivity is not a characteristic restricted to executives or leaders. All followers are empowered to act. Servant leaders create the environment for action taking. They make it easy for followers to be proactive because the desired direction and the behavioural boundaries are communicated to them and modelled for them.

In his best-selling book *Good to Great* Jim Collins describes the Level 5 leadership style that his research identified as necessary for turning a good company into a great one.

> Compared to high-profile leaders with big personalities who make headlines and become celebrities, the good-to-great leaders seem to come from Mars. Self-effacing, quiet, reserved, even shy–these leaders are a paradoxical blend of personal humility and professional will (Collins 2001, 12-13).

Collins goes on to describe further the professional will of these leaders to take action and produce results. He writes,

> Level 5 leaders are fanatically driven, infected with an incurable need to produce sustained results. They are resolved to do whatever it takes to

make the company great, no matter how big or hard the decisions (2001, 39).

Also, he discusses how Level 5 leaders display compelling modesty. When asked to explain their organization's success, Level 5 leaders attribute achievements to others. Typically, they downplay their personal contributions. They credit their proactive staff and other followers for accomplishing great things on their own.

There are many parallels between Level 5 leaders and servant leaders. As we have seen in this discussion, effective leaders create the environment in which followers can flourish. One way they do so is by expecting constituents to make things happen guided by the organization's vision (future direction) as well as values and beliefs (boundaries). Once this playing field for success is established, servant leaders, like Collins' Level 5 leaders, feel comfortable letting followers exercise their proactivity. There is no temptation to micromanage. There is no compulsion to look over shoulders. Followers are empowered to take action and produce expected results. Leaders monitor progress by fervently measuring results, confident that their team understands and is committed to vision and values. The servant leader role is educator, then facilitator and coach.

Examining organizational results more closely, let's attend to Drucker's effectiveness practice of focusing on opportunities rather than problems. Within this book it has already been argued that servant leaders practice the skill of being optimistic. Concentrating on opportunities instead of problems is certainly a form of optimism, but it's also a very effective approach for leaders committed to achieving outstanding results.

Problems must be addressed, of course. They cannot be ignored by leaders. Commonly, however, problem solving is about containing damage to performance. Recognizing and exploiting opportunities can produce growth and exceptional outcomes.

Good servant leaders institute processes that focus on opportunities and, at the same time, provide avenues for followers' personal growth and development. Instead of falling into a familiar management trap of assigning one's best people to an organization's most pressing problems, some servant leaders put their best people on the enterprise's most promising opportunities. For example, every six months or so leaders prepare two lists: 1) current or developing opportunities and 2) team members and their skills and interests. Then they match opportunities to team members and challenge individuals to develop action plans for innovating, improving and growing. Successful new actions aimed at specific opportunities hold the promise of remarkable results.

Helpfully, Drucker (and many others) provides a few guidelines for identifying opportunities. To adopt the most direct approach, look for opportunity anywhere change touches an enterprise. Identifying change both inside and outside the organization can focus attention on a potential opportunity for growth and get the grey cells firing. Some types of change could be: new knowledge or a new technology; shifts in demographics; alterations in industry structure or market structure; innovations in processes, products or services both within and outside one's own industry; unexpected successes or failures within one's own organization or a competitor's organization; and any unexplained gap between what is and what could be in a market, product or service.

The behaviour of being proactive calls for adopting at least the following servant leader attitudes: think and say "we," not "I"; value statements are meant to be put into practice, not stored on a shelf; vision isn't everything, but it's the beginning of everything; I am committed to your (staff's) success; as well as it's useful to give my power away. Being proactive also calls for applying these servant leader skills: knowing and sharing one's personal values; saying "we"; being optimistic (focusing on opportunities rather than problems); visioning; and running a meeting.

Servant Leader Tips – Being proactive
Be aware that passive people wait for events to occur, then respond to them; proactive people are much more likely to create or control events; proactive people are more effective in organizations than passive people
Support proactive behaviour; it will lead to more workers taking bold action and championing new initiatives
According to Peter Drucker, individuals aren't confident developing action plans before they have answers to the questions: "What needs to be done?" and "What is right for the enterprise?"
Set the stage for followers' proactive behaviour by communicating clearly and continuously the organization's vision (desired future) and values (behavioural guidelines, boundaries, constraints)
Follow progress by fervently measuring results; do not micromanage or look over workers' shoulders
To achieve outstanding results focus on opportunities rather than problems
Help achieve outstanding results and support followers' personal growth by assigning people to organizational opportunities, not problems
Look for opportunities where changes are occurring

Establishing credibility

It would be encouraging to say this particular servant leader habitual behaviour can be developed quickly and is guaranteed to be long-lasting. Alas, exactly the opposite is true concerning the single most important behaviour relevant to servant leadership, establishing one's credibility. A reputation for being believable and trustworthy takes a long time to build, and it can be forfeited in a heartbeat. Establishing credibility isn't easy or convenient, but it is necessary for servant leaders.

The concept of establishing credibility is derived directly from James Kouzes and Barry Posner's practical, accessible and inspirational leadership research published in their books *Credibility* and *The Leadership Challenge*. Citing the reciprocal relationship between those who lead and those who choose to follow in *Credibility*, Kouzes and Posner state:

> Credibility is about how leaders earn the trust and confidence of their constituents. It's about what people demand of their leaders as a prerequisite to willingly contributing their hearts, minds, bodies and souls. It's about the actions leaders must take in order to intensify their constituents' commitment to a common cause (2003, xiii).

In *The Leadership Challenge*, the authors refer to credibility as "the foundation of leadership." Followers need to be able to trust their leaders, and leaders' actions must reinforce what they say and believe. As stated in their First Law of leadership: "If you don't believe in the messenger, you won't believe the message." Leaders make clear to their followers what they stand for, believe in and care about.

How do leaders establish credibility? According to Kouzes and Posner's research, there are four major contributors. Leaders must be perceived by followers as *honest, forward looking, competent and inspiring*.

Honesty

This is the most important element of the leader-constituent relationship. "Character" and "integrity" are frequently used as synonyms for this vital leadership attribute. Leaders' behaviours, not their words alone, evidence their honesty. From a follower's perspective there must be consistency between their leader's words and deeds. "If leaders espouse one set of values but personally practice another, we find them to be duplicitous" (Kouzes and Posner 2003, 37.) Leaders walk the talk; they do what they say they will do. Sounds straightforward, doesn't it?

Of all the leadership characteristics, honesty is the most personal. Values, the standards that guide conduct in a variety of situations, are not just for preaching. They are for acting out. People expect one to practice what one preaches, and they notice if their leaders don't. Followers expect leaders to keep their promises, and they fail to trust leaders who don't. Many elements of good leadership are just common sense, not rocket science.

Honesty starts by knowing oneself. For leaders this is evidenced by awareness of personal values. Servant leaders are in touch with their behavioural guidelines and the sources of those guidelines. They communicate their values through stories they tell about their personal experiences, demonstrating that they deeply understand their beliefs about right and wrong, good and bad, fairness and unfairness. Stories also communicate how those personal principles were learned from parents, family members, teachers, coaches, clergy, mentors, leadership role models, past successes and failures as well as a variety of other people and life experiences. Leaders make clear that they follow in others' footsteps, and they appreciate the important lessons that have been passed along to them.

Also, servant leaders emphasize how their personal values coincide with their organization's values. Every opportunity is taken to talk about and, importantly, demonstrate consistency between their personal life and their work life. Of course, leaders ensure their behaviours mirror their values because they realize followers are always observing.

Leaders understand their promises should never be made casually because broken promises brand leaders as dishonest and result in forfeited credibility. While this is always true, one special situation deserves attention. When leaders first assume their authoritative position, some followers employ a strategy of bringing up in discussion some of their favourite improvement ideas or pet projects (probably ones that past leaders have not supported). In doing so, they try to get the new leader to agree with them. Simple, innocuous responses such as, "Yes, that sounds like a good idea," "We'll have to look into that" or even "Maybe" can be interpreted as a promise by hopeful workers trying to win the new boss over to their side. Leaders who want to avoid any appearance of giving promises that later may be interpreted as "broken" are cautious with their language.

Therefore, it's often an effective policy for new leaders to state to all that the first few weeks or months on the job will be spent listening and "getting the lay of the land," and no major changes will be contemplated or commitments made until the listening period has concluded. This or a similar approach can help avoid any minefields associated with perceived broken promises during the early days of a new leader's tenure.

Admitting mistakes, in many (but not all) cultures, is another common means of establishing a reputation for honesty. Servant leaders adopt the attitude that we are all imperfect; we all make mistakes. They don't attempt to deny or hide their errors. Instead, they admit fallibility and model the behaviour of learning and growing from mistakes.

Holding people accountable for their behaviour and job performance is another contributor to a leader's reputation for honesty. In his discussions of servant leadership James Hunter discusses the linkage between honesty and accountability. He writes:

> A major aspect of honesty and being free from deception is in how we hold people accountable for their actions. If we fail to do so, we are not leading honestly, because accountability is our responsibility as leaders, along with helping people be the best they can be. It is deceptive behaviour because failure to hold people accountable creates an illusion that everything is okay, and everything is *not* okay (2004, 106).

Sometimes holding followers accountable is referred to as telling the "hard truth" because confronting under-performers can be a challenging and uncomfortable task for leaders. Hunter (2004, 118) continues:

> Who benefits when the manager does not hold people accountable? Certainly not the employees, because they will not be better off when they leave than when they got there. In fact, they will probably be worse off because they, like the rest of us, are moving in a direction, either getting better or getting worse. The organization certainly does not benefit, although the competition probably will. About the only one who benefits is the manager, because he or she doesn't have to deal with it and can avoid the hassle.
>
> Just think how self-serving and dishonest that is! Someday, an honest leader may follow this self-serving manager, and now the employee can discount the truth: "They've told me I'm great around here for ten years, and now you're telling me I'm not? *You* must be the problem!

People practicing servant leadership don't make excuses for accepting below-standard performance. They don't, as many do, avoid the situation by trying to convince themselves that a certain under-performer is "otherwise a really nice person," or "takes criticism too personally," or "might quit" or is "intimidating."

Servant leaders address under-performing situations directly by discussing the gap between high expectations and actual outcome assessments. They work with the employee to discover causes and jointly seek to identify remedies. They act as facilitator in discussing resources that can be provided to support better performance. And they act as coach in expressing confidence that the worker can meet high expectations in the future.

If performance remains sub-standard after remedies have been attempted, credible leaders remove individuals who fail to perform. In other words, they recognize their responsibility to be fair to other workers and to ensure high performance for the organization and a variety of stakeholders.

Another form of honesty among servant leaders is the willingness to deliver bad news to superiors. The organizational phenomenon of "filtering" is based on workers' unwillingness to pass along bad news such as poor job performance, product/service quality issues, customer complaints and the like to people in higher positions because they don't want to deal with the consequences of taking the blame or upsetting the boss. In organizations where filtering occurs, people at the top of the hierarchy are "protected" from the truth and develop a false view of their organization's performance. Honest leaders pass along the bad news as well as the good. They tell the truth–the whole truth.

Also, this well-known human tendency to filter out bad news in organizations is the reason servant leaders say "thank you" whenever bad news is delivered to them. They don't blame the messenger. Rather, they express appreciation that the messenger has told the whole truth. As a result, servant leaders are much more likely to get *all* the news in the future.

Some servant leader skills that can contribute to establishing a reputation for honesty are: being aware of personal values; telling stories to demonstrate how leaders live their values and where those values came from; and forgiving themselves and others for mistakes.

Servant Leader Tips – Establishing a reputation for honesty
Be aware of your personal values
Tell stories to demonstrate your values and how you learned them from others
Tell stories that include examples of how your personal values match organizational values
Be sure your personal and work behaviours model your values; understand that followers notice
Keep your promises; be careful to avoid making promises you cannot keep

Admit your mistakes; demonstrate the attitude that no one is perfect and we all have room for improvement
Tell the hard truth; inform people when their job performance is below standard or their behaviour does not conform to shared values; hold them accountable
Tell the whole truth; pass along bad news when necessary; don't filter bad news to avoid dealing with an unhappy boss
Say "thank you for telling me" when people give you bad news

Forward-looking

Exemplary leaders exhibit a concern for the future and are able to articulate a sense of direction. After all, followers can only join leaders on a shared journey if leaders seem to know where everyone is going. "An expectation that their leaders be *forward-looking* is what sets leaders apart from other credible individuals" (Kouzes and Posner 2012, 37). Constituents want to know what will be better in the future. They want to understand the reasons for their hard work and sacrifice. Forward-looking leaders have a talent for expressing a positive, optimistic and worthy view of tomorrow.

Being forward-looking doesn't mean leaders have to imitate Nostradamus and divine future events. Kouzes and Posner (2003, 29) tell us:

> By the ability to be forward-looking, people don't mean the magical powers of a prescient visionary. The reality is far more down-to-earth: it's the ability to set or select a desirable destination toward which the company, agency, congregation, or community should head. Visions reveal the beckoning summit that provides others with the capacity to chart their course toward the future. As constituents, we ask that a leader have a well-defined orientation toward the future. We want to know what the organization will look like, feel like, be like when it arrives at its destination in six quarters or six years. We want to have it described for us in rich detail so that we'll know when we've arrived and so that we can select the proper route for getting there.

A significant finding from Kouzes and Posner's research involves the relationship between a leader's hierarchical level and followers' expectation of the forward-looking leadership attribute. Clearly, for leaders at senior levels, there is almost universal expectation that leaders be forward-looking because it's understood that their job responsibilities include planning for the long-term organizational future. At the other end of the spectrum, let's say frontline supervisors, the forward-looking expectation still exists, but it is less strong. Leaders in lower-level roles are understood to have a more problem-solving than forward-looking focus. Still, however, followers expect even their lower-level supervisors to be forward-looking.

Are you perceived by others as forward-looking? Audit your own conversations. How often do you speak in the future tense as opposed to the past and present? How often do you articulate what can be right rather than what is wrong? Do people refer to you as optimistic?

To be perceived as forward-looking, polish your skills for visioning and being optimistic. You will be better prepared for creating the impression that you think and care about the future.

Competent

A reputation for competence is supported by a leader's track record, the demonstrated ability to get things done. To attain credibility, constituents must perceive their leaders as capable and effective in their organization's significant tasks. Competence inspires followers' confidence that the leader will be qualified to guide the organization in the espoused forward-looking direction. Followers ask, "Can this leader get us there?"

Here, leaders can demonstrate relevant experience in their organization and/or in their profession. Formal education, licensing, certification, development of job-related knowledge as well as a variety of career and life experiences can also be evidence that leaders possess competence. In many cases, time and patience are required in developing a track record of success and skill attainment. One does not become competent overnight.

Kouzes and Posner state, "The most important competency a leader brings to the role is the ability to work well with others" (2002, 30-31). Servant leaders facilitate others' success. They must be able to bring out the best in followers. Well-polished interpersonal skills and a history of working productively in team experiences–as both a leader and a follower–will go a long way in demonstrating competence for servant leadership in any industry, market, professional service environment or any other work-related context.

Skills that confirm the ability to work productively with others will demonstrate competence. These proficiencies include listening, asking questions, telling stories, saying "we," stimulating informal conversations, managing time, running a meeting and forgiving.

Inspiring

Leaders inspire others when they are enthusiastic, energetic and positive about the future. They encourage others to join them in pursuing a vision through their passion. Their emotions are contagious. Body language is emotionally expressive.

> (Inspiring) people lean forward in their chairs, they move their arms about, their eyes light up, their voices sing with emotion, and they smile. They are enthusiastic, articulate, optimistic, and uplifting. In short, people are inspiring! (Kouzes and Posner 2002, 144)

If leaders cannot display passion for their cause, why should anyone else?

Expressing a positive view and sincere passion for the future can be very uncomfortable for some individuals. Many people are sceptical of their own ability to inspire others, so they simply hesitate to "stick their neck out" by exposing their personal vision for a better future. After all, what if no one cares and nobody follows?

Leading is not easy, convenient or free from risk. However, the rewards can be great. As Kouzes and Posner (2002, 31) write:

> Inspiring leadership speaks to our need to have meaning and purpose in our lives. Further, being upbeat, positive, and optimistic about the future offers people hope. This is crucial at any time, but in times of great uncertainty, leading with positive emotions is absolutely essential to moving people upward and forward. When people are worried, discouraged, frightened, and uncertain about the future, the *last* thing needed is a leader who feeds those negative emotions. Instead, we need leaders who communicate in words, demeanour, and actions that they believe we *will* overcome. To get *extraordinary* things done in *extraordinary* times, leaders must inspire optimal performance–and that can only be fuelled with positive emotions.

Similar to the forward-looking attribute, skills that support inspiring others include visioning and being optimistic. Also, leaders should recall Warren Bennis' admonition that leadership and the performance arts have much in common. To inspire others to act, leaders may find it necessary to tap their personal passion and apply it to whatever Shakespeare they can find in their souls.

Establishing and maintaining credibility is vital for servant leadership success. And those who aspire to lead must know that this precious personal attribute is all about perception. Leaders can't declare themselves to be credible or demand that others recognize credibility in them based upon facts or rational thinking. Followers have to perceive credibility in their leaders. Credibility is attributed to leaders by followers who perceive them to be honest, forward-looking, competent and inspiring.

Servant leaders should attend well to what James Kouzes and Barry Posner say about leadership and credibility. Leadership is a relationship; it is personal; it is about you and me. Leaders serve. Leaders sacrifice. Leaders keep hope alive. And credibility is the foundation of leadership.

Building trust

As has been discussed, to a large measure establishing personal credibility for a leader is about being believed and perceived as honest (or possessing integrity or character) by followers. In other words, it's about being trusted by constituents on a personal basis. Servant leaders seek to develop trust between themselves and followers, and they strive to build an environment of trust among all in an open, honest workplace.

Trust is the lynchpin of leadership. Without it, power is lost. Without it, leaders will fail to drive any team or organization forward. Practically every topic addressed in this book either contributes to trust building or is a result of a trusting environment. Let's examine what leadership authors say about trust.

Peter Drucker writes simply that the final requirement of effective leadership is to earn trust. Otherwise, there won't be any followers–and the only definition of a leader is someone who has followers.

Stephen Covey describes trust as a stimulus for taking initiative and attaining self-sufficiency. However, he cautions that trust cannot be developed overnight and that people who are trusted to accomplish work may still need support. Covey writes,

> Trust is the highest form of human motivation. It brings out the very best in people. But it takes time and patience, and it doesn't preclude the necessity to train and develop people so that their competency can rise to the level of that trust. (1989, 178).

Trust provides motivation for followers to go beyond simple compliance with a leader's authority. It stimulates them to reach for the best within themselves, their work group and their organization.

In discussing the importance of leaders adopting the "We, not I" philosophy, Kouzes and Posner (2012, 219) state:

However, "we" can't happen without trust. It's the central issue in human relationships. Without trust you cannot lead. Without trust you can't get people to believe in you or in each other. Without trust you cannot accomplish extraordinary things. Individuals who are unable to trust others fail to become leaders, precisely because they can't bear to be dependent on the words and works of others. They either end up doing all the work themselves or supervising work so closely that they become overcontrolling. Their obvious lack of trust in others results in others' lack of trust in them. To build and sustain social connections, you have to be able to trust others, and others have to trust you. Trust is not just what's in your mind; it's also what's in your heart.

Nancy Ortberg remarks on the importance of trust and observes, like Drucker, that trust is not awarded to leaders just because they have been promoted to positional authority by their organization. Ortberg says,

> Trust is the foundational element of any good leader, and it has to be earned. You have to lay a foundation of trust before people can individually do their best (2004, 89).

Also, she suggests that in regard to task accomplishment and teamwork there is a need to be comfortable trusting others as we trust ourselves.

> Teamwork and collaboration can only happen when people trust each other. As leaders, we have no trouble trusting ourselves. We have to learn to put the same trust in other people that we put in ourselves and then release them to do the work (2004, 89).

One of John Maxwell's 21 irrefutable laws of leadership is the Law of Solid Ground. Maxwell offers several noteworthy thoughts on how trust connects to influence, decision-making and character:

> How important is trust for a leader? It is *the most important thing*. Trust is the foundation of leadership. It is the glue that holds an organization together. Leaders cannot repeatedly break trust with people and continue to influence them. It just doesn't happen (2007, 61).

> Trust is like change in a leader's pocket. Each time you make good leadership decisions, you earn more change. Each time you make poor decisions, you pay out some of your change to the people. All leaders have a certain amount of change in their pocket when they start in a new leadership position. Whatever they do either builds up their change or depletes it ... When you're out of change, you're out as the leader (2007, 63).

How does a leader build trust? By consistently exemplifying competence, connection, and character. People will forgive occasional mistakes based on ability, especially if they can see that you're still growing as a leader. And they will give you some time to connect. But they won't trust someone who slips in character. In that area, even occasional lapses are lethal (2007, 63-64).

In discussing the values of servant leaders and their associated workplaces, James Autry writes:

> If one of the personal values is trust, this means the leaders must trust the people and, in turn, must be trustworthy. Again, one thing leads to another. Creating a trusting environment means a workplace in which people are part of the decisions about the goals to be accomplished, then are trusted to do the work without constant supervision (looking over their shoulders), in which rewards and recognition are based on results and not on favouritism, in which rules and policies are as few as possible and as flexible as possible in accommodating individual human needs. And so on (2001, 33).

As Autry points out, it's important to realize that trustworthiness is not only a personal characteristic of leaders but also, by logical extension, an attribute of the organizational systems and processes a leader employs. It's not sufficient for leaders to be worthy of trust. The communication systems, human resource policies, goal-setting processes and so forth they employ must also be consistent with leaders' values. For example, communication systems that deliver information that can be believed (accurate, consistent, timely) are part of leaders' trustworthiness. And workers must have confidence in all systems–such as planning, financial, performance review and the like–that impact their work.

Autry goes on to make this claim about the qualification to be a servant leader:

> One of the basic foundations of servant leadership is trust. Far too many managers try to operate without trust between managers and employees as a basic value. I suggest that a manager who does not believe that most people will do a good job if trusted to do a good job is not a candidate for servant leadership (2001, 42-43).

Hopefully, it is clear that trust involves relying on others and having confidence in them to accomplish their work. Of course, this is true for all team members, not just leaders. However, when leaders trust others, leaders retain responsibility for everyone's activities and performance outcomes. So the leader's credibility remains on the line even though the work is done by their constituents. Leaders are constantly exposed to the consequences of others' shortcomings or failures. Being a trusting leader means acknowledging and accepting this fact. So be it; this risk can be viewed as a cost of leadership. Some are never comfortable with it, and they are poor aspirants for leading. Those accepting of this risk may balance it against the reward of enjoying their leadership role in big accomplishments that could only be achieved by many working together successfully.

Trust is about openness, and trust can only be established by building relationships in which all parties feel safe enough to risk being open and honest with each other. Building trust involves creating and sustaining an environment in which all feel comfortable sharing information, opinions, emotions, control, resources and the like with each other.

However, openness creates vulnerability. When you trust, you take a chance. And in most situations many people are hesitant to share anything that might somehow be used against them. Once people know what you think, how you feel, how you work, what resources you possess or control, what you desire to achieve and the like, it may be possible to embarrass you, harass you, harm your reputation, steal your ideas or methods, surpass your accomplishments, block or subvert your goal achievements, let you down and disappoint you. Thus, many experience a natural first tendency to protect against vulnerability by avoiding openness.

Because openness can be scary, Kouzes and Posner say, quite rightly, that leaders need to *go first*; to set the stage for openness by *trusting first*. Once leaders accept the risks of candidness and honesty, others will feel safer in dropping their guards, listening to and accepting others, demonstrating respect for and valuing others' opinions and perspectives and moving outside their comfort zones by letting go of their own ways of doing things and appreciating others' ways of thinking and working. They will feel safe to share.

Once leaders trust first, people can start to believe in the goodwill and intentions of others. They will find it unnecessary to make promises they can't keep just to impress others. And even if someone does let them down, try to subvert their efforts or work to block their achievements, the responsibility for such despicable behaviour will be theirs, it will not fall on the shoulders of the worker who trusted. Once leaders trust first, the entire workplace environment becomes more supportive of mutual trust.

How can leaders be first to trust? Ten approaches will be discussed here. Each approach contributes bit by bit to the overall environment in which leaders and their followers work each day.

Readers will recognize many of the steps that help leaders be first to trust, because, as mentioned earlier, practically every topic addressed in this book contributes to trust building. That's a fundamental reason this book contains *servant leader* attitudes and skills. Servant leaders put others' needs ahead of their own. They act as educators, facilitators and coaches. In every attitude they demonstrate and every skill they practice, servant leaders create trust. They establish a supportive environment in which people can be comfortable working together and in which productivity can be achieved.

Be first to trust

- Self-disclosure; reveal yourself to others
- Show concern for others
- Freely share information and knowledge
- Acknowledge the need for self-improvement
- Include interested parties in important meetings, events, experiences
- Admit needing help and making mistakes
- Acknowledge the contributions of others
- Be willing to be influenced by others (let them change your mind)
- Ask for feedback
- Avoid speaking negatively about others

Self-disclosure; reveal yourself to others

Let others know what you stand for, what you believe, what you value, what you need and hope for, what you are willing to do and not to do. In other words, disclose your values and dreams to followers. The more constituents believe they know their leader–how he or she thinks and feels and visions and decides–the easier it will be for them to trust their leader.

Leaders can reveal themselves to others by getting in touch with their own values and telling stories about how those values were formed and applied in their work and life experiences. They can tell stories about past successes and failures, their personal heroes and the like. People learn important lessons from stories, and they start to feel closer to the storyteller.

Once a leader opens up and takes the risk of trusting others with personal information, the more likely others will be to embrace openness.

Show concern for others

When leaders demonstrate that their own personal interests are subservient to followers' interests, followers will reward leaders with their trust. However, they have to see it to believe it. They won't accept the leader's word that they are concerned.

Leaders show concern by being available to others and listening to them. They walk the shop, meet their people in neutral sites for informal conversations by arriving early for meetings, attending organizational events and the like. When engaging followers concerned leaders ask questions to get to know them better. They apply their skills for empathetic and non-judgmental listening. Servant leaders put themselves in their constituents' shoes. They demonstrate compassion. They show respect by paying attention to peoples' ideas and concerns. Leaders make connections with constituents' aspirations and experiences. They develop an understanding of what motivates their people in life and at work–and followers notice.

When necessary and possible, leaders help others solve their problems. They show they are on the other's side. Being empathetic and compassionate creates interpersonal bonds which, in turn, make it easier for followers to accept leaders' advice and guidance. Trust builds.

Another way to show concern involves sharing the pain when necessary. That is one reason why servant leaders should be prepared to suffer first. If anyone in the organization has to take a "hit" during troubled times, the leader should be first in line.

Freely share information and knowledge

Servant leaders communicate clearly; they are as forthright and candid as possible. They demonstrate the attitude that their job is to ensure people get the information they need or want when they need or want it and in a form they can understand and use. In other words, leaders build trust by making sure organizational information flows freely. Secret meetings, closed doors and hushed conversations are avoided. They treat information as the important asset it is within their organization.

When occasional situations occur, as they will, when leaders cannot be forthcoming with current information due to confidentiality or timing issues, at least leaders explain the valid obstacles encountered and then provide complete information as soon as possible.

Also, as discussed previously, competence is a vital element of trust and confidence in leaders. Constituents have to believe that leaders know what they are talking about and that they have the necessary abilities to accomplish the organization's vision. One way leaders demonstrate competence is to share their knowledge freely with others. They convey their insights, share lessons learned from professional experiences and help connect constituents to experts and advisors. Leaders who fulfil this knowledge-builder role set the example for how people should treat each other. As a consequence, followers' trust in one another and in the leader increases–along with their performance.

Acknowledge the need for self-improvement

It's relatively simple for everyone to agree that people require regular skill upgrades if they are to remain competent in our modern, fast-changing times. This goes for leaders, too. If you have ever encountered a situation where leaders require (or at least encourage) workers to attend training sessions but never take the training themselves, you are familiar with a less-than-trusting environment. Behaviour that evidences the leader attitude, "Training is good for you, but it's not good enough for me," does not engender trust.

Servant leaders bolster organizational trust by acknowledging their own need for continuous self-improvement. They know that if it is necessary for followers, it's necessary for them. In fact, many servant leaders insist they attend the first offering of a training session that all workers will be required to complete. It's a corollary to the "suffer first" rule. Leaders who want to build and sustain a trusting environment should "train first."

Include interested parties in important meetings, events, experiences

An environment where information flows freely, opinions are welcome and mutual respect is shown to all is characterized by a rule of thumb such as "when in doubt, invite." That is, leaders concerned with building trust ensure that invitations are extended to individuals and/or group representatives who share a stake in important meetings, events and learning or development experiences.

Inclusion is the rule. Appearance of exclusion or selectivity is avoided. This is true for organizational celebrations as well as training or growth and development activities, but it is especially relevant for meetings in which future plans will be considered, goals and strategies discussed, meaningful decisions made and major projects or activities coordinated. Building trust requires a culture of inclusion.

Admit needing help and making mistakes

"I need help" is a phrase used freely by servant leaders. It communicates their humility and demonstrates respect for workers' abilities to deliver valuable assistance to their hierarchical superior. Because a leader asks for assistance, it is clear that she or he recognizes the individual from whom help is sought possesses valuable skills.

Personal humility, respect for others, recognizing competence in others: these three magic words communicate many important trust-building messages. They are used often outside workplaces because they typically produce very helpful responses, even from total strangers, and they should be used unreservedly by leaders inside organizations as well.

Servant leaders know that recognizing their need for help is a personal strength, not a weakness. They don't worry about being perceived as dependent on others. They welcome the opportunity to acknowledge their willingness to work with others to address significant problems. In return, they demonstrate their willingness to offer support for others when their help is needed. Teamwork often starts with the simple phrase, "I need help."

Trust invites self-disclosure. Therefore, trust tolerates mistakes, since we all make them. People within a trusting environment are not embarrassed by admitting they have erred. Nancy Ortberg writes about her personal leadership experience with businessman, great writer and her informal mentor, Max De Pree.

> I called Max De Pree one day. I was in a tizzy about something, and he let me ramble for a while: then he said, 'You know, Nancy, leaders are only right 50 percent of the time.' I remember thinking, *Oh my gosh! I can do 50 percent!* I was trying to be right all the time, or 90 percent of the time, and it was wearing me out. Allowing your people to see your human side–hearing you say, 'I'm sorry' or 'I was wrong'–will take you off the pedestal (on which you can be admired but never emulated) and put you down on the ground with them, where they will say, 'If she can do it, I can do it' or 'If he can make it work, I can, too.' That's powerful leadership, but it only comes when you fill an organization with trust (Ortberg 2004, 90).

Mistakes are par for the course. When leaders admit they make mistakes, they enhance their reputation for honesty, therefore they build personal credibility, and they contribute to organizational trust. The potential harm a few mistakes may do to their reputation for competence is usually minimal, especially if they have an impressive track record for getting things done. Do your personal math; the plus side of the equation typically falls on admitting you made a mistake.

Since servant leaders fulfil the role of educator, consider how effective leaders encourage their followers to learn. Did any good instructor ever tell a learner they should never make a mistake? Of course not. Educators know the only way people learn is by doing things they've never done before. Those who stick to only what they know well enough to avoid mistakes will not learn anything new.

If people believe they will be punished for mistakes, they will stop trying anything new. Promoting learning and improvement calls for a tolerance for errors. And, importantly, it includes a framework for forgiveness, another servant leader skill. Great leaders are educators. Great educators encourage learners to try new things. Trying new things leads to mistakes. People learn from mistakes and develop new knowledge and skills. Great leaders forgive mistakes and enjoy improved performance from their people. Great leaders build trust by admitting they make mistakes, too.

Servant leaders are first on their team to say, "I need help" and "I have fallen short, I made a mistake."

Acknowledge the contributions of others

Do good work, get credit for a job well done. That's fair. That's what people expect: nothing more, and certainly nothing less. Trust is developed when followers see and hear leaders give credit to everyone who contributes to success. Constituents quickly come to realize their leaders are not "sponges" who try to absorb all the credit for jobs done well. Rather, they become more trusting when they recognize their leaders are distributors of praise and appreciation for their good work. They can count on the fact that their reputations will be bolstered as a result of their winning efforts. They don't have to ask, they don't have to wonder. They trust their leader.

A significant element of a leader's reputation for both honesty and humility derives from the way they acknowledge the contributions of others. Servant leaders are more likely to deflect personal credit for success, playing down the significance of their own role. They are quick to point outward and mention by name the many other team members who participated in a successful effort.

In *Good to Great* Jim Collins referred to this behaviour as Level 5 leaders' "compelling modesty."

> In contrast to the very *I*-centric style of the comparison leaders, we were struck by how the good-to-great leaders *didn't* talk about themselves. During interviews with the good-to-great leaders, they'd talk about the company and the contributions of other executives as long as we'd like but would deflect discussion about their own contributions (2001, 27).

> Level 5 leaders look out the window to attribute success to factors other than themselves. When things go poorly, however, they look in the mirror and blame themselves, taking full responsibility (2001, 39).

If you have ever attended the opening performance of a Broadway play, you have seen the curtain calls that follow the performance. Commonly, the greatest ovations are offered for the leading actors. After a while, the producer is called out to take a bow. The producer envisioned the project, recruited the stars as well as all other personnel, raised the financing, booked the theatre, approved the sets and props and oversaw every other aspect of the production. Yet the producer never appeared on stage. Who is this person, anyway, the audience wonders. A smattering of applause results.

But the producer rarely expects applause. The audiences' enjoyment and the ovations they offered for the performers were the producer's psychic reward. In some ways servant leaders are like Broadway producers. They don't seek stage appearances, they don't insist on sharing credit. They like to give it all away. They go out of their way to ensure their people are credited with success achieved by the team.

When followers know they can count on receiving credit for the good work they do, trust builds.

Be willing to be influenced by others
(let them change your mind)

Aware of the advantages of trusting first so that others will be more comfortable to trust in an open, honest environment, servant leaders know it is useful to listen to and consider alternative viewpoints. They are happy to gather and employ other people's expertise and abilities.

Once followers see that leaders use their information, ideas and opinions in decision making, the openness of the environment comes into focus. They feel respected and effective. Constituents become more willing to listen to and accept input from leaders and others. Servant leaders are also willing to allow others to exert influence over group decisions.

According to Kouzes and Posner, there is a clear reciprocal process.

> By demonstrating an openness to influence, leaders contribute to building the trust that enables their constituents to be more open to their influence. Trust begets trust (2002, 247).

Leaders who serve first make themselves susceptible to influence. They listen first and trust first. They thank followers for inputs then go out of their way to make sure people know that their input influenced eventual decisions and actions.

Ask for feedback

When considering effective strategies for self-improvement and growth, servant leaders rely on many sources for input. Already in this book the attitude that "feedback is a gift" has been discussed. Among other useful skills that pertain to receiving feedback, servant leaders sit quietly and listen without explaining or defending themselves when feedback is offered, and they say "thank you" when the feedback concludes.

One of the most valuable inputs for leaders' potential improvements involves followers' perceptions. How do people who work for you on a daily basis, interacting with you on your bad days as well as good, think you can improve your leadership attitudes, skills and behaviours? It's helpful to know.

> If you are going to grow your leadership skills, you have to rely on people around you to let you know about the impact of your behaviors and actions (Kouzes and Posner 2016, 166).

Leaders have to go first by asking for feedback from followers. It is quite unlikely that direct feedback will be offered without a request because telling the boss how she or he can improve can be intimidating. Followers need assurance leaders want their feedback, and they want to know what form of feedback is desired and how it will be used. It requires everyone's agreement that they operate within a very open, honest environment. Thus, leaders' requests for input must get the trust ball rolling.

> Because you don't know what people are going to say when you ask for feedback, most likely you're going to seek feedback from people you trust.

The same goes for others. They are much more likely to be open and honest with you if they trust you. It's a reciprocal process ... So if you're going to put asking for feedback on your agenda, you're also going to have to put trust building on your agenda (Kouzes and Posner 2016, 163.)

In this instance the reciprocal nature of the trust building process is key. Followers will offer feedback to leaders if they trust the leaders to use both their praise and criticism for only the intended purpose–to identify areas for leader improvement. No ill will or retaliation will result.

In turn, a leader's request for feedback demonstrates to followers that followers are trusted. Their opinions are respected and valued. This opens the environment for the leader's feedback to followers regarding their performances and potential areas for improvement. The trust snowball continues to roll downhill. But leaders have to be first to trust.

Avoid speaking negatively about others

All steps for building trust discussed so far have been proactive in nature. They are things leaders can do to help create and sustain workplaces characterized by mutual trust. However, it is probably necessary to take the negative view at least once and discuss poor behaviours that should be avoided to prevent destroying trust. Unfortunately, the type of environment described here exists all too often in organizations.

Duplicitous behaviour such as gossiping, backstabbing and pairing can destroy trust in short order. It doesn't matter whether leaders participate directly in such activities or just tolerate them without swiftly intervening. Mutual trust will be destroyed. Spreading false or unsubstantiated rumours about others can never be accepted by those who want to trust. Character assassination is not a component of anyone's open, honest workplace. Pairing, a destructive alliance between two or more who choose to break off and talk about their group rather than bringing issues to the group for discussion, is dishonest behaviour that destroys teamwork.

Any servant led work culture should include a norm of speaking up early whenever such negative activities are noticed. Swift and direct action is required to stop them before they may be interpreted as accepted behaviour by others.

Preventing such destructive behaviours from poisoning an organization's culture of trust does not necessarily mean leaders must act threateningly toward those who gossip, backstab or pair. But it does mean such behaviours have to be addressed openly and identified as toxic and unwelcome. Once addressed, leaders can reinforce desired norms of trust, openness and honesty that will surely be more in line with any organization's values.

As a final thought, let's refer to James Hunter's wonderful discussion and consider the simplest possible approach for servant leaders desiring to build trust among their workers. Trust is built by doing the right thing to others. If others expect their leaders to do the right thing, they will trust their leaders.

So what is the right thing? It's very clear. There is universal acceptance on doing what is right. The right thing to do to others is be patient, kind, humble, respectful, selfless, forgiving, honest and committed. If people expect that of you and your organization in mutual relationships, an environment of trust will be built.

Building networks

Servant leaders recognize the importance of networking to improve their *own* and their *followers'*:

- job performance
- personal growth
- career development, and
- time management skills.

Because networks are such valuable personal assets, successful leaders develop the habit of meeting others and establishing mutually supportive relationships with them. They put networking on their schedule. They practice it regularly. In their roles as their followers' educators, facilitators and coaches, servant leaders nurture networking behaviour in others so that they, too, reap the numerous benefits networking offers.

The most effective networks are built through a purposeful strategy, not through meetings that occur as happenstance. Over time effective leaders build sets of person-to-person links that are wide in coverage and deep in talent.

> **Building networks**
>
> Servant leaders:
> - build their own networks to prepare for leadership success
> - support followers in developing their own networks
>
> **Types of networks (Ibarra and Hunter, 2007)**
> - operational
> - personal
> - strategic

In the Skills chapter a leader's use of networks to save time has been discussed. Here the focus will be on job performance, personal growth and leadership career development. Individuals who appreciate the importance of networking are more likely to move beyond their functional specialties, typically the early-career focus of most workers, and continue on the path toward broader organizational leadership.

Because servant leaders appreciate the challenging demands and numerous pitfalls encountered by their followers in their own network building activities, they mentor constituents in the process. Servant leaders stress the different needs to network at various career stages, the different types of networks and the attitudes that support and typically hinder networking efforts. Helpful leaders offer tips and techniques for building networks. Especially, servant leaders support their followers by providing introductions and referrals that can help jump start the network building process, and they may even serve as a member of their followers' personal board of advisors.

Networking involves creating personal contacts through relationship building to help provide a variety of valuable support, feedback, insight, information and resources. These various products of networking help to accomplish current tasks, solve unique, developing problems and address highly uncertain strategic challenges. The specific need a worker is likely to have depends on her or his career stage and level in an organizational hierarchy.

Servant leaders consider meeting new people and forming professional and social relationships one of the important tasks in which they engage continuously throughout their careers. Check their monthly calendars and daily to-do lists. You will find time scheduled to attend meetings and events sponsored by professional societies, local associations of businesses, not-for-profits and governmental agencies, personal interest groups, and the like. At each opportunity they renew old acquaintances and forge new ones. They exchange contact information with the people they meet along with invitations to "lean on me" in my areas of expertise "whenever I can be of assistance" with the implied reciprocal relationship that "I'll contact you whenever I need your help."

In this manner leaders build a cadre of supporters who can offer specific advice when a problem outside their own experience occurs or, alternatively, help identify other (third, fourth, fifth or sixth degrees of separation) connections who can provide necessary counsel or add their influence to a cause. Servant leaders know how to use the three magic words, "I need help," and, when necessary, they are capable of marshalling that help. Networks are their tools.

The best way of building a professional network is similar to the best way of building a personal retirement nest egg. Start early (that is, early in one's career) and add a little each month. But the key is "start early"–to form the habitual networking behaviour and add names, one by one, to a network membership list.

Researchers and Professors Herminia Ibarra and Mark Hunter write very helpfully on the topic of networking. They point out that many workers, especially the inexperienced, may resist the notion that networking is necessary because for some people it requires stepping outside their comfort zone and engaging in a practice that can carry the stigma of succeeding through "who you know, not what you know." Ibarra and Hunter's research leads them to the conclusion that a significant number of workers view networking as one of their most dreaded personal development challenges. For some it is even seen very negatively as an elegant way of using people that smacks of insincere and manipulative "string pulling." However, nothing could be farther from the truth.

Servant leaders know that mind set matters, and they help followers see networking as a way of building an invaluable personal resource that can support an individual in accomplishing work tasks, enhancing social skills and solving problems efficiently and effectively.

Networking can also help extend limited personal perspectives in a wide variety of unfamiliar contexts to appreciate fully a "big picture." The behaviour of relationship building can even serve to shape the external environment to a leader's or organization's advantage. In their excellent *Harvard Business Review* article, "How Leaders Create and Use Networks," Ibarra and Hunter (2007, 41) claim, "The alternative to networking is to fail–either in reaching for a leadership position or in succeeding at all."

And, of course, due to the reciprocal responsibilities of network members, building a wide and deep personal network provides servant leaders with opportunities to offer their help to others and apply their own expertise to a very high number of situations.

Ibarra and Hunter propose a decidedly useful framework for understanding three distinct but interdependent forms of networking that extend throughout various stages of a typical professional career. Their three forms of networking are: *operational*, *personal* and *strategic*.

It's vital to understand that as individuals move into leadership roles, their relationships and networks must reorient themselves from internal (inside the organization) to external, from present to future, from problem-solving to opportunity-framing (visioning) and from understanding their organization's environment to shaping that environment.

As servant leaders develop their own networking approaches and assist their followers in comprehending the networking process, this framework can be extremely beneficial.

Operational networking

All workers, including leaders, need to establish and maintain good relationships with the organizational colleagues who can assist them in accomplishing their jobs. These people could include peers within an operational unit, direct subordinates and superiors. Also, the list could include other internal stakeholders from different operational units who can support (or hinder) a project and key outsiders like customers, suppliers and distributors.

Operational networking serves to ensure cooperation and coordination among all such individuals and groups who must come together in various combinations to accomplish the immediate tasks for which the worker is responsible. Simply, operational networking addresses the objective of completing an individual's current work responsibilities both effectively and efficiently. An operational network involves using a worker's internal contacts to help manage internal responsibilities. Coordination, cooperation and trust among interdependent internal contacts drive the need for operational networks.

First, operational networking provides direct support for completing a worker's or leader's tasks. Second, according to Ibarra and Hunter,

> it is relatively straightforward because the task provides focus and a clear criterion for membership in the network: either you're necessary to the job and helping to get it done, or you're not (2007, 41).

When developing an operational network, it is imperative not to overlook individuals that may be important to the outcome of the task. Keen observation is vital to the creation of operational networks.

Overall, the vast majority of operational networking occurs within a worker's organization, and necessary relationships are determined by routine, short-term demands. Therefore, the networking approach is straightforward: meet and form mutually supportive relationships with fellow workers who have the information, skills, expertise, resources or cooperation you need to accomplish your work assignments. Get to know them on a work-related basis, a social basis or both. Since most organizational assignments involve dependencies on fellow workers, the better your relationships with colleagues, the higher your job performance is likely to be.

Operational networks
(Ibarra and Hunter 2007)

- purpose: accomplish job tasks through cooperation and coordination
- focus: primarily internal (inside the organization)
- typical members: direct subordinates, superiors, peers within an operational unit, internal stakeholders from different operational units who can support (or block) a project, some key outsiders like customers, suppliers and distributors

---

If your job assignments typically involve working with people external to the organization, such as customers, suppliers or distributors, get to know them as well as practicable. Good relationships with members of the organization's environment often lead to highly valued job performance.

Workers who spend their careers within a single organizational function, and who maintain a corresponding internal focus, can perform effectively with only operational networks. Many people believe their success will be built on working very hard and remaining focused on the technical skills their jobs require. They may well see no need for additional networking.

However, things change for workers who aspire to a leadership role. A move into leadership presents new challenges, particularly strategy-making, that supports the organization as a whole entity, not simply the functional specialities workers had previously relied upon.

If individuals set their sights on leading others and organizations, the internal focus of operational networking is not sufficient. Lack of external focus and relationships will tend to disqualify people from consideration for leadership positions. Common ground with people outside their usual circles will be noticeably absent. Lack of "big picture" thinking, vague knowledge about professional domains beyond their own, and perhaps even limitations in social skills, will be evident to those who choose and train the next generation of leaders. Therefore, servant leaders who delight in preparing future generations of servants see the network building behaviour as something they must encourage in others.

Personal networking

Learning to lead necessitates obtaining help from others. Social support is one required condition for growth and development.

Personal networking extends an individual's network beyond internal contacts, allowing an aspiring leader to enhance personal and professional development, expand social skills and increase his or her ability to gain knowledge. Through professional societies, industry associations, social clubs, charitable organizations, alumni groups, communities of special interests and the like, individuals gain new perspectives that help them advance their careers.

Largely, personal networks are external to an employing organization, comprised of discretionary links to others with whom aspiring leaders share a common interest. That interest could be work-related, as in professional societies or industry associations, or personal, as in social groups or hobby-related activities.

Personal networks enable individuals to reach other people quickly and easily. And these people may be the ones with helpful information, expertise or influence. To be sure, personal networks offer high potential for attaining valuable referrals.

One particularly interesting example of a personal network is offered by Kouzes and Posner in their book *Learning Leadership: The Five Fundamentals of Becoming an Exemplary Leader*. It involves making connections by building a personal board of advisors. They suggest working to build a personal board that can provide custom support and encouragement.

> Your personal board should have four to seven people whom you respect and trust and to whom you can turn when you need counsel on tough questions and ethical dilemmas, guidance during transitions, advice about personal development needs, and help in staying true to your values and

beliefs. They should represent a diverse set of skills and experiences and be role models of many of the skills you'd like to develop ... Start by asking one person to be on your board. Tell that person what you're up to, and ask whether they'd be available for a cup of coffee every so often to offer advice and counsel. You can then go out and find a second board member (Kouzes and Posner 2016, 158).

Unfortunately, according to Ibarra and Hunter, many people fail to recognize the importance of personal networking, viewing it as a time waster. This disabling attitude develops because many people do not see the immediate benefits they hope personal networking will offer in carrying out their current responsibilities. They may pose a question like, "Why bother spending time widening my circle of acquaintances when there isn't even time for my most urgent tasks?" They don't view using their time in network building as an investment in their own growth and development and in a more opportunistic leadership future.

Another potential misconception regarding personal networking involves a sentiment that personal lives and business/organizational lives should be kept separate. However, personal networking is not only about using personal contacts. The greatest strength of personal networking is creating flexible linkages to other people who share common interests. Relationships built with them can have business and/or personal benefits.

Servant leaders facilitate followers by helping to dispel attitudes that building personal networks may be a waste of time. They can also help aspiring leaders appreciate the value of amassing numerous network entry points into webs of resources. Further, servant leaders can encourage their constituents to establish their own personal board of advisors–and even sit on some personal boards themselves.

Personal networking through professional societies, associations, groups, clubs, communities, etc. helps develop knowledge in areas beyond an individual's own domain of proficiency, greater understanding of self and deeper perspective of the environments in which a person operates.

All this can be developed along with access to important information, support for growth and development as well as referrals. In terms of referrals and information, Ibarra and Hunter write,

According to the famous six degrees of separation principle, our personal contacts are valuable to the extent that they help us reach, in as few connections as possible, the far-off person who has the information we need (2007, 42).

> **Personal networks**
> **(Ibarra and Hunter 2007)**
>
> - purpose: enhance personal and professional development, expand social skills and increase ability to gain knowledge through social support and referrals
> - focus: external (outside the organization)
> - typical members: acquaintances within professional societies, industry associations, social clubs, charitable organizations, alumni groups, communities of special interests, friendship groups and so on
>
> Special case (Kouzes and Posner 2016):
> - personal board of advisors
> - focus: mentors
> - typical members: 4-7 trustworthy acquaintances who can provide occasional counsel on ethical dilemmas, life and career transitions, personal growth and development needs and help in staying true to personal values and beliefs

Obviously, the six degrees of separation principle does not apply to those who remain steadfastly internally-focused and decide not to pursue new professional and personal relationships on a regular basis.

Of course, in order for personal networking to improve job performance and leadership abilities, workers need to apply the information and knowledge gained through personal networking to their organizational activities.

Strategic networking

When people begin the challenging transition from functional worker or manager to organizational leader, they need to begin thinking strategically. No longer primarily focussed on solving today's problems, their activities evolve into the realm of future opportunity recognition, balance of multiple stakeholder interests, environment management and resource attainment.

A leader's job includes recruiting stakeholders, engaging allies, appreciating the political landscape and organizing conversations among unconnected parties. Internally, their relationships with other functional managers, outside their direct control, become important.

Strategic networking opens an individual's eyes to potential new directions–for herself or himself, the organization and its stakeholders–that are necessary to achieve success.

> (It) plugs the aspiring leader into a set of relationships and information sources that collectively embody the power to achieve personal and organizational goals (Ibarra and Hunter 2007, 43).

Members of one's strategic network are found both within and outside the work organization. A successful leader develops the foresight and ability to be future-oriented and recruit people needed to make things happen.

> The key to a good strategic network is leverage: the ability to marshal information, support and resources from one sector of a network to achieve results in another (Ibarra and Hunter 2007, 44).

Strategic networks do not necessarily require direct influence to achieve future successes. Rather, indirect influence, persuading one individual to convince another individual, is necessary.

**Strategic networks
(Ibarra and Hunter 2007)**

- purpose: think strategically, recognize future opportunities, recruit stakeholders, balance multiple stakeholder interests, engage allies, manage the environment, understand the political landscape and attain resources through a variety of connections and referrals
- focus: external and internal
- typical members: associates from operational and personal networks, other organizational managers of functional and business units outside immediate authority, mentors, heads of business, not-for-profit and governmental organizations, leaders of professional societies and industry associations, political office holders (federal, state and local) and so on

Strategic networking demands significant time and energy, leading some individuals to feel costs may outweigh benefits. However, determined aspiring leaders, aided by their servant leader coaches, recognize the long-term payback of their investment.

As discussed, typically workers rise through the ranks due to their strong command of the technical aspects of their jobs and a shoulder-to-the-wheel determination to accomplish their own and their team's goals. But when given the opportunity to move beyond functional expertise and address the organization's strategic issues, many people fail to realize their challenge will involve relational, not analytical, tasks. Only those prepared for leadership success understand that contacts and relationships with an array of stakeholders, both current and potential, are not diversions from their "real work" but actually form the core of their new leadership roles. Those with well-developed networks are prepared to handle the challenge.

It's important to remember that operational, personal and strategic networking are not mutually exclusive. That is, all forms of networking can occur at the same time, and one form of networking is not dependent on outcomes from another form. The first helps workers manage current internal responsibilities, the second boosts their personal growth and development, and the third opens their eyes to new organizational directions and the stakeholders they need to enlist.

Successful leaders establish a simple system for recording and organizing the information they collect about their network members' contact addresses/numbers and areas of expertise. They are savvy enough to join new groups periodically, recognizing the necessity to rotate memberships occasionally to keep alive opportunities to meet new people. They are aware that maintaining one's networks is equally important as building them. Reaching out to the individuals in their networks, even when they do not require specific support or information, allows leaders to maintain contacts and further solidify relationships. Therefore, connections will be there when needed.

Servant leaders commit to the behaviour of building networks by putting the activity on their schedule. They spend a few hours each week establishing and maintaining their relationships. They attend events and meetings of professional societies, industry and market associations, alumni groups, special interest clubs and the like to meet new people. They grow their number of relationships and keep old ones alive through regular contact.

Leaders consider their time well invested when they forge relationships with people new to their sphere of contacts. They appreciate that networking serves different purposes as their career advances–from gaining cooperation and achieving coordination among fellow workers to enhancing personal and professional growth to envisioning new directions and developing new resources for their organization.

In their network building behaviour servant leaders apply skills for listening, asking questions, being optimistic and stimulating informal conversations as they engage others and recruit them as network members. They help convert strangers to connections by demonstrating the personal values and beliefs by which they live.

Aspiring leaders who want to excel at network building let shine their servant leader attitudes that "everyone is good at something," "I am committed to your success" and "I don't have to be right all the time." Perhaps most noticeably they demonstrate the attitude that "I am a community builder," and they welcome into their personal community a variety of people who appreciate the value in forming relationships that offer mutual support, feedback, insight, information and resources.

Servant Leader Tips – Building networks
Understand the three types of networks (operational, personal, strategic) and their roles in various stages of your career
Commit to network building behaviour; put it on your schedule and to-do lists; view network building as a valuable investment of your time and energy
Establish a simple e-system or paper system for recording and organizing information related to network members' contact addresses/numbers and each member's areas of expertise, support, feedback, insight, resources
Start building networks by establishing friendly, mutually supportive relationships between yourself and colleagues at work
Join relevant professional societies, industry associations, alumni groups, charitable organizations, personal interest clubs and so on; build your networks among their memberships
Ensure you have opportunities to meet new people; attend a variety of events and meetings; join new groups periodically; if necessary, rotate memberships
When meeting new people, use servant leader skills like listening, asking questions, telling personal stories, being optimistic, stimulating informal conversations
When recruiting network members, demonstrate servant leader attitudes such as "everyone is good at something," "I am committed to your success," "I don't have to be right all the time," "I am a community builder"

> When meeting new people and recruiting them to be members of your network, remember that servant leaders demonstrate their personal values and beliefs through their attitudes and behaviours and through the stories they tell; identify people who share your values and beliefs; they will become your strongest network members

Importantly, servant leaders understand how challenging it can be for their followers to build networks. Therefore, servants see their duty as encouraging followers to develop this habitual behaviour from the early stages of their careers. And they educate followers regarding the different career stages and needs for relationships. Servant leaders facilitate followers' network building efforts by providing encouragement, reinforcing positive attitudes about this challenging and time-consuming behaviour, sharing their own contacts, providing introductions and suggesting memberships that are likely to be fruitful.

Servant Leader Tips – Facilitating followers in developing network building behaviour
Encourage followers to develop the habit of network building early in their careers and to maintain it throughout their work lives
Educate followers regarding different types of networks they will need: operational, personal, strategic
Coach followers on the different and valuable supports each type of network provides
Help followers overcome negative attitudes about network building, such as: "it takes me out of my comfort zone," "networking is insincere and manipulative 'string pulling' and I want to succeed through what I know, not who I know," "networking wastes too much time," "personal lives and business/organizational lives should be kept separate"
Share your own contacts and resources with followers to jump start their network building activity
Provide personal introductions so followers can expand their internal and external networks
Suggest memberships in specific professional and social associations, societies, groups and clubs

Finally, it's important to realize that active and effective networks empower those who build them. Leaders' and followers' confidence is bolstered when they know all the support they need to perform well is available to them. Feeling connected to support, feedback, insight, information and resources enables people to vision, to plan and to act with the confidence that they can bring their visions to fruition. Being connected to necessary resources and sufficient authority is one of the fundamental elements of empowerment.

Empowering others to act

As discussed in the introduction to this Behaviours section, much of what servant leaders accomplish through their followers occurs due to the empowering organizational environment they establish. Servant leaders' behaviours create an enabling work climate by:

- facilitating workers' proactive approaches
  - leaders provide vision (direction, knowing what to accomplish) and values (behavioural guidelines) which empower followers to create action plans
- establishing and maintaining their credibility as leaders
  - leaders build their reputations for being honest, forward-looking, competent and inspiring, which earns followers' trust and confidence and intensifies constituents' commitment to a common cause
- building trust throughout the organization
  - leaders make it safe for all to share information and resources, take risks and make mistakes, admit weaknesses as well as pursue personal growth and development; an open, honest workplace stimulates taking action and attaining self-sufficiency, and it supports teamwork and collaboration, and
- facilitating workers' connections to resources and power through networking
  - leaders help followers build networks to engender their confidence and competence, improving their job performance, personal growth, career development and time management capabilities.

One major and vital conclusion about servant leadership is offered here: just about everything servant leaders do contributes to creating a workplace climate that supports workers' independent action-taking and achieving. Since the previously discussed behaviours detail how servant leaders contribute to "empowering others to act," no other specific behaviours will be described in this section. Instead, a summary of what other authors have written about the servant-led empowering work environment will be presented.

Nancy Ortberg (2004, 96-97) writes about servant leader approaches to worker motivation:

> The leader who tells everybody what to do and expects immediate obedience, without the motivation that comes from watching a servant leader at work, creates a workforce of implementers. This type of leader creates what has been called malicious compliance. You get the behaviour you want on the outside, but nothing changes on the inside. Although this kind of action looks good on the surface, in reality, it breeds undesirable qualities like cynicism and lack of trust–subtly powerful forces that may not initially affect the outcome but eventually weaken the goal, the team, the organization. But when you lead out of a servant's heart, you tap into the best level of motivation in a person. Without the element of servant leadership, the farthest you will get into someone's motivation is the 'have to' level. Over time, that will build a narrow, thin organization.
>
> When a leader is able to drive down deeper and get to the 'I want to' motivation, the organization becomes a type of perpetual motion machine. It no longer takes as much energy from you as a leader because you've built into those around you the zeal to do a job well. The 'sustain' you've tapped in your team will carry all of you, collectively, well into the future. But remember, you can never develop other people as long as you hold onto the power. The power base has to be shared.

Ortberg goes on to suggest four values for an empowering work environment. They are integrity, authenticity, joy and dignity of work. "If you as a leader can build an environment around those four values, you will create a place where people want to work" (2004, 97).

Servant leaders' empowering work environment
Nancy Ortberg (2004, 96-97)

"Without the element of servant leadership, the farthest you will get into someone's motivation is the 'have to' level. Over time, that will build a narrow, thin organization.

When a leader is able to drive down deeper and get to the 'I want to' motivation, the organization becomes a type of perpetual motion machine."

4 suggested values for an empowering work environment:
Integrity   Authenticity   Joy   Dignity of work

Kouzes and Posner (2004, 29) discuss enabling others to act through empowerment:

> Leaders strengthen others by sharing power and discretion. Creating a climate in which people are involved and feel that what they are doing is important is at the core of strengthening others. It's essentially the process of turning constituents into leaders themselves–making people capable of acting on their own initiative. Leaders give people the latitude to make their own decisions and create an environment that both builds requisite capabilities and promotes a sense of self-confidence. People who experience a sense of personal accountability feel ownership for their achievements. Exemplary leaders know that they must use their own power in service of others, so they readily give their power away instead of hoarding it for themselves.

Kouzes and Posner (2002) claim that enabling self-leadership, providing choice, developing competence and confidence as well as fostering accountability are necessary factors in strengthening others to act. Individual workers who feel a sense of empowerment, ownership, responsibility and involvement are more satisfied and more productive. Of course, long-term organizational success is dependent upon satisfied and productive workers. Therefore, a relationship can be seen between empowered employees and positive organizational outcomes.

Servant leaders recognize that "leaders accept and act on the paradox of power: we become more powerful when we give our power away" (Kouzes and Posner 2002, 284). The authors suggest that empowering others to act can be achieved by:

- creating an environment of trust
- listening to others
- connecting others to sources of power
- educating, and
- creating a learning environment.

As previously presented, trust is the central theme in successful relationships. Creating an open, honest, trusting environment in the workplace begins with a leader's self-disclosure. It also includes showing concern for others, sharing information and knowledge, acknowledging the need for self-improvement, inviting other parties to meetings and other events and experiences, admitting the need for help and conceding mistakes, acknowledging others' contributions to success, accepting influence from others, asking for feedback and avoiding speaking negatively about others.

Listening to others demonstrates caring. Followers become convinced that leaders are sensitive to their needs and interests. Listening strengthens trust. When followers believe leaders care about them and feel safe investing their trust, motivation to contribute to team success increases.

Effective leaders ask questions twice as often as they give instructions or orders. And they listen attentively to answers to their questions. By doing what Kouzes and Posner term "listening deeply," leaders simultaneously build trust and take the pulse of the organization and its members.

Servant leaders benefit from auditing their listening habits. How often do they ask questions? Do they really listen to what others are saying or are they just waiting for their chance to speak again? Do they take constituents' information and opinions into account in future decisions and actions?

"Making something happen is not only a function of what we know. It's also a function of who we are and who we know" (Kouzes and Posner 2002, 260). Connecting others to resources and sources of power is one of a leader's most effective contributions to empowering others to act. Not only do great leaders have their own effective personal networks, but they also encourage and aid their constituents in developing their own networks to build social capital.

Leaders help others "connect" by making assignments that will expose workers to a variety of organizational members and external stakeholders, as well as facilitating introductions to a variety of powerholders at every possible occasion. Well-connected workers feel confident they can access the information, expertise and authority they need to complete their tasks effectively.

Educating people through formal training and development programs is also vital to building competencies. Followers must be confident that they have the necessary skills to succeed if they are to feel empowered to act. Developing competence and confidence in others is important to align the goals of the organization and the goals of individuals. Kouzes and Posner (2002, 292) tell us:

> Organizations that have invested more than the average amount of money on training enjoy higher levels of employee involvement and commitment and better levels of customer service, along with greater understanding of and alignment with company visions and values.

Therefore, personally and regularly participating in training opportunities and encouraging followers to do so helps establish one's credentials as a servant leader and helps empower others to take action.

Another very useful approach to empowering others through education deserves mention here. Servant leaders realize that one learns the most about a topic when one teaches it to others. Delegating duties as a trainer to others in appropriate circumstances will contribute much to deepening knowledge and skills and increasing self-confidence through education.

Creating a learning environment involves a leader's efforts to foster trust, problem-solving and effectiveness. Without the safety of a trusting and open environment, people are very likely to be defensive, less willing to take risks and make mistakes and more likely to expend effort deflecting blame to others.

Servant leaders don't support an environment for punishing failure, assigning blame for mistakes or introducing a plethora of rules to control worker actions. Rather, sharing information and making resources available to others are important instruments for personal development and enabling others to become problem-solvers. Providing choices allows workers to feel a sense of responsibility. "People can't lead and can't make a difference unless they have a choice" (Kouzes and Posner 2002, 290). Choices empower others to act.

If leaders want higher levels of performance and greater initiative, they must be proactive in designing work that allows people discretion and choice (Kouzes and Posner 2002, 291).

Servant leaders' empowering work environment
James M. Kouzes and Barry Z. Posner (2002, 282)

"People everywhere seem to share this: when we feel able to determine our own destiny, when we believe we're able to mobilize the resources and support necessary to complete a task, then we persist in our efforts to achieve. But when we feel we're controlled by others, when we believe that we lack support or resources, we show no commitment to excel (although we may comply)."

Servant leaders take advantage of opportunities to let others decide for themselves and do for themselves. To empower followers servant leaders relax control, provide support and allow others to make their own decisions whenever possible.

To contribute to a learning environment leaders encourage (sometimes require) project teams to hold post-mortems or after-action reviews following completion of work. Honest and open group discussions generate lessons about what went well, what was poorly executed, what people learned and what participants can do better the next time. Through such meetings or retreats, followers come to realize that learning is part of the work. The final element of every project is learning from their experiences and mistakes.

Being a servant leader means empowering and enabling others to take action. As discussed by Drucker (2006) and Kouzes and Posner (2012) and as suggested earlier in this book as a necessary attitude for servant leaders, it is imperative to think and say "we," not "I." Effective leaders realize that they possess authority only because they have the trust of their followers. This trust is earned, according to Drucker, because leaders demonstrate that they think of the needs and opportunities of the business, agency, society, community or assembly and its members before they think of their own personal needs and opportunities. In *Good to Great* Jim Collins describes the compelling modesty of his Level 5 leaders who talk very little about themselves, but rather prefer to emphasize the contributions of others to their organization's successes.

In his book *The World's Most Powerful Leadership Principle: How to Become a Servant Leader*, James Hunter provides two versions of his *Leadership Skills Inventory* (Hunter 2004, 216-217). One version is for a leader to complete as an audit of his or her self-perceived leadership skills, and the second format is for workers to complete regarding their perceptions of their leader. In this inventory there are 25 statements about the leader and two open-ended questions.

Using this very helpful questionnaire to understand and close any perception gaps between leader and followers is a quite useful exercise for leader development. For our purposes the inventory provides keen insight into the empowering work environment Hunter expects to see in a servant-led organization. From the employee's perspective, some of the questionnaire items describing the leader's contribution to an enabling climate are included below.

My leader:

- is someone people can trust
- is a good listener
- is actively involved in the development of subordinates
- gives credit to those who deserve it
- gives positive feedback to subordinates when appropriate

- is a leader people feel confident following
- sets high goals for self, subordinates, and department
- confronts people with problems/situations when they arise
- makes clear to subordinates what is expected on the job
- holds people accountable for meeting the standards set
- gives appreciation to others
- gives encouragement to others
- coaches/counsels employees to ensure compliance with goals
- treats people with respect (i.e., like they are important people).

John Maxwell, in his book *The 21 Irrefutable Laws of Leadership,* addresses several leader actions and approaches that significantly affect the overall work climate. The laws of empowerment, solid ground, addition and connection will be discussed with a focus on how workers' motivation to take action is impacted through a leader-created empowering work environment.

- In his *Law of Empowerment* Maxwell says leaders empower followers by being on their side, encouraging them, giving them power and helping them succeed. Also, the author observes that only secure leaders give power to others. He cautions that leaders need to adopt the attitude that power is not a zero-sum game.

  … the assumption often is that you need to fight others to maintain your leadership. But that reflects a scarcity mind-set. The truth is that if you give some of your power away to others, there is still plenty to go around (Maxwell 2007, 146).

- We have seen that in his *Law of Solid Ground* Maxwell tells us trust forms the foundation of leadership. Leaders build trust by consistently demonstrating their competence, connection and character. Importantly, it is the leader's character that communicates to followers the leader's consistency, potential and respect.
- Maxwell's *Law of Addition* refers to leaders adding value to workers by serving them. This is servant leadership.

  When you add value to people, you lift them up, help them advance, make them a part of something bigger than themselves, and assist them in becoming who they were made to be (Maxwell 2007, 53).

Value is added when leaders are willing to be open, trusting and caring, when they offer their help, and when they are willing to be vulnerable. Leaders also add value to others when they teach skills, provide opportunities and offer their personal insight and perspective. Maxwell summarizes well his concept of the Law of Addition by stating that inexperienced leaders may be too quick to start leading before they know anything about the people they expect to lead. Instead, mature leaders listen to followers first, learn about their hopes and dreams, become acquainted with their aspirations and pay attention to their emotions. Only then do mature leaders try to lead.

- In the *Law of Connection* the importance of a leader contributing emotion and empathy to a work environment is discussed. Maxwell says, "You can't move people to action unless you first move them with emotion" (2007, 115). Leaders connect on an emotional basis in many ways. Among others, some of the most significant ways leaders create a climate of connection is by just "being themselves" in their relationships with constituents, communicating with openness and sincerity, learning people's names and using them in conversation, knowing followers' histories and dreams as well as *adapting to followers* in language, culture, education, and so on instead of expecting followers to adapt to them. Most importantly, leaders who want to connect practice what they preach. Living one's message supports a leader's credibility and thus facilitates connection. Maxwell suggests how important it is for leaders to be initiators of relationships. Some leaders, he says, have trouble connecting because they feel that they are the boss so others should come to them. But the Law of Connection means leaders should always make the effort to build relationships.

In his book *The Servant Leader: How to Build a Creative Team, Develop Great Morale, and Improve Bottom-Line Performance* James Autry shares his thoughts about what leadership is about and what it is not about as well as his ideas regarding the work environment created by a servant leader.

Autry writes that leadership is not about controlling others, but more about caring for them and serving as a useful resource for them. Leadership isn't about being the boss. Rather it's about being present for followers and building a community at work. Leadership is not about holding onto one's territory, but about letting go of one's ego. It's more concerned with bringing your spirit to work and being your best and authentic self in relationships with others.

Leadership is less about pep talks and motivation techniques, and, as stated earlier in the introduction to this Behaviours section, it's more about creating a place where people can do good work, can find meaning in their work and can bring their spirits to work. This type of climate, Autry describes, is where leaders are inspired by the concepts of servant leadership and the community of work and where there is shared decision-making, honest and open communication, trust, elimination of destructive competition and an environment of mutual respect.

To conclude this treatment of empowering others to act, let's attend to another quotation from James Kouzes and Barry Posner's *The Leadership Challenge*. It serves as a strong justification for servant leadership and the establishment of an enabling work environment.

> As we examine powerless and powerful times, we're struck by one clear and consistent message: *feeling powerful–literally feeling "able"–comes from a deep sense of being in control of life*. People everywhere seem to share this: when we feel able to determine our own destiny, when we believe we're able to mobilize the resources and support necessary to complete a task, then we persist in our efforts to achieve. But when we feel we're controlled by others, when we believe that we lack support or resources, we show no commitment to excel (although we may comply). Thus any leadership practice that increases another's sense of self-confidence, self-determination, and personal effectiveness makes that person more powerful and greatly enhances the possibility of success (2002, 282-283).

Servant leaders make followers "feel able" through their behaviours of facilitating workers' proactive approaches, establishing and maintaining their credibility as leaders, building trust throughout the organization and facilitating workers' connections to resources and power through networking.

Embracing change

The great philosopher Alfred North Whitehead wrote that the art of progress is to preserve order amid change and to preserve change amid order. Progress requires a change in the way things are perceived or done. If people are to do things better, they must do them differently in one form or another. This is the fundamental nature of progress. Although change is necessary for improvement, the implementation of change must not overwhelm the sense of order that underpins our sanity. Excessive change that disturbs our sense of well-being is fertile ground for controversy and resistance. However, change is necessary to achieve progress. For leaders navigating between order and change is always challenging.

Servant leaders strike a comfortable and productive relationship with change. They don't resist change like so many individuals and organizations that become ineffective over the long term due to their failure to improve. They don't over commit to change since it would be counterproductive to engulf people with too much disorder. Rather, servant leaders embrace change as a highly useful tool to serve the diverse, often conflicting needs of their followers and their organizational stakeholders.

Sipe and Frick discuss the important relationship between vision within a servant-led organization and change. Vision provides a necessary shared and unifying direction for the future. Servant leaders know there are many paths, many potential changes that can lead to their vision, therefore they allow for flexibility in how their vision is attained.

With an eye toward a better tomorrow, servant leaders and their followers take part in numerous iterations of change strategies and results assessments, then more changes and results, and so on. Each round of strategy introduces change in the forms of new methods, processes, relationships, etc. Some succeed, some fail, some open different paths. Kouzes and Posner refer to the fruitful strategic changes on the vision road as "small wins." Step-by-step progress takes servant-led organizations toward their compelling visions.

Sipe and Frick (2009, 149-150) describe the vision-strategic change relationship this way:

> Vision provides an organization with the stability of moving in the right direction. Strategy helps it get there.
>
> Notice that the first sentence above includes two seemingly contradictory words: "stability" and "moving." The kind of stability provided by a Servant-Leader systems thinker is more vibrant than the stability of things that never change. It is a stability with surprises.
>
> Part of the human makeup seeks harmony, balance, and some level of predictable security ... Servant-Leaders find harmony in moving toward the shared vision rather than in embracing the security of once-and-for-all answers. They do not confuse vision with goals. Many others do, though, and that is why managing change is so difficult.
>
> ... a Servant-Leader continues to communicate the relationship between changes and the shared vision. He personally *lives* the change even while

he is honest about his own inner pull to do things the same way for the sake of tradition or harmony or just plain comfort. This is where the "lead" emerges from a Servant-Leader.

These highly respected and valued writers on servant leadership propose that a "systems thinking" servant leader manages change in three dimensions: organizational (or systemic), relational (or interpersonal) and individual (or personal). They advise that if any dimension is overlooked, the leader will fail to manage change effectively and systemically.

Sipe and Frick also suggest that in the normal course of events followers view organizational change as something that starts external to the community. It is "out there" and forcing its way in. The change stimulus can often be upsetting because people will have to alter the ways they have been doing things.

Common reactions to change involve disbelief, denial and active attempts to resist by rationally justifying the status quo. Servant leaders are empathetic to the fear change engenders in people. They are cognizant of the need to channel fear and resistance productively.

They start by listening to their followers. Then they listen some more. Calmly and dispassionately they explain why there is a need for change and how it will be accommodated. They avoid preaching, coercing or seeking buy-in to situations or conditions followers had no opportunity to affect through participation. Instead, over time servants guide and empower people to explore positive possibilities for achieving mission and vision within the new context. It takes patience. There are no strong directives "from above."

> **Categories of change**
> Thomas L. Saaty and Larry W. Boone
> *Embracing the Future: Meeting the Challenge of Our Changing World*, 1990
>
> Sudden change
> Slow change
> Subtle change
> Cyclical change
> Selective change

Perhaps vision can be likened to a ship's rudder as the vessel sails on choppy waters. As the winds of change blow and strong waves rock the hull, the rudder influences the ship's eventual direction rather than exerting complete control over the course the craft takes.

As often described by numerous writers, servant leadership is quite different in this particular way from the traditional command-and-control leadership style. Servant leaders provide vision as a strategic guide and values as behavioural guides, and they see their role as facilitating followers' actions. Servant leaders do not, as so many command-and-control leaders do, see their role as supplying the "right" strategy that followers are merely expected to carry out.

James Autry writes:

> The servant leader understands that nothing positive can be accomplished in an organization without the support of those who are to do the hard work. So, in contemplating organizational or structural changes, the employees–those closest to the process, the product, or the people (the customers)–should participate in the decision. After all, they are the ones who'll have to make it work; thus, the major factor in making it work is their commitment. To paraphrase W. L. Gore, founder of Gore-Tex, productivity comes from commitment, not from control (2001, 116).

Besides the role of vision in embracing change there is also the vital matter of supporting followers' participation. It's easier for people to commit to change decisions if they participate in them. What do servant leaders do to facilitate workers' journeys into doing things differently? This can be viewed as a special case of empowering others to act. It's not just about a leader motivating constituents to devise and implement action plans–that is, to make things happen. It's about inspiring them to experiment, take risks and innovate in an atmosphere of ambiguity and uncertainty–to make *new* things happen. After all, new ideas and methods are tenuous. Resource usage may not be optimized. Mistakes are likely to be made. Failures will inevitably be encountered.

There are many well-recognized factors that create resistance to change in both individuals and organizations. Individuals develop habits to cope with complexities in life and at work, but change threatens the effectiveness of some programmed behaviours they have adopted to simplify their day-to-day activities. Resisting change helps preserve the relevance of their comfortable habits and relieves them of the burden of developing new ones.

Some individuals with a high need for security resist change because it threatens their personal feelings of safety.

Alterations in job tasks or work routines can give rise to economic/financial fears because workers may not be capable of learning new methods, or perhaps pay systems might be affected by new standards or productivity measures. The financial security of maintaining systems already in place is attractive to many people.

Other people resist change directly out of fear of the unknown; they have low tolerance for ambiguity and uncertainty and prefer the comfort of the status quo.

Sources of resistance to change also exist at the organizational level because enterprises have built-in mechanisms intended to maintain stability.

For example, over time selection processes tend to bring in certain people and remove certain others, and training systems reinforce specific role requirements and skills.

Formalized systems provide job descriptions, rules and procedures workers get used to following.

Constraints on behaviour exist as group norms or organizational culture; therefore, change adopters may find themselves ostracized from social groups at work.

Some departmental groups may resist change because they perceive a threat to their status emanating from their valued expertise or specialization.

Finally, any potential redistribution of decision authority may stimulate resistance to change because long-established power relationships within the organization may be disrupted.

Categories of change
Sudden change

When we encounter sudden, unexpected change, be it the death of a loved one, loss of a job, or involvement in an accident, we usually react with disbelief and shock: "Why did it happen to me?" Placing this event in a proper perspective is not easy: it may call for some new ways of viewing ourselves and the world around us. This kind of reorientation may take some time and much careful, realistic thinking.

While important sudden changes alter the rules of life's game, they do not defeat us unless we permit them to. They are not failures but setbacks that can be overcome with determination. It is easy to fail the test of sudden change, but a positive attitude can be a powerful ally. Sudden changes can be viewed as opportunities for growth.

Fortunately, Kouzes and Posner write elegantly about creating a special climate that supports change and innovation. It is their third practice of exemplary leadership, and they title it "challenge the process."

As these authors describe, exemplary leaders venture out knowing progress requires change from the status quo. Leaders accept being pioneers as one of their many roles. They are willing to step into the unknown. They are aware that part of leaders' duties involves destroying existing individual and organizational routines by replacing them with new and better ones. Leaders also encourage followers to do likewise.

Kouzes and Posner say that leaders challenge the existing process through 1) searching for opportunities by seizing the initiative and looking outward for innovative ways to improve and 2) experimenting and taking risks by constantly generating small wins and learning from experience.

Kouzes and Posner write:

> Times change, problems change, technologies change, and people change. Leadership endures. Teams, organizations, and communities need people to step up and take charge. ... Change is the province of leaders. It is the work of leaders to inspire people to do things differently, to struggle against uncertain odds, and to persevere toward a misty image of a better future (2012, 1).

And these authors add:

> Because innovation and change involve *experimenting and taking risks*, your major contribution will be to create a climate for experimentation in which there is recognition of good ideas, support of those ideas, and the willingness to change the system. ... When you take risks, mistakes and failures are inevitable. Proceed anyway. One way of dealing with the potential failures of experimentation is *by constantly generating small wins and learning from experience* (2012, 20).

Leaders help identify opportunities and seek ways to change and grow by being open to receiving ideas from anyone and anywhere. In Kouzes and Posner's terms, leaders who seek opportunity see themselves as net importers of ideas; they use their "outsight."

Astute leaders know their best source of innovation may be their own followers so they ask questions about what people see going on around them and pay attention to even the fuzziest mentions and weakest signals that something different is on the horizon. Besides listening attentively and respectfully in one-on-one conversations, leaders may create systems for followers' ideas to be collected and evaluated. For example, they may institute an "innovation board" comprised of workers and managers to help evaluate and develop followers' suggestions for new processes, products and services. They may even supply resources to start new internal ventures that are approved by the board.

To support change and innovation leaders treat every project and task as an adventure–and they encourage constituents to do the same. They adopt the role of active explorer. They get out of their office and visit any places in their organization they have not been. They make regular field trips a habit to ensure exposing themselves to anything that has changed or anyone who is doing things differently.

They find and create meaningful challenges for people. As discussed previously, leaders assign followers to opportunities, not necessarily to problems. Every six months or so they create a list of potential opportunities facing the organization and match workers to each opportunity based on personal interests and skills.

Leaders make sure the organization's work teams are renewed regularly. Aware that groups go through typical life cycles, servants seeking innovation insist that a new member or two be added to each team every couple of years–or sooner. Even top-performing teams get stale and need to be refreshed. Rotating members in and out of groups helps introduce fresh perspectives, assumptions and knowledge as well as connect to different networks, stimulating innovation.

New ideas and approaches can be generated through structures such as focus groups, advisory boards and junior boards (especially if leaders seek to engage and empower "new blood") or through use of mystery shoppers, suggestion sites on employee intranets, worker visits to customers or competitors, brainstorming sessions and the like.

The point is that lots of different approaches are used by leaders committed to searching for opportunities. There is no single best method. People notice that leaders are serious about change when they try so many different things.

Servant leaders who desire to support worker experimenting and risk-taking make it safe for others to take chances. They are aware that grand visions are achieved through incremental changes so they support breaking down big plans into small, achievable steps. Of course, leaders recognize failure is inevitable in some of the steps so they adopt practices that recognize and reward risk-taking and make sure failures are not punished.

> **Categories of change**
> **Slow change**
>
> Slow change is experienced without being recognized. It happens to all of us. Those who fail to notice this type of insidious change may one day be shocked by its cumulative effects. Hairs turn grey one at a time until one day some young pup describes us as grey-haired. For years we hear about, but manage to ignore, the oncoming age of artificial intelligence, when all at once our boss calls us into the office to explain that a very small device can do our job much better than we can—and we still don't know how this technology works or what it can do to help us.
>
> Slow change may seem imperceptible because our brain and senses are not calibrated to detect very small differences. But an accumulation of very small changes can be noticed by stepping away from the situation and assuming the viewpoint of an outsider. Parents do not notice the day-to-day changes in their young children, but a comparison of this year's birthday picture with last year's will reveal significant alterations. Infrequently seen relatives are quick to point out the magnitude of the slow change because they have the advantage of an outsider's view: "My, how Johnny has grown!" Slow transitions are noticeable if the necessary time and care are taken to look for them. Only the unobservant are taken by total surprise.

Frequently, new ideas are nurtured on a small scale with trusted groups in an incubator or test site where the probability of success is maximized. Those in charge of experiments collect feedback, make improvements and learn transferrable lessons before rolling out the idea on a grander scale. In Kouzes and Posner's terms, a small win is created and can be celebrated. The success becomes a story that makes heroes out of the participants and can be told to inspire others. In case the new idea does not pan out, keeping it small at first limits the cost of failure.

Leaders who support their constituents in venturing out and taking chances watch their language carefully. They want people to be comfortable proposing new ideas so they avoid spirit-deflating phrases like, "It's not in the budget," "That will never work," "We've tried that before, and it didn't work," or "We've never done that before" (inferring it must not be worth doing).

Staying on the communication theme, leaders can really surprise followers, as well as garner a lot of attention, by rewarding people for failing. The "shock value" of such an announcement alone can signal that leaders actually expect workers to do things differently. Of course, failure is not rewarded directly. It's the risk-taking behaviour that leaders want to recognize and support. But people learn quickly that leaders are serious about supporting the behaviour of experimenting with new ideas when even a failed attempt is publicly praised because it was something that offered a big payoff and presented at least a reasonable possibility of succeeding. "Congratulations on the attempt. Taking the risk is appreciated. We celebrate your creativity and effort. Better luck on the next idea."

Honesty and prudence demand recognition of the difficulties leaders encounter when, with good intentions, they incite a sense of restlessness in their teams and organizations by encouraging people to challenge "the way things are done around here." Assuming one's necessary role as leader *and* change agent can be quite uncomfortable. To be sure, not every individual welcomes change. Without doubt, many "owners" of existing organizational processes don't appreciate challenges.

Patrick Lencioni discusses extremely well the difficulties faced by leaders and the personal attributes needed to persevere as change agents. He writes:

> If you were searching for leaders to change the world for the better, what qualities would you look for? Courage and intelligence would certainly be prime candidates. Charisma might make the list. Or even creativity.
>
> As important–even essential–as these characteristics might be, I would rank two others ahead of them ... In fact, in my work with leaders, I have found many courageous, intelligent, charismatic, and creative people. But few of them possessed the two qualities that I'm thinking of: humility and pain tolerance.
>
> ... Before setting out on a quest to challenge the process and change the world, ... leaders should probably ask themselves two questions: "Who am I really serving?" and "Am I ready to suffer?" (2004, 71-72)

The first question is relatively easy to answer. Servant leaders see themselves serving others, not themselves. Otherwise, they wouldn't sign up for servant leadership. Humility is a built-in characteristic. Servants set their personal needs in line behind all others' needs. They meet the first requirement to be embracers of change.

Leaders in traditional command-and-control organizations tend to see themselves at the top of a hierarchy. They merit high salaries and perks. They enjoy being the boss. Formal authority is their most effective tool. Humility may be lacking. Therefore, when some form of resistance is inevitably encountered to their proposed strategic or structural changes, they tend to push harder. They may try to impose change on both individuals and organizations, and it rarely works. Recall one of Peter Senge's 11 Laws of Systems Thinking: the harder you push, the harder the system pushes back.

> **Categories of change**
> **Subtle change**
>
> Subtle changes are not easily detected by casual observation. Some probing may be required to find the change at all. A log by the side of the road appears solid and sturdy, yet one's foot drops straight through it when one is playfully mounting the "wood." The log has undergone subtle change as weather, fungus and termites have altered its internal structure.
>
> We build our knowledge through subtle change. In small increments the mind is gradually strengthened through learning; its capacity for reason grows. Simple facts become complex thoughts. Several old ideas become one new relationship. Transformation from novice to expert takes place gradually over a lifetime.

Why, though, must servant leaders be prepared to suffer? Why must they be fortified by a high tolerance for pain?

As advocates for vision-driven change, servant leaders will be ridiculed for being optimistic and for trying to reach too far. They will be chided for not being realistic, for failing to acquiesce to the already discussed individual and organizational factors that erect and sustain resistance to change. They will be criticized verbally to their faces and behind their backs. The changes they support will be opposed openly by some. And so they will be subject to suffering some traumatic impact to their self-esteem.

Therefore, servant leaders require what Kouzes and Posner refer to as "psychological hardiness." They need to be people who take in stride the rigors of change, risk and turmoil as well as the strains of work and life. When confronted with stressful change or personal encounters, they consider the experience engaging, they believe they can influence change (even though they cannot completely control it), and they see it as an opportunity for both personal and organizational development. In other words, they require the skill of being optimistic. Psychological hardiness is the attribute that permits servant leaders to be ready to suffer.

> **Categories of change**
> **Cyclical change**
>
> From the cycles of nature we learn that timing is an important issue if change is to be managed successfully. What appears to have changed may simply have entered a different part of a natural cycle. For example, isn't it foolish to cut down a barren tree in the middle of winter? With the warmth of spring the "dead" tree will begin another season of growth.
>
> Personal progress can be viewed similarly. One need not expect to grow in a well-defined linear fashion. There are times for expansion and times for consolidation. A master of change appreciates the cycle and is not disheartened by periods of seemingly slow progress.

One particular form of psychological hardiness is needed when servant leaders build their teams to pursue the organization's mission and vision. As Jim Collins advised in *Good to Great*, one of the most vital things leaders have to do is "get the right people on the bus." Sometimes this involves getting the current and wrong people, those who cannot commit wholeheartedly to mission and vision, off the bus.

Patrick Lencioni offers valuable advice for dealing with followers who are not energized by mission and vision. He suggests:

> A leader who is uncertain, even doubtful, about whether a team member is appropriately motivated would be well advised to take the most naked, obvious approach: come right out and say so. There is nothing wrong with saying, 'I am deeply passionate about the challenge our team is taking on, and I want everyone on the team to share that passion. Not that it has to look and feel the same for you as it does for me, because we're all different. But commitment has to be there. And if, after we talk about this and completely understand it, you don't think that this is interesting and personally motivating, that's okay. Let's just be clear about it and find another organization or issue that fires you up.'
>
> If, after hearing this message, they decide to enlist in the challenge, terrific. If they decide they can't commit with the level of passion and energy you need, they'll often opt out without the bitterness and resentment that accompanies most separations. In those cases of separation when bitterness and resentment are unavoidable, you'll know you've given the person an honest chance to find a way to get on the bus. Remember, if you're really motivated by the challenge of serving others, then you owe it to yourself,

your team, and the people you're serving to make sure everyone on the bus is committed (2004, 79).

It should be relatively simple to conclude that servant leaders are well prepared to enact the behaviour of embracing change. Attitudes and skills that support saying "we," visioning, committing to others' success, giving power away, not having to be right all the time, appreciating feedback, building community, asking questions, listening, telling stories, being optimistic, delegating and forgiving prepare and strengthen servant leaders to accomplish amazing new things in their enterprises, to view their pioneering work as a calling and to have the tenacity to hang on during turbulent times.

Servant leaders know that accepting the status quo promulgates mediocrity in performance and people. It is the playing field of ordinary supervisors and managers, not leaders.

Servants apply their special attitudes and skills to inspire others to do things differently and achieve improved results through new methods, processes, products and relationships. Servants embrace change because they understand that the real work of leaders is change. To carry out their responsibilities they don't have to change history, but they do have to change "business as usual." They know that leaders whose purpose is to serve others have to challenge the process by searching for opportunities as well as experimenting and taking risks. And they are aware that they will have to make personal sacrifices in service of higher purpose.

Categories of change
Selective change

Selective change is the heart of the matter: to succeed in the future we need to take an active and informed role in selecting the changes we desire. Do we possess a vision of ourselves and our organization at some future time? Do we have dreams? Do we aspire to be better in some ways? Although it is easy to predict failure and disappointment, what value does pessimism offer?

Selective change is deciding what one wants and creating a means to attain it. Look within for inspiration. Listen to other's hopes and dreams. Challenge yourself and followers. Embrace change.

Servant Leader Tips – Embracing change
Be someone others see embracing change; facilitate continuous innovation; welcome experimentation; celebrate improvement; at the same time take care not to overwhelm followers with too much change occurring too fast ("the art of progress is to preserve order amid change and preserve change amid order")
Provide a compelling, shared vision so that all followers will be moving in the desired direction
Achieve progress toward the vision through many incremental change strategies that followers initiate and implement
Ensure change occurs in three dimensions: organizational (systemic), relational (interpersonal) and individual (personal)
Continuously measure results to ensure change strategies are successful
Constantly communicate the relationship between changes and the shared vision
Expect naturally-occurring individual and organizational resistance to change
Empathize with followers; change creates fear; be prepared to listen, then listen some more; explain why there is a need for change; guide and empower people to explore positive possibilities for achieving mission and vision; be patient; call people to change rather than order them
Be open to ideas from anyone and anywhere; use your "outsight;" be a "net importer of ideas"
Be an active explorer; make regular field trips; see for yourself how things are being done differently
Create meaningful challenges for followers; match opportunities to people with relevant interests and skills
Renew teams regularly; rotate members to add fresh perspectives, assumptions and knowledge to groups
Support new idea generation and collection through focus groups, advisory boards, junior advisory boards, mystery shoppers, intranet suggestion sites, visits to customers and competitors, brainstorming sessions, …
Make it safe for others to take chances; praise and reward risk-taking; do not punish failure
Nurture new ideas by introducing them on a small scale in incubators or test sites with trusted groups; maximize the probability of success
Celebrate small wins (successful change strategies); make heroes of innovators; tell their stories

Use language that supports change; don't say "It's not in the budget," "We've tried that before," "That will never work," "We've never done that before"
Reward people for risk-taking behaviour even if their effort fails; use language like "Congratulations for trying," "We know every effort will not succeed," "Thanks for your creativity and effort," "Better luck with your next idea"
Remember that servant leaders facilitating change require humility and high pain tolerance; "be prepared to suffer"
Get the right people on the bus; ensure that everyone on the bus is committed to and energized by mission and vision
Exercise "psychological hardiness;" be optimistic; consider change engaging; believe you can influence change even if you can't fully control it; see change as opportunity for personal and organizational development

Planning the future

Effective leaders engage in planning behaviour. They know they cannot control the future, but they don't just let it happen to them. They establish shared visions for a better tomorrow, collaborate with others to set goals that lead to those visions, facilitate strategies to achieve those goals, seek always to integrate and coordinate activities and keep an eye on financial performance as well. As the old saying goes, if you have no particular destination in mind, any road will do. Servant leaders have an energizing, compelling destination to be sure. And they share their vision with others through planning because leaders can't get there unless followers are aware of it and commit to it.

Thinking about a preferred future, considering scenarios that take into account various uncontrollable factors and events, plotting a variety of contingent paths to bring aspirations to fruition and communicating to followers about a desired tomorrow become customary practices that evolve into parts of a leader's routines. They are recognized by others as elements of a leader's character.

The importance of visioning for servant leaders as both an attitude (vision isn't everything, but it's the beginning of everything) and as a skill has been mentioned numerous times in this book. A vision is a mental picture of success shared by leaders and followers. It expresses high ideals and values and gives focus to human energy. A well-developed vision connects workers' personal dreams and aspirations with the organization's identity. Its compelling power lures constituents forward to action.

However, visioning doesn't stand alone and apart as a leadership activity. Visioning is practiced in a planning context.

There are many excellent books and materials covering topics like strategic planning, planning methods, and forecasting techniques. In this short space it is not prudent to attempt to cover every area included under the broad leadership function of planning. Discussion will necessarily be limited.

The purposes of this section are to describe what a plan is from a servant leader's perspective, explain why servant leaders engage naturally in planning behaviour, examine typical contents of a plan, discuss some helpful ways servant leaders can manage the organizational planning process and consider how servants start planning by thinking about "who we serve." Also, another purpose is to help place visioning in its proper perspective as one of many elements of a leader's planning behaviour. So servant leader planning behaviour will be organized by addressing several basic questions:

- What is (and is not) a plan?
- Why develop a plan?
- What is included within a typical plan?
- Who is involved in planning? and
- Where does planning start?

What is (and is not) a plan?

A plan is a roadmap to an organization's future. Some like to think of it as a passage to opportunities. Typically, a plan covers the next 3-5 years because that's about how far out anyone can look with even a small degree of certainty, comfort and reasonableness.

Usually, a planning process leads to writing and publishing a document. The published plan serves as a communication tool. It's easier for followers and stakeholders to review planners' thinking and expected directions if the plan exists in written form. However, any published document should be accepted by all as essentially obsolete as soon as it is printed because planning is a continuous process in which leaders and followers are unceasingly involved. The written plan is a snapshot of the planning effort at a point in time.

If a company, agency, congregation or community is engaged in its first planning process, it usually takes several months to produce a plan, and dozens of people from all over the organization become involved in various roles. They could be engaged in internal assessment of strengths and weaknesses, environmental scanning of opportunities and threats, trend identification and forecasting, goal setting, strategy development, performance assessment (including financial performance) or other necessary activities. Of course, the leader maintains responsibility for all steps and for the final plan. Commonly, a plan is anywhere between 10-25 pages in length depending on the degree of detail an organization desires to communicate. Lengthier documents include specific goals and strategies.

Let's examine a plan's useful roadmap analogy. As any roadmap will demonstrate, there are various paths from one's current position to a distant destination. If one route that appears open when a journey begins is discovered blocked, an alternative way can be taken. But the destination is still reachable. Flexibility along the way is necessary. It may take a bit more time than originally expected or the road taken may be bumpier than anticipated, but the traveller can still get where she or he is going. So it is with planning.

Planning is a commitment to a destination. It is an allegiance to a future state, a desired place, as well as a call to followers to work hard on the changes necessary to get there. A written plan contains a *perceived* path, a set of goals and lists of strategies for attaining those goals. But inherent in every plan is an understanding that unexpected things will happen over the planning horizon and, therefore, adaptations will be necessary. When one path is found closed, another will be chosen.

A plan is:
- a roadmap to an organization's future
- a passage to opportunities
- a snapshot of the continuous planning effort at a point in time
- a shared commitment to a destination
- a call to followers to participate in change
- based on an organization's history, mission, values and vision
- a 3-5 year outlook
- 10-25 pages in length (depending on level of detail)

Planning requires courage to change what is necessary and to preserve what should be cherished and esteemed.

A plan is not:
- a contract
- starting over from scratch

Many misperceptions exist about plans and planning. For example, a plan is not a contract. It is not a document that spells out in detail how an organization will move step-by-step from where it is today to where it wants to be. Because the future always presents uncertainties and ambiguities, only a very courageous (or a very foolish) planner would expect to detail every goal and every strategy that's needed to achieve the successful future identified in a plan. There will have to be many mid-course corrections.

One reason many managers (they can't be called "leaders" if they fail to plan for the future) hesitate to commit to formal plan discussion, development and publication is that they know some of what they say they will do in today's plan will have to be changed in the future. And they believe those changes are likely to be interpreted by others as mistakes they have made or promises they have broken. No one can detail what needs to be done a year from now or in three years or five years. No plan can be "perfect" in laying out specific goals and strategies that will be required in the future. Adaptability will always be necessary. That understanding must always be part of every planning process. Leaders and followers commit to the plan's vision, not the specific means of achieving the vision.

Also, planning is not about forgetting everything that is important to an enterprise–like its history, mission and values–and starting from scratch to give birth to something new. In fact, most good plans celebrate an organization's past, purpose and behavioural guidelines. A well-developed plan proudly shows how a community is retaining what's most important, its character. Good plans demonstrate how "we" are not changing who we are, but we are becoming better in certain necessary ways.

Developing a plan requires courage to change what is necessary and to preserve what should be cherished and esteemed. To be effective planners leaders have to apply their foresight, know their organization's history well, respect its values and be in touch with their own and their followers' hopes, dreams and aspirations. (More is mentioned about foresight in the Reflecting behaviour discussion.)

It's always helpful to remember that in planning leaders have to exercise their psychological hardiness. As already discussed, it assists leaders greatly to be prepared to suffer and to have a high tolerance for pain because communicating a plan entails leaders "sticking their neck out" and declaring "this is where we want to go." Once any plan is made public, some others will start casting doubt. They will disparage any plan because it's easier to resist change than commit to it. They will be sceptical because they are pessimists or because they have difficulty committing to improvement. It is much easier to be a naysayer than a leader.

A plan is a roadmap to an organization's future. It is based upon an enterprise's history, mission and values. It serves as a call to followers to conceive and commit to the changes necessary to achieve the vision expressed within it.

Why develop a plan?

A multitude of reasons exist for servant leaders to engage in planning behaviour. As mentioned earlier, leaders are expected by their constituents to be forward-looking. Having a plan fulfils a major expectation workers have for their leaders. It adds to the leader's credibility.

Servant leaders call followers to a better tomorrow. They provide vision, direction and priorities for the future. They are not hesitant or embarrassed to express high expectations. Once committed to a plan, the vision is clear for all to access.

Servant leaders don't pretend they have all the answers. They energize followers to join in the hard work of change, and they pledge to facilitate that work. Servants do not demand compliance to prescribed action plans. They issue an invitation to followers to join the community's unified effort by bringing to the task their own ideas and creativity. The plan is the call, the vision, the direction, the priorities, the pledge and the invitation.

A plan answers the "why?" question. That is, plans help leaders avoid the perception of "arbitrariness." Bosses should anticipate their workers asking "why?" whenever decisions are made and directives given. "Because I'm the boss" should not be the response. In other words, good leaders are philosophers in part. They provide the fundamental nature of organizational knowledge, the core logic of their decisions and actions.

Servant leaders demonstrate respect for people by making them aware of the basic rationale for all actions. Workers typically resent feeling that they do things because the boss wants to or says so. (In a worst case scenario workers come to perceive that the boss wants something different every day; they have no way to predict what direction they may be told to pursue next.)

> **Servant leaders engage in planning to:**
>
> - demonstrate they are forward-looking
> - enhance their leadership credibility
> - provide a vision, a call, direction, priorities
> - invite followers to join in the hard work of change
> - pledge to facilitate change
> - answer the "why?" question
> - avoid the perception of arbitrariness
> - institutionalize a process for structured listening
> - help strengthen community
> - engage followers

A good plan helps explain "why?" by providing mission (our purpose), values (our behavioural guidelines), vision (where we are headed together) and priorities (what's most important at present). Additional detail is provided when goals and strategies are included in a plan.

Expected performance outcomes (the way an organization keeps score to determine if they are "winning") can supply even more detail for workers because they can keep score themselves to determine if they are succeeding. If workers ask why a new initiative is being undertaken, why one product or service is offered but not another or why a budget is as small or as large as it is, the place to look for an explanation is the organization's plan. Everyone, if interested, can reference the organization's philosophy: its mission, values, vision and priorities.

Servant leaders listen. It is both an important servant attitude and skill. Planning behaviour includes a "structured listening" element so planning formalizes listening throughout an enterprise. In an effective planning process multiple channels of communication are utilized to listen to peoples' aspirations, personal goals and ideas through face-to-face conversations, surveys, forums and meetings, intranet site suggestion boxes and any other means available. Planning underscores servant leaders' commitment to listen. In addition, multiple channels of communication are utilized to make the planning process a two-way communication effort. Regular updates and milestone achievements are reported to constituents to keep them informed of progress attained as planning efforts proceed.

Planning behaviour helps strengthen community. Servant leaders build community by emphasizing what diverse constituents have in common–

shared mission, values and vision. "We are bound together by the same purpose, beliefs and aspirations." Community can be enhanced through planning because the entire process accentuates "who we are, what we believe and where we are going together."

Planning provides a process for not only engaging followers but also for developing new leaders. Servant leaders see themselves as facilitators of fully engaged workers and as educators and coaches of new generations of leaders.

A good planning process is a way of getting constituents involved by adding them to the planning group directly or engaging them in two-way communication about the organization's future. Followers feel their input is valued, their work is important and they are kept informed about future directions.

Also, servant leaders use planning as a platform to develop new leaders by providing opportunity to demonstrate their abilities. Some workers get a chance to serve on various planning committees with current leadership personnel so they can showcase their leadership potential. Other workers can highlight their capabilities by communicating their ideas for new initiatives or improvements.

All workers can learn about servant leadership by observing the planning behaviours modelled by their leaders.

Why do servant leaders develop a plan? A plan demonstrates that leaders are forward-looking. A plan provides to followers a vision and a call, a direction, priorities, a pledge that leaders will facilitate change and an invitation to join the community's change efforts. A plan answers the "why?" question and avoids the perception of a leader's arbitrariness. A planning process provides opportunity to institutionalize structured listening, helps strengthen community, engages followers and develops new servant leaders.

What is included within a typical plan?

Although leaders choose many different topics and materials to put into their planning documents, some common *primary* contents of an institution's plan include:

- **Mission**
  Who we are; purpose; what we do
  A mission statement is a formal expression of an organization's or community's reason for being. It describes the work of the enterprise and why the work matters. Commonly 1-3 sentences in

length, a mission statement establishes parameters for organizational activity, helps identify priorities for members and helps non-members decide whether or not they wish to join. Mission statements are often compared to the North Star; they help members stay on track, keep their bearings. If every activity leaders and followers consider pursuing is tested against the group's mission, the enterprise will never stray too far from its purpose.

- **Values**

What community members believe collectively; principles that serve as common ground for all members; enduring beliefs about the way things should be done or about the ends members desire; standards that bind members together in community; truths that guide decisions and actions

Typically, an organization's values statement identifies 4-6 individual values and includes a brief explanatory statement about each. Within the values statement values are listed in *priority* order. Therefore, planners necessarily communicate their judgments about which values are more important than others. Since many organizational decisions are complex and require consideration of conflicting values (for example, safety versus service versus productivity), the order infers which values take precedence over others, even though all are important.

- **Vision**

Aspirations; future direction(s); what we aspire to be or to do; the "big picture"

Describes where an organization sees itself in the future. It is a word picture of a future state in which either key problems are resolved or in which ideals are more fully realised–or both. A vision statement may be written in the present tense as if it had already been accomplished. This helps the reader experience the look and feel of what the organization and its environment will be like when the vision is fully achieved.

Presented together mission, values and vision can be viewed as the organization's "story." It communicates "who we are" to readers no matter how familiar or unfamiliar they may be with the enterprise. The entire story can be presented easily on a single page. Readers can obtain a meaningful overview of the enterprise's character and decide whether or not there is compatibility between themselves and the organization. It helps them decide whether or not they want to join, align with or do business with the group.

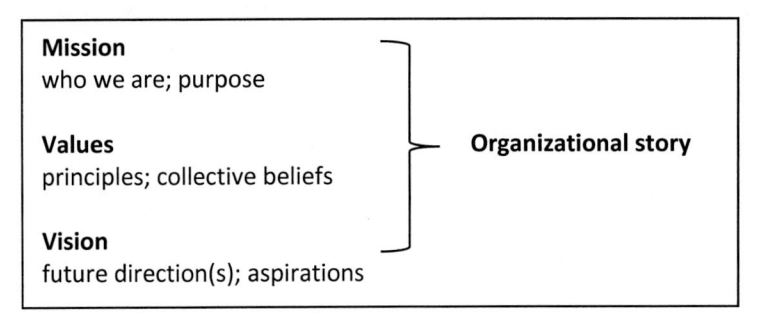

Mission who we are; purpose **Values**   **Organizational story** principles; collective beliefs **Vision** future direction(s); aspirations

Some people involved in planning ask reasonably why it's necessary to communicate mission, values and vision during a planning process and within a written plan since it may be assumed that all constituents are aware of their enterprise's defining characteristics. To address this question, one may envision any large population of workers, students, alumni, patients, stockholders, subscribers, congregation members or whatever term applies to the population. Consider classifying members into three categories: "engaged," "not engaged" and "disengaged."

"Engaged" members have a strong psychological connection with the organization and demonstrate loyalty. They are the faces leaders commonly see at meetings and other events. They are more committed than other members, more likely to invite non-members to accompany them to events and more likely to volunteer to provide assistance, make contributions and the like.

Members who fall into the "not engaged" category form the majority of almost every large population. Their participation can best be described as lukewarm. They may attend events sporadically, but they have no strong connection or commitment. They "straddle the fence" with one foot in the organization and one foot out. Their link to the organization may be more social than mission-related. If a friend attends an event with them, they may go. Otherwise, non-participation is a comfortable choice. They volunteer moderately or not at all. They are not likely to invite or recruit non-members and are somewhat likely to leave.

The "disengaged" members do not show up. Perhaps they used to be members and decided to leave or they are current members about ready to leave. They have decided that they and the organization are incompatible.

Any typical sizable population of organization members tends to consist of approximately 20-25 percent engaged individuals, 70-75 percent who are not engaged and 0-10 percent disengaged.

Now consider who needs to have mission, values and vision spelled out for them.

Engaged members don't need a detailed organizational story. They know it already; it is in their hearts. It drives their loyal behaviour.

The story is most useful to the majority of members who fall into the "not engaged" category. The information serves to deepen their understanding of the enterprise with which they have a tepid association. It helps educate them, and it may assist in converting them into engaged members.

An organization's documented mission, values and vision may be helpful to disengaged members–if they see it. That outcome may be problematic because the disengaged may never bother to access the information. However, it exists should disengaged members seek it.

Therefore, one may conclude that the major purposes for formalizing an organization's mission, values and vision and communicating them within a documented plan are: 1) to help move the "not engaged" members into the "engaged" category and 2) to celebrate the enterprise for the sake of "engaged" members. These very useful results are likely to benefit any institution.

- **Priorities or focus areas**
  Desired areas of growth; opportunities to pursue; operational aspects that require improvement
  Priorities or focus areas represent desired areas of growth or opportunities for improvement in any of the institution's aspects of operation. They are what the enterprise needs to pay attention to in order to achieve its vision. Typically, 8-12 priorities or focus areas are identified in the early stages of a planning effort. Examples of priorities may be: improve the quality of services to customers, renovate and expand physical facilities, strengthen administrative skills of first- and second-level managers, consolidate the balance sheet or increase supply chain coordination. Once planners have articulated their priorities or focus areas, direction is clarified. Then the means of attaining priorities through the institution's pillars can be discussed and organizational resources and energy concentrated.
- **Pillars**
  Primary organizational functions or strengths; enterprise building blocks; change levers
  Pillars provide strength and support. In the case of strategy formulation, strategic pillars hold up the vision. In planners' minds they are building blocks for successful change. They may form the

foundation of two or more priorities or focus areas. They represent basic needs for growing or improving the enterprise. Some planners like to think of pillars as the levers they will use for accomplishing the desired changes identified as priorities or focus areas. For example, an organization can achieve its priority of improving customer services by introducing changes in its marketing area, information technology function and HR training system. Typically, 4-6 pillars are identified during a planning process and closely managed during future operations.

- **Goals**

Desired outcomes or targets; criteria against which results are measured

A plan may include annual as well as more short-term (3-month, 6-month) goals. Goals should be specific and measurable. By identifying goals leaders communicate high expectations for performance and establish outcomes standards for which followers will be held accountable. Everyone knows what results are expected. There are no surprises, no misunderstandings about targets. Each goal should be broken down into a sequence of tasks or actionable steps. Action plans for each goal should specify who is responsible for implementing each step, a timeline for starting and achieving the action and how the outcome will be evaluated.

- **Timeline**

A graphic representation of expected and actual goal accomplishments

Within a plan it's helpful to include a simple overall timeline to provide an administrative overview of the plan's expected progress. Leaders and planners can become increasingly involved in plan implementation if goals are not being accomplished by responsible personnel in accordance with expectations. It is important to remember that organizational changes and improvements need not be made all at once. Planners should consider the enterprise's ability to embrace planned change. Too much change introduced too quickly can generate problems. And, of course, the effect of resource limitations (for example, personnel and funding) must be considered when deciding which action steps can be undertaken during any specific period. Effective servant leaders are "forward-looking." That is, they plan for the future, but they don't try to make everything happen immediately! Consider that a good plan is a multi-year event.

- **Resources needed**
  People; facilities; equipment; materials; systems; programs; policies; funding
  Planners are encouraged to consider the widest possible set of resources that may be applied or developed to support goal accomplishment. The planning process will be helpful in identifying the highest priority resource needs as well as where resource scarcity is affecting mission and vision achievement.

Some common *secondary* contents of an enterprise's plan include:

- **Cover page**
  Typically, the leader's name and/or signature is included indicating approval of the plan.
- **Leader's letter to followers** or **Introduction**
  An introductory statement is commonly provided to explain the need for planning and its role in the organization's future. Expectations for followers can also be described. A summary of environmental changes, anticipated opportunities and evolving challenges may also help set the stage for plan details.
- **Table of contents**

Plan structure and contents (basic)

Cover page
Leader's introductory letter
Table of contents
Organizational story: mission, values, vision
Planning process description
Assumptions
Outcomes measurements
Priorities or Focus Areas
Pillars: goals, strategies and resources needed for each pillar
Timeline
Appendix materials

- **Process description**
  A brief description of how the plan was developed, such as who was involved and when major planning activities took place, helps orient readers to the multiple steps taken in producing the plan over a considerable period of time.
- **Assumptions**
  All plans are based on a set of assumptions about the future. Major assumptions planners adopted regarding potential competitors' actions, market demand fluctuations, government policies, technology developments, sources of funding and so forth can be identified succinctly. Readers can assess the reasonableness of assumptions used by planners and can understand when mid-course corrections may be needed due to original assumptions requiring revisions.
- **Outcomes measures**
  Planners may wish to specify how major outcomes will be assessed to verify goal accomplishment.
- **Appendix**
  A wide variety of appended materials are included in plans to provide results of research efforts and analyses carried out by planners, an enterprise's historical milestones, financial trends and so on.

Who is involved in planning?

One of many possible approaches to planning involves the servant leader naming a steering committee of 10-12 people who represent the overall population of organization members. That is, men and women of various ages and years of experience in the enterprise, from different hierarchical ranks and with different specialties will be invited to bring their perspectives to the planning effort. Steering committee members will be responsible for listening to their constituents while gathering assessments and opinions on current operations as well as aspirations for the future. Typically, the servant leader heads the steering committee.

Often divided into sub-committees working simultaneously, the steering group will draft and/or edit statements of mission, values, vision, priorities and pillars. Each draft document will be made available to all organization members for review and comment. Planning elements take shape through numerous iterations of document drafts and revisions, which often include small group meetings and large organizational discussion forums.

Servant leaders are well aware that the organizational members' discussions of mission, values, vision, priorities and pillars bring the real value of planning to their communities. This is where education takes place. Followers learn what leaders are thinking and vice versa. Visions are formed, tested and forged into final shape. Participation and community-building are strong. Commitment is developed among constituents. Everything necessary to facilitate future success becomes clearer to the servant leader. Process is the thing! Leader-driven planning is what creates value for the organization. It's not the eventual written plan which will be obsolete upon printing. The published plan itself serves best as a focal point for discussions and as a communication tool for letting followers and stakeholders see the results of their discussions.

Once the steering committee has produced the plan's mission, values, vision, priorities and pillars, it's time to recruit many more planning participants. A typical approach is to create a sub-committee of 10-12 individuals for each pillar, therefore there may be 4-6 sub-committees consisting of dozens of organization members. Each sub-group is responsible for adding necessary detail to the plan. It is the sub-committees who identify specific goals and action plans as well as necessary resources and time to completion. The targets of their devised actions steps are the priorities or focus areas the steering committee previously wrote into the plan. These are the enterprise's desired areas of growth, significant opportunities to pursue and aspects of operations that require improvement. Also, one or two members of the steering committee often sit on each sub-committee to enhance communication between the steering group and its sub-groups as all the details of the final plan are worked out and implemented.

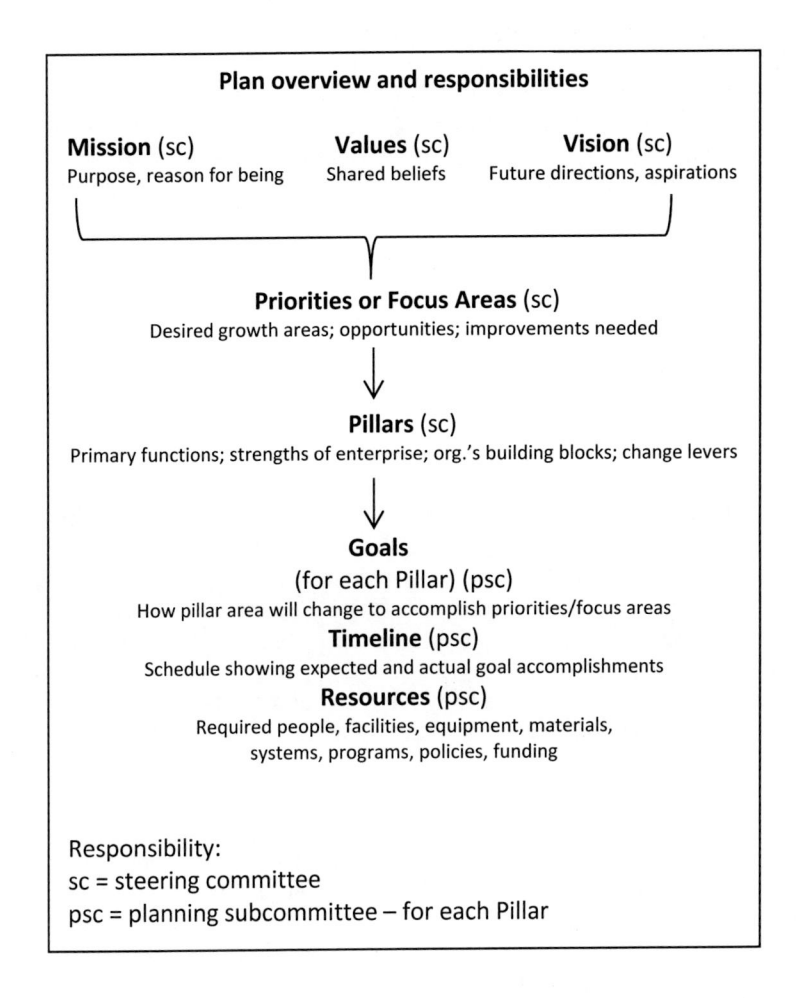

```
┌─────────────────────────────────────────────────────────────────┐
│                  Plan overview and responsibilities             │
│                                                                 │
│   Mission (sc)           Values (sc)           Vision (sc)      │
│   Purpose, reason for being  Shared beliefs   Future directions, aspirations │
│         └──────────────────────┬──────────────────────┘         │
│                                ▼                                │
│                  Priorities or Focus Areas (sc)                 │
│          Desired growth areas; opportunities; improvements needed │
│                                ▼                                │
│                          Pillars (sc)                           │
│   Primary functions; strengths of enterprise; org.'s building blocks; change levers │
│                                ▼                                │
│                            Goals                                │
│                      (for each Pillar) (psc)                    │
│        How pillar area will change to accomplish priorities/focus areas │
│                         Timeline (psc)                          │
│        Schedule showing expected and actual goal accomplishments │
│                        Resources (psc)                          │
│            Required people, facilities, equipment, materials,   │
│                  systems, programs, policies, funding           │
│                                                                 │
│   Responsibility:                                               │
│   sc = steering committee                                       │
│   psc = planning subcommittee – for each Pillar                 │
└─────────────────────────────────────────────────────────────────┘
```

On the steering committee and the multiple pillar sub-committees, especially, new generations of servant leaders are developed by educating them on how the enterprise works and how all operations integrate as well as coaching them on the practices and benefits of the servant leadership approach.

Where does planning start?

The final aspect of a servant leader's planning behaviour to be covered here regards answering the question about the origin of planning. From a servant's perspective where do all questions and answers about any organization's future begin? Simply, and expectedly, with the ones being served by the institution.

The most basic and most important lesson to learn about planning is to start by developing deep understanding of who is served by the organization and what their needs are. All planning decisions derive from this focus and this knowledge. Servant leaders know this and future servant leaders need to know it.

Through the planning process every follower comes to know that all future plans emanate from basic information about those served: who they are, where they are, how their numbers are growing or declining, what segments they can be divided into reasonably based on common needs, what their needs are currently and how their needs may be expected to change in the future.

Armed with this information, organizations can begin to plan how big they have to be, where they should be located, what human resource skills they require, what facilities and equipment they need, what systems, programs and policies will serve best, how much financing they must attain, and on and on. It all starts by focussing on who the enterprise serves and how the enterprise meets their current and future needs.

Reflecting

On a regular basis servant leaders spend time listening to others. But it is also important that leaders develop the behaviour of listening effectively to themselves. As mentioned previously in the listening skill discussion, servant leaders habitually spend time alone, inviting silence so they may better sense what is in their own minds and hearts. This practice is vital to their long-term success because leaders need to get in touch with their own inner voice. So servant leaders entice silence and summon their quiet heart. They spend 10-15 minutes each day clearing their minds to focus on questions designed to produce insights into what they believe, how they act, the health of their relationships, where they and their organizations are going and other topics with which servant leaders need to stay in touch.

Reflecting helps leaders examine their values and beliefs, visions, information, knowledge, priorities, goals, process and progress. Servant leaders need to understand themselves well so that they can make sense of the sometimes contradictory and perplexing information, requests and guidance they receive at an exceedingly fast pace. They need to steady themselves in the turmoil and keep a clear head. Stillness feeds their perspective. Reflecting leads to greater self-awareness. Self-awareness produces stronger self-confidence.

> The instrument of leadership is the self, and mastery of the art of leadership comes from mastery of the self. Leadership development is self-development ... It's about leading out of what is already in your soul. It's about liberating the leader within you. And it starts with taking a look inside (Kouzes and Posner 2012, 337).

Looking inward permits leaders to recognize with assurance their own strengths, weaknesses, capabilities and needs for improvement. Self-awareness deepens understanding of what is important to them and what they stand for. With the clarity that derives from self-knowledge leaders are able to communicate and connect with followers more effectively, and the authenticity of their leadership grows.

Leaders who spend silent time listening to themselves stay in touch with their answers to important questions. They better understand how personal values guide their decisions and actions. They appreciate their beliefs about how others should be called to conduct the affairs of their organizations. Their own attributes can be evaluated with honesty, and they can realise any differences that might exist between the ways they see themselves and how others see them. Courage can be summoned to face disappointments and setbacks, to admit mistakes and to forgive those who have wronged them. The true strength of their relationships with constituents can be perceived. Reflecting helps reveal whether or not leaders need to recommit to trust-building between themselves and those who follow them. And, among many other things, servants can appreciate how much they depend on other people and how important it is to say "thank you," celebrate their successes and share credit with them.

Typically, reflecting behaviour consists of spending 10-15 minutes each day experiencing solitude and engaging in consideration of self. It can be done at a quiet desk, within a closed-door office, during a commute, at a coffee break, while walking the dog (or otherwise exercising), before falling asleep at night or in any circumstances where an individual finds it comfortable to relax, experience solitude and enter silence. It's a habit of regularly turning off the noise and looking inward.

But reflecting can be an anxiety-inducing trial for some people. At first it may be easier to sit alone in a quiet room and practice Sipe and Frick's "quieting the mind" exercise until reflecting abilities can be further developed. Once skills mature, it becomes much easier to engage in reflecting behaviour just about anywhere and anytime.

Quieting the mind
James W. Sipe and Don M. Frick
Seven Pillars of Servant Leadership (2009, 116)

"Sit with your feet on the floor, hands resting comfortably by your side or on your legs. Close your eyes and take three long, deep breaths. As you inhale, imagine you are breathing in quietness; as you exhale, imagine breathing out your pressing concerns of the moment.

Before long, current thoughts, images, or anxieties will try to intrude. Do not drive them away; simply accept and observe them. Some people find it helpful to imagine putting those distractions on a floating log and watching them drift downstream.

Next, imagine a place of natural beauty and peace, perhaps a mountain scene, a forest or an ocean view, someplace where you feel safe and content. See, hear and smell the environment. Expect nothing and force nothing; simply experience what unfolds. Perhaps nothing will happen or animals will appear or a surprising scene will emerge.

Now empty your mind of everything. No images or sounds.

When you are ready, bring yourself back to the present.

What did you see and hear? How do you feel now? What did you gain from the experience of silence?"

While a few minutes of daily reflecting is a highly useful routine for servant leaders to practice in support of continuous self-examination, occasional full-day, weekend or even week-long retreats will deepen the reflecting experience and help leaders explore complex personal issues like reinstituting work-life balance, making career changes, emotional healing and renewing one's spiritual life. However, the focus here is on the helpful behaviour of reflecting for a few minutes each day.

While reflecting, leaders can focus on structured materials from leadership publications to stimulate their thinking. The excellent leadership books on which this book is based are filled with highly useful resources. For example, consider the "Think about the past" exercise which helps leaders get in touch with their visions for the future as well as, perhaps, their own personal value formation processes which may have been affected by the peak and valley events in their lives. The Kouzes and Posner exercise included here was adapted from Shepard and Hawley and can be very helpful as a source of leaders' personal "who I am" stories that help leaders reveal their values to followers.

> **Think about the past**
> James M. Kouzes and Barry Z. Posner
> *The Leadership Challenge*, 3rd edition (2002, 132)
>
> "Before you attempt to write your vision statement, look to your past for key messages about the direction you have chosen and the future to which you aspire. We especially like the 'lifeline' exercise developed by Herb Shepard and Jack Hawley. Here's an abbreviated version:
>
> Look backward in your past and record significant events in your life—turning points that have influenced the direction you have taken. Start as far back as you can remember and stop at the present time.
>
> Briefly record key events in your life that represent turning points or significant learning experiences. Many people find it useful to draw this as a *lifeline*—a graph that maps both the peaks and valleys, the highs and the lows. Others prefer to just list events. Whichever method works for you, give the technique a try.
>
> Next to each event, write a word or two identifying the experience.
>
> Now go back and review each peak event, making a few notes on why each was a high point for you.
>
> Analyse your notes. What dominant themes emerge? What patterns are revealed? What important personal strengths? What do these themes and patterns tell you about what you're likely to find personally compelling in the future?"

Once this exercise for thinking about one's own past has been completed, servant leaders can do the same thing while focusing on their organization's past. What have been the organization's peaks and valleys, highs and lows? What dominant themes emerge? What patterns are revealed? What important organizational strengths? What do these themes and patterns tell you about what you're likely to find compelling for the organization in the future?

Servant leadership journeys necessarily include examining what leaders are doing, why they are doing it and how they are doing it. Leaders who don't take the time to reflect regularly on their own character and abilities, priorities, directions and teams risk running off the rails–perhaps just a little at first but then more and more as small missteps lead to bigger and bigger misdirection.

Reflecting is a humbling yet powerful behaviour that helps leaders improve their performance. It requires servants to take an honest look at themselves through answers to a series of questions that test their application of servant leadership. Included at the end of this section are examples of useful questions that can be asked a few at a time. They examine various elements of effective servant leader attitudes, skills and behaviours. They are intended to be a starting point for reflecting. Servants can refine the list over time to include additional questions that focus on areas of special interests and needs depending on leaders' specific situations.

Reflecting and foresight

In the introduction to their book, *The Seven Pillars of Servant Leadership*, under the bolded title "The Psychology of Change," James Sipe and Don Frick integrate the important topics of character, decision-making, analysing and reflecting. The perspective they provide on the behaviour of reflecting is well worth our attention. Sipe and Frick (2009, 9) write:

> Aristotle believed that moral character is the result of consistently acting on virtues like courage, temperance, and modesty. Every time a choice presents itself, one considers all the variables, determines the best course of action in the situation–what Aristotle calls the Good–and chooses it, day after day, week after week. Eventually, the *process* of analysis and reflection becomes a habit, and so does the *outcome* of choosing Good. Character is a result of the right habits.
>
> The analysis component of decision making is not a problem for most people. We analyse, categorize, and prioritize an issue to within an inch of its life, because that is what is rewarded in most organizations. The *reflection* part of problem solving is more challenging. It often requires taking time away from the matter to gain perspective and to draw upon the *wisdom of intuition* (italics added). This element of the process does not

come naturally to most people. It requires a bit of one's precious time, a slight leap of faith, and some loss of control–something that produces anxiety in many people.

The authors go on to explain that Robert Greenleaf offered a major contribution to leadership thought by discussing the need for reflection and intuition. Basically, he termed this part of leaders' decision-making processes "foresight."

Following the text book description, when a decision is needed, information is gathered, priorities established, alternatives identified, consequences forecast then a choice is made. Right? No, wait. Foresight has been omitted. Reflection has been ignored. In applying foresight a decision maker may walk away from the issue for a while. Sleep on it to let the brain replenish its neurotransmitters. Then allow the neurons, programmed in the language of electricity and chemistry, to fire on multitudes of connections. Cogitate. Let the mind play with other ideas, activities and issues. Allow the subconscious to function. Let the servant's heart have a chance to chime in. Then decide.

Greenleaf discussed how foresight plays a major role in planning. Based upon Greenleaf's thinking, Larry Spears, past President and CEO of the Robert K. Greenleaf Center for Servant-Leadership, defines foresight as:

> the ability to foresee the likely outcome of a given situation, enabling the Servant-Leader to understand lessons from the past, realities of the present, and likely consequences of a decision for the future. It is deeply rooted in the intuitive mind (Spears 2004, 15).

Sipe and Frick explain that foresight is not the same as planning, positioning or forecasting. Rather, it is "a practical strategy for making decisions and leading" (2009, 106). Summarized here are some steps the authors suggest for harnessing one's power for foresight:

1. *Analyse the past*
   History repeats its patterns. Foresight relies on bringing to consciousness some deep patterns already recognized and generated in the brain.
2. *Learn everything there is to know about the issue at hand*
   Accurate information is necessary for accurate foresight. Do all the research, absorb the data, speak with knowledgeable colleagues and consult with many people all over the organization's hierarchy and

departments. Apply analytical reasoning as far as it will possibly take you.
3. *Let the information incubate*
Spend considerable time away from the issue. Do not rush; stop thinking about the decision that is waiting to be made. Put off rationality so that your brain can play with solutions.
4. *Be open for breakthrough*
Patterns of foresight occur to different leaders in different ways. Welcome hunches, fleeting suggestions and incomplete ideas. They are the raw materials of answers. Find what helps you fill in the missing pieces; some people like to doodle, some still themselves to clear their minds, some prefer to engage in dialogue with others to breakthrough to solution. No matter the method you choose, patience is required.
5. *Share your insights with trusted colleagues*
Exercise a servant's humility. Seek informed feedback. Your idea may or may not be useful, or it may generate resistance to change. Exercise care in choosing a confidant. Choose one with perspective different than yours and who is sensitive to the practical challenges of implementing new ideas in the organization. Listen to their reactions and suggestions.

Foresight can be viewed as helpful to servant leaders in many ways. It contributes to the visioning process. Servants spend time listening to followers' dreams and aspirations, internalizing them, assimilating and distilling them, then mingling them with the organization's mission to identify a compelling shared vision. Foresight may also be seen coming into play as servant leaders recognize constituents' best talents and realise how they can be connected in the long term to vision achievement. Also, servants can apply foresight to appreciate how future benefits will accrue to their current practices of giving their power away, building community, developing trust, establishing networks and embracing change. Leaders who do not adopt the attitudes, develop the skills and practice the behaviours of the servant very often deny the usefulness of the servant leadership style because they fail to foresee how the future will be better through servant leadership.

Silence and reflection form the fertile ground foresight requires for incubating the ingredients of decisions and actions. Servant leaders who practice reflecting know how to quiet their minds and hearts. They may well be more capable than others at accessing foresight and more gifted at applying the "wisdom of intuition."

Following are some questions that can be asked a few at a time while reflecting. They are intended to call to mind many of the servant leader attitudes, skills and behaviours for the silent leader's consideration.

Servant Leader Tips – Reflecting questions to ask myself about my servant leadership
What are my greatest leadership strengths and weaknesses?
Do I exemplify the servant leader attitudes described in this book?
Do I possess the servant leader skills described in this book?
Do I engage in the servant leader behaviours described in this book?
What are my greatest needs for improvement?
Do the people I work with see the same strengths and weaknesses? If not, are problems created by the different perceptions?
Do I have a plan for self-improvement? Am I working the plan?
Am I clear about the values that guide my life and leadership?
Do I live my values? Do others see me behave in accord with my values? Do I lead by example?
Is the way I spend my time aligned with my values? Am I spending my time on the most important things for my organization and for myself?
Do I talk enough about my values to others?
Am I effective at telling stories that reveal "who I am," "who we are" and "our shared vision," that make heroes of others and that teach important lessons?
Is there agreement on values within the group I lead?
How clear am I about the shared vision for our organization? Do I truly understand where we want to go?
How clear are others about our shared vision? How do I know?
What have been the peaks and valleys, the highs and lows in the organization's history? What dominant themes emerge? What patterns are revealed? What important organizational strengths? What do these themes and patterns tell us about what we are likely to find compelling in the future?
How has this organization struggled and survived? What is the story of organizational struggle? What are the teachable lessons from this story?
What would inspiring success look like for this organization? What can I do to make everyone proud to work here?
What imagery represents the organization's success? What are the most inspiring stories of hope and transformation?
How effectively do I ask questions to learn about the people I lead? How can I improve the way I ask questions of others?

How well do I understand the hopes, dreams and stories of those I lead? How can we create a future that includes our common aspirations?
How prepared am I to address the numerous challenges that confront the organization?
Am I good at facing ambiguity, uncertainty and adversity? Do I possess sufficient courage and humility?
How well do I handle disappointments, mistakes and failures?
What are my sources of personal strength and courage?
Am I ready to suffer?
Do I possess sufficient psychological hardiness?
How well do I break down the long journey to the organization's vision into small steps that can be achieved to move us forward and create momentum?
How effectively do I celebrate small wins to encourage followers?
Do I encourage risk-taking and experimentation sufficiently?
Am I careful to support creativity and not to punish failure?
How do I create a learning environment where people accept the mistakes that are unavoidable while achieving breakthrough performance?
Do I make sure the organization is hiring people with the right values and skills?
How effective are my relationships with constituents?
Do I empower others to act? Is sufficient initiative demonstrated by followers?
Do constituents trust me and trust each other? What evidence of trust do I see?
Do I share credit for successes? Do I say "thank you" to others for their contributions to success?
How often do I walk the shop looking for people doing things right?
Do I pay enough attention to the positive things happening in the organization?
Do I share my power with others? How can I share more power?
Do I share information with others? How can I share more information?
Have I increased my personal networks recently?
How well do I help others connect to the sources of information, expertise and authority they need to make things happen for the organization?
How can I increase followers' discretion and choice?
Are there people whose talents and potential I have overlooked? How can I engage them?

Do I use my "talent radar"? Do I act as if I believe that everyone is good at something? Do I show people how they can apply their best talents to help achieve the organization's vision?
Are others convinced that I am committed to their success?
Do others believe that I have to be right all the time?
Do others see me as a community builder? What evidence do they see?
Am I achieving my personal goals?
Do I make time for those closest to me?
Have I thought sufficiently about my legacy? What do I want to leave behind when I move on? What do I need to do now to create my preferred legacy?
Do I communicate high expectations to others?
Do people agree that I am an optimistic leader?
Do I always say "we"?
How do I stimulate informal communications and conversations among followers?
Am I getting the important things done? What improvements can I make in my personal time management?
How can I delegate more effectively?
Do I manage meetings effectively? How can I improve?
In meetings, do I put other people on the agenda so they can demonstrate their abilities and gain leadership experience?
Do I hold people accountable for their performance and behaviour?
Do I address underperformance, problems and situations as they occur?
Do I ignore problems because it's easier than confronting others?
Do I make clear to people what results and behaviours are expected on the job?
Am I a good listener? What evidence do I have? How can I improve my listening abilities?
Do I act as an effective coach to others? Are there other people I should be training and encouraging?
Am I involved actively in developing others?
Do I treat people with respect? Do they agree I treat them with respect?
Do I demonstrate enough patience with others?
Do I practice self-control when necessary?
How do I know people have confidence in my leadership?
Do I forgive others when necessary? Even when I'm sure I'm right?
How can I be more forgiving?
Do I ever say unkind things about others behind their backs?
Do I spend enough time and effort giving feedback to others?

Do I spend enough time and effort collecting others' feedback about my leadership performance?
Do I praise others in public to demonstrate what good performance and behaviour looks like?
Do I ever embarrass or criticize people in front of others?
Do people agree that I bring a positive attitude to my job?
Am I sensitive to the implications of my decisions on other groups and individuals?
Do followers agree that I am honest, forward-looking, competent and inspiring?
Do followers agree that I embrace change? How can I better demonstrate the courage to change what is necessary and to preserve what should be cherished and esteemed?
Do I have and participate in an effective process for planning the organization's future?
Do I spend enough time reflecting to focus on questions designed to produce insights into what I believe, how I act, the health of my relationships, where my followers and I are going, and other topics that are important to my servant leadership?

BIBLIOGRAPHY

Chapter One

"A Leader's Prayer." Accessed August 25, 2018. https://cpco.on.ca/files/6213/8437/4870/A_Leaders_Prayer.pdf.

Autry, James A. 2001. *The Servant Leader: How to Build a Creative Team, Develop Great Morale, and Improve Bottom-Line Performance.* Roseville, CA: Prima Publishing.

Barbuto Jr., John E. and Daniel W. Wheeler. 2006. "Scale Development and Construct Clarification of Servant Leadership." *Group & Organization Management* 31 (3): 300-326.

Blanchard, Ken. 2004. "Reflections on Encourage the Heart." In *Christian Reflections on The Leadership Challenge*, edited by James M. Kouzes and Barry Z. Posner, 101-118. Jossey-Bass.

Blanchard, Ken and Phil Hodges. 2003. *The Servant Leader: Transforming Your Heart, Head, Hands and Habits.* Nashville, TN: Thomas Nelson.

Boone, Larry W. and Sanya Makhani. 2013. "Five Necessary Attitudes of a Servant Leader." *Review of Business* 33 (1): 83-96.

Boone, Larry W. and Monica S. Peborde. 2009. "Developing Leadership Skills in College and Early Career Positions." *Review of Business* 28 (3): 3-13.

Burrell, Darrell N. and Brian C. Grizzell. 2010. "Do You Have the Skills of a Servant-Leader?" *Nonprofit World* 28 (6): 16-17.

Collins, Jim. 2001. *Good to Great: Why Some Companies Make the Leap and Others Don't.* New York: Harper Collins.

Covey, Steven R. 1998. "Servant-leadership from the inside out." In *Insights on Leadership: Service, Stewardship, Spirit, and Servant-Leadership*, edited by Larry C. Spears, xi-xviii. New York: Wiley.

Drucker, Peter F. 2006. *The Effective Executive: The Definitive Guide to Getting the Right Things Done.* New York: HarperCollins.

Drucker, Peter F. 2005. "Managing Oneself." *Harvard Business Review* 83, (1): 100-109.

Ebener, Dan R. 2010. *Servant Leadership Models for Your Parish.* New York: Paulist Press.

"Fortune's Best Companies to Work for with Servant Leadership." Modern Servant Leader. Accessed August 18, 2018. http://www.modernservantleader.com/servant-leadership/fortunes-best-companies-to-work-for-with-servant-leadership/

Graham, Jill W. 1991. "Servant-Leadership in Organizations: Inspirational and Moral." *The Leadership Quarterly* 2 (2): 105-119.

Greenleaf, Robert K. 2002. *Servant Leadership: A Journey into the Nature of Legitimate Power and Greatness.* New York: Paulist Press.

Greenleaf, Robert K. 2008 (originally published in 1970). *The Servant as Leader.* Atlanta, GA: The Greenleaf Center for Servant Leadership.

Hunter, James C. 2012. *The Servant: A Simple Story about the True Essence of Leadership.* New York: Crown Business.

Hunter, James C. 2004. *The World's Most Powerful Leadership Principle: How to Become a Servant Leader.* Colorado Springs, CO: Waterbrook Press.

Jaramillo, Fernando, Douglas B. Grisaffe, Lawrence B. Chonko, and James A. Roberts. 2009. "Examining the Impact of Servant Leadership on Salesperson's Turnover Intention." *Journal of Personal Selling & Sales Management* 29 (4): 351-365.

Keith, Kent M. 2010. *The Meaning of the Compound Word "Servant-Leader."* Atlanta, GA: Greenleaf Center for Servant Leadership.

Kelly, Margaret J. 2010. "Leadership." In *A Concise Guide to Catholic Church Management*, edited by The Vincentian Center for Church and Society, 5-22. Notre Dame, IN: Ave Maria Press.

Kouzes, James M. and Barry Z. Posner. 2016. *Learning Leadership: The Five Fundamentals of Becoming an Exemplary Leader.* New York: Wiley.

Kouzes, James M. and Barry Z. Posner. 2012. The Leadership Challenge, 5th edition. San Francisco, CA: Jossey-Bass.

Kouzes, James M. and Barry Z. Posner. 2010. *The Truth About Leadership.* San Francisco, CA: Jossey-Bass.

Kouzes, James M. and Barry Z. Posner. 2004. "The Five Practices of Exemplary Leadership." In *Christian Reflections on The Leadership Challenge*, edited by James M. Kouzes and Barry Z. Posner, 7-38. San Francisco, CA: Jossey-Bass.

"Leadership Styles: Choosing the Right Approach for the Situation." Mindtools. Accessed August 15, 2018. https://www.mindtools.com/pages/article/newLDR_84.htm.

"Leadership Styles: Understanding and Using the Right One for Your Situation." June 5, 2015. Informa. https://www.informa.com.au/insight

/leadership-styles-understanding-and-using-the-right-one-for-your-situation/.

Lencioni, Patrick. 2016. *The Ideal Team Player: How to Recognize and Cultivate the Three Essential Virtues.* San Francisco, CA: Jossey-Bass.

Lichtenwalner, Ben. 2017. "Servant Leadership Companies List." Last modified April 29, 2017. https://www.modernservantleader.com/featured/servant-leadership-companies-list/.

Liden, Robert C., Sandy J. Wayne, Hao Zhao, and David J. Henderson. 2008. "Servant Leadership: Development of a Multidimensional Measure and Multi-level Assessment." *The Leadership Quarterly* 19 (2): 161-177.

Maxwell, John C. 2007. *The 21 Irrefutable Laws of Leadership, 10th Anniversary Edition.* Nashville: Thomas Nelson.

Maxwell, John C. 1998. *The 21 Irrefutable Laws of Leadership.* Nashville: Thomas Nelson.

Mayer, David M., Mary Bardes, and Ronald F. Piccolo. 2008. "Do Servant-Leaders Help Satisfy Follower Needs? An Organizational Justice Perspective." *European Journal of Work and Organizational Psychology* 17 (2): 180-197.

McAllister-Wilson, David. 2004. "Reflections on Inspire a Shared Vision." In *Christian Reflections on The Leadership Challenge*, edited by James M. Kouzes and Barry Z. Posner, 55-68. San Francisco, CA: Jossey-Bass.

Neubert, Mitchell J., Michelle K. Kacmar, Dawn S. Carlson, Lawrence B. Chonko, and James A. Roberts. 2008. "Regulatory Focus as a Mediator of the Influence of Initiating Structure and Servant Leadership on Employee Behavior." *The Journal of Applied Psychology* 93 (6): 1220-1233.

Ortberg, Nancy. 2004. "Reflections on Enable Others to Act." In *Christian Reflections on The Leadership Challenge*, edited by James M. Kouzes and Barry Z. Posner, 85-98. San Francisco, CA: Jossey-Bass.

Robbins, Stephen P. and Timothy A. Judge. 2015. *Organizational Behavior, 16th edition.* Pearson Education.

Robbins, Stephen P. 2013. *The Truth About Managing People, 3rd edition.* FT Press.

Russell, Robert F. and A. Gregory Stone. 2002. "A Review of Servant Leadership Attributes: Developing a Practical Model." *Leadership & Organization Development Journal* 23 (3): 145-157.

Searle, Travis P. and John E. Barbuto, Jr. 2011. "Servant Leadership, Hope, and Organizational Virtuousness: A Framework Exploring

Positive Micro and Macro Behaviors and Performance Impact." *Journal of Leadership & Organizational Studies* 18 (1): 107-117.
Sendjaya, Sen and James C. Sarros. 2002. "Servant Leadership: Its Origin, Development, and Application in Organizations." *Journal of Leadership & Organizational Studies* 9 (2): 57-64.
"Servant Leadership: Putting Your Team First and Yourself Second." MindTools. Accessed August 4, 2018. https://www.mindtools.com/pages/article/servant-leadership.htm.
Sipe, James W. and Don M. Frick. 2009. *Seven Pillars of Servant Leadership: Practicing the Wisdom of Leading by Serving.* New York: Paulist Press.
Sivasubramaniam, Jeevan. "5 Companies that Embrace Servant Leadership." August 22, 2017. https://ideas.bkconnection.com/five-surprising-companies-that-embrace-servant-leadership.
Smith, Brien N., Ray V. Montagno, and Tatiana N. Kuzmenko. 2004. "Transformational and Servant Leadership: Content and Contextual Comparisons." *Journal of Leadership & Organizational Studies* 10 (4): 80-91.
Spears, Larry C. 2010. "Character and Servant Leadership: Ten Characteristics of Effective, Caring Leaders." *The Journal of Virtues & Leadership* 1 (1): 25-30.
Van Dierendonck, Dirk and Inge Nuijten. 2011. "The Servant Leadership Survey: Development and Validation of a Multidimensional Measure." *Journal of Business Psychology* 26 (3): 249-267.
Vinod, Sangeetha and B. Sudhakar. 2011. "Servant Leadership: A Unique Art of Leadership!" *Interdisciplinary Journal of Contemporary Research in Business* 2 (11): 456-467.

Chapter Two

Think and say "We" not "I"
Drucker, Peter F. 2006. *The Effective Executive: The Definitive Guide to Getting the Right Things Done.* New York: HarperCollins.
Kouzes, James M. and Barry Z. Posner. 2002. *The Leadership Challenge, 3rd edition.* Jossey-Bass.
Lencioni, Patrick. 2016. *The Ideal Team Player: How to Recognize and Cultivate the Three Essential Virtues.* Jossey-Bass.

Value statements are meant to be practiced, not stored on a shelf
Blanchard, Ken. 2004. "Reflections on Encourage the Heart." In *Christian Reflections on The Leadership Challenge*, edited by James M. Kouzes and Barry Z. Posner, 101-118. Jossey-Bass.
Kouzes, James M. and Barry Z. Posner. 2007. *The Leadership Challenge, 4th edition*. Jossey-Bass.
Robbins, Stephen P. and Timothy A. Judge. 2015. *Organizational Behavior, 16th edition*. Pearson Education.
Robbins, Stephen P. 2013. *The Truth About Managing People, 3rd edition*. FT Press.
Sipe, James W. and Don M. Frick. 2009. *Seven Pillars of Servant Leadership: Practicing the Wisdom of Leading by Serving*. New York: Paulist Press.

Vision isn't everything, but it's the beginning of everything
Covey, Steven R. 1998. "Servant-leadership from the inside out." In *Insights on Leadership: Service, Stewardship, Spirit, and Servant-Leadership*, edited by Larry C. Spears, xi-xviii, Wiley.
Greenleaf, Robert K. 1970. *The Servant as Leader*. The Greenleaf Center for Servant Leadership.
Kelly, Margaret J. 2010. "Leadership." In *A Concise Guide to Catholic Church Management*, edited by The Vincentian Center for Church and Society, 5-22. Notre Dame, IN: Ave Maria Press.
Kouzes, James, M. and Barry Z. Posner. 2010. *The Truth About Leadership*. Jossey-Bass.
Kouzes, James M. and Barry Z. Posner. 2004. "The Five Practices of Exemplary Leadership." In *Christian Reflections on The Leadership Challenge*, edited by James M. Kouzes and Barry Z. Posner, 7-38. Jossey-Bass.
Kouzes, James M. and Barry Z. Posner. 2002. *The Leadership Challenge, 3rd edition*. Jossey-Bass.
McAllister-Wilson, David. 2004. "Reflections on Inspire a Shared Vision." In *Christian Reflections on The Leadership Challenge*, edited by James M. Kouzes and Barry Z. Posner, 55-68. Jossey-Bass.
Sipe, James W. and Don M. Frick. 2009. *Seven Pillars of Servant Leadership: Practicing the Wisdom of Leading by Serving*. New York: Paulist Press.

Everyone is good at something
Ortberg, Nancy. 2004. "Reflections on Enable Others to Act." In *Christian Reflections on The Leadership Challenge*, edited by James M. Kouzes and Barry Z. Posner, 85-98. Jossey-Bass.

I am committed to your success
Blanchard, Ken. 2004. "Reflections on Encourage the Heart." In *Christian Reflections on The Leadership Challenge*, edited by James M. Kouzes and Barry Z. Posner, 101-118. Jossey-Bass.
Blanchard, Ken and Sheldon Bowles. 1998. *Gung Ho!* William Morrow.
Greenleaf, Robert K. 1970. *The Servant as Leader*. The Greenleaf Center for Servant Leadership.
Kouzes, James M. and Barry Z. Posner. 2007. *The Leadership Challenge, 4th edition*. Jossey-Bass.
Liden, Robert C., Sandy J. Wayne, Hao Zhao, and David J. Henderson. 2008. "Servant Leadership: Development of a Multidimensional Measure and Multi-level Assessment." *The Leadership Quarterly* 19 (2): 161-177.
Maxwell, John C. 1998. *The 21 Irrefutable Laws of Leadership*. Nashville: Thomas Nelson.
Ortberg, Nancy. 2004. "Reflections on Enable Others to Act." In *Christian Reflections on The Leadership Challenge*, edited by James M. Kouzes and Barry Z. Posner, 85-98. Jossey-Bass.

It's useful to give my power away
Autry, J.A. 2001. *The Servant Leader*. Prima Publishing.
Blanchard, Ken. 2004. "Reflections on Encourage the Heart." In *Christian Reflections on The Leadership Challenge*, edited by James M. Kouzes and Barry Z. Posner, 101-118. Jossey-Bass.
Blanchard, Ken and Phil Hodges. 2003. *The Servant Leader: Transforming Your Heart, Head, Hands and Habits*. Thomas Nelson.
Hunter, James C. 2004. *The World's Most Powerful Leadership Principle: How to Become a Servant Leader*. Waterbrook Press.
Kouzes, James M. and Barry Z. Posner. 2007. *The Leadership Challenge, 4th edition*. Jossey-Bass.
Lencioni, Patrick. 2016. *The Ideal Team Player: How to Recognize and Cultivate the Three Essential Virtues*. Jossey-Bass.
Maxwell, John C. 1998. *The 21 Irrefutable Laws of Leadership*. Nashville: Thomas Nelson.

Ortberg, Nancy. 2004. "Reflections on Enable Others to Act." In *Christian Reflections on The Leadership Challenge*, edited by James M. Kouzes and Barry Z. Posner, 85-98. Jossey-Bass.

I don't have to be right all the time
Blanchard, Ken. 2004. "Reflections on Encourage the Heart." In *Christian Reflections on The Leadership Challenge*, edited by James M. Kouzes and Barry Z. Posner, 101-118. Jossey-Bass.
Blanchard, Ken and Phil Hodges. 2003. *The Servant Leader: Transforming Your Heart, Head, Hands and Habits*. Thomas Nelson.
Ortberg, Nancy. 2004. "Reflections on Enable Others to Act." In *Christian Reflections on The Leadership Challenge*, edited by James M. Kouzes and Barry Z. Posner, 85-98. Jossey-Bass.

Listening is hard work–and it's worth the effort
Drucker, Peter F. 2006. *The Effective Executive: The Definitive Guide to Getting the Right Things Done*. New York: HarperCollins.
Greenleaf, Robert K. 1970. *The Servant as Leader*. The Greenleaf Center for Servant Leadership.
Kouzes, James M. and Barry Z. Posner. 2016. *Learning Leadership: The Five Fundamentals of Becoming an Exemplary Leader*. Wiley.
Kouzes, James M. and Barry Z. Posner. 2002. *The Leadership Challenge, 3rd edition*. Jossey-Bass.
Maxwell, John C. 2007. *The 21 Irrefutable Laws of Leadership, 10th Anniversary Edition*. Nashville: Thomas Nelson.

Feedback is a gift
Blanchard, Ken. 2004. "Reflections on Encourage the Heart." In *Christian Reflections on The Leadership Challenge*, edited by James M. Kouzes and Barry Z. Posner, 101-118. Jossey-Bass.
Blanchard, Ken and Phil Hodges. 2003. *The Servant Leader: Transforming Your Heart, Head, Hands and Habits*. Thomas Nelson.
Nickols, Fred. 1995. "Feedback about Feedback." *Human Resources Development Quarterly* 6 (3): 289-296.
Sipe, James W. and Don M. Frick. 2009. *Seven Pillars of Servant Leadership: Practicing the Wisdom of Leading by Serving*. New York: Paulist Press.

I am a community builder
Collins, Jim. 2001. *Good to Great: Why Some Companies Make the Leap and Others Don't*. New York: Harper Collins.
Drucker, Peter F. 2006. *The Effective Executive: The Definitive Guide to Getting the Right Things Done*. New York: HarperCollins.
Drucker, Peter F. 2005. "Managing Oneself." *Harvard Business Review* 83, (1): 100-109.
Hunter, James C. 2004. *The World's Most Powerful Leadership Principle: How to Become a Servant Leader*. Waterbrook Press.
Kouzes, James M. and Barry Z. Posner. 2016. *Learning Leadership: The Five Fundamentals of Becoming an Exemplary Leader*. Wiley.
Kouzes, James M. and Barry Z. Posner. 2007. *The Leadership Challenge, 4th edition*. Jossey-Bass.
Kouzes, James M. and Barry Z. Posner. 2002. *The Leadership Challenge, 3rd edition*. Jossey-Bass.
Maxwell, John C. 1998. *The 21 Irrefutable Laws of Leadership*. Nashville: Thomas Nelson.

Chapter Three

Knowing and sharing personal values
Jeffrey, Scott. 2018. "The Ultimate List of Core Values." Accessed May 14, 2018. https://scottjeffrey.com/core-values-list/
Kouzes, James M. and Barry Z. Posner. 2012. *The Leadership Challenge, 5th edition*. Jossey-Bass.
Kouzes, James, M. and Barry Z. Posner. 2010. *The Truth About Leadership*. Jossey-Bass.
Kouzes, James M. and Barry Z. Posner (editors). 2004. *Christian Reflections on The Leadership Challenge*. Jossey-Bass.
Kouzes, James M. and Barry Z. Posner. 2002. *The Leadership Challenge, 3rd edition*. Jossey-Bass.
Massey, Morris. 1979. *The People Puzzle: Understanding Yourself and Others*. Brady.
Rokeach, Milton. 1973. *The Nature of Human Values*. New York: Free Press.
Sipe, James W. and Don M. Frick. 2009. *Seven Pillars of Servant Leadership: Practicing the Wisdom of Leading by Serving*. New York: Paulist Press.

Listening
Covey, Stephen. 1989. *Seven Habits of Highly Effective People*. New York: Fireside.
Greenleaf, Robert K. 1977. *Servant Leadership: A Journey into the Nature of Legitimate Power & Greatness*. New York: Paulist Press.
Greenleaf, Robert K. 1970. *The Servant as Leader*. The Greenleaf Center for Servant Leadership.
Hunter, James C. 2004. *The World's Most Powerful Leadership Principle: How to Become a Servant Leader*. Waterbrook Press.
Kouzes, James M and Barry Z. Posner. 2012. *The Leadership Challenge, 5th edition*. Jossey-Bass.
Robbins, Stephen P. 2013. *The Truth about Managing People, 3rd edition*. FT Press.
Robbins, Stephen P. 2003. *Essentials of Organizational Behavior, 7th edition*. Prentice Hall.
Sipe, James W. and Don M. Frick. 2009. *Seven Pillars of Servant Leadership: Practicing the Wisdom of Leading by Serving*. New York: Paulist Press.

Asking questions
Hunter, James C. 2004. *The World's Most Powerful Leadership Principle: How to Become a Servant Leader*. Waterbrook Press.
Kouzes, James M. and Barry Z. Posner. 2012. *The Leadership Challenge, 5th edition*. Jossey-Bass.
Kouzes, James M. and Barry Z. Posner. 2002. *The Leadership Challenge, 3rd edition*. Jossey-Bass.

Telling stories
Gardner, Howard. 1995. *Leading Minds*. New York: Basic Books.
Kouzes, James M. and Barry Z. Posner. 2012. *The Leadership Challenge, 5th edition*. Jossey-Bass.
Kouzes, James, M. and Barry Z. Posner. 2010. *The Truth About Leadership*. Jossey-Bass.
Kouzes, James M. and Barry Z. Posner. 2003. *Credibility*. Jossey-Bass.
Kouzes, James M. and Barry Z. Posner. 2002. *The Leadership Challenge, 3rd edition*. Jossey-Bass.
Sipe, James W. and Don M. Frick. 2009. *Seven Pillars of Servant Leadership: Practicing the Wisdom of Leading by Serving*. New York: Paulist Press.
Tichy, Noel M. 1997. *The Leadership Engine: How Winning Companies Build Leaders at Every Level*. Harper Business.

Being optimistic
Blanchard, Ken. 2004. "Reflections on Encourage the Heart." In *Christian Reflections on The Leadership Challenge*, edited by James M. Kouzes and Barry Z. Posner, 101-118. Jossey-Bass.
Fredrickson, Barbara L. 2009. *Positivity: Groundbreaking Research Reveals How to Embrace the Hidden Strength of Positive Emotions, Overcome Negativity, and Thrive*. New York: Crown.
Kouzes, James M. and Barry Z. Posner. 2016. *Learning Leadership: The Five Fundamentals of Becoming an Exemplary Leader*. Wiley.
Kouzes, James M. and Barry Z. Posner. 2010. *The Truth About Leadership*. Jossey-Bass.
Kouzes, James M. and Barry Z. Posner. 2004. "Leadership is a Relationship." In *Christian Reflections on The Leadership Challenge*, edited by James M. Kouzes and Barry Z. Posner, 119-126. Jossey-Bass.
Kouzes, James M. and Barry Z. Posner. 2003. *Credibility: How Leaders Gain and Lose it, Why People Demand It*. Jossey-Bass.
Martinuzzi, Bruna. 2018. "Optimism." Accessed March 26, 2018. https://www.mindtools.com/pages/article/newLDR_72.htm.
McGinnis, Alan Loy. 1990. *The Power of Optimism*. San Francisco: Harper.

Saying "we"
Drucker, Peter F. 2004. "What Makes and Effective Executive." *Harvard Business Review* June: 58-63.
Kouzes, James M. and Barry Z. Posner. 2002. *The Leadership Challenge, 3rd edition*. Jossey-Bass.
Maxwell, John C. 2007. *The 21 Irrefutable Laws of Leadership, 10th Anniversary Edition*. Nashville: Thomas Nelson.

Stimulating informal conversations
Kouzes, James M. and Barry Z. Posner. 2012. *The Leadership Challenge, 5th edition*. Jossey-Bass.
Kouzes, James M. and Barry Z. Posner. 2002. *The Leadership Challenge, 3rd edition*. Jossey-Bass.

Visioning
Kouzes, James M. and Barry Z. Posner. 2012. *The Leadership Challenge Workbook, 3rd edition*. Jossey-Bass.
Kouzes, James M. and Barry Z. Posner. 2002. *The Leadership Challenge, 3rd edition*. Jossey-Bass.

Sipe, James W. and Don M. Frick. 2009. *Seven Pillars of Servant Leadership: Practicing the Wisdom of Leading by Serving*. New York: Paulist Press.

Tichy, Noel M. 1997. *The Leadership Engine: How Winning Companies Build Leaders at Every Level*. Harper Business.

Von Oech, Roger. 1990. *A Whack on the Side of the Head: How You Can be More Creative*. New York: Warner Books,

Managing time

Atkinson, Barbara. 2017. "The Most and Least Productive Hours of the Day." *Evernote*, https://blog.evernote.com/blog/2017/10/20/the-most-and-least-productive-hours-of-the-day/. Accessed April 22, 2018.

Covey, Stephen. 1989. *Seven Habits of Highly Effective People*. New York: Fireside.

Drucker, Peter F. 2006. *The Effective Executive: The Definitive Guide to Getting the Right Things Done*. New York: HarperCollins.

Kotter, John P. 1999. "What Effective General Managers Really Do." *Harvard Business Review* March-April. Accessed September 24, 2019. https://hbr.org/1999/03/what-effective-general-managers-really-do

Kouzes, James M. and Barry Z. Posner. 2002. *The Leadership Challenge, 3rd edition*. Jossey-Bass.

Onken, Jr., William and Donald L. Wass. 1974. "Management Time: Who's Got the Monkey?" *Harvard Business Review* November-December. Reprinted with Stephen R. Covey. 1999. *Harvard Business Review* November-December: 1-8.

Slevin, Dennis P. 1989. *The Whole Manager: How to Increase Your Professional and Personal Effectiveness*. New York: American Management Association, AMACOM.

Running a meeting

"10 ground rules for meetings." MeetingSift. meetingsift.com Accessed April 26, 2018.

Drucker, Peter F. 2004. "What Makes and Effective Executive." *Harvard Business Review* June: 58-63.

Keith, Elise. "The 16 types of business meetings (and why they matter)." https://blog.lucidmeetings.com/blog/16-types-of-business-meetings. September 23, 2017.

Kelly, Margaret J. 2010. "Meetings." In *A Concise Guide to Catholic Church Management*, edited by The Vincentian Center for Church and Society, 83-104. Notre Dame, IN: Ave Maria Press.

Kouzes, James M. and Barry Z. Posner. 2002. *The Leadership Challenge,*

3rd edition. Jossey-Bass.
"The six most common types of meetings." MeetingSift. Meetingsift.com/the-six-types-of-meetings Accessed April 24, 2108.

Forgiving
Hunter, James C. 2004. *The World's Most Powerful Leadership Principle: How to Become a Servant Leader.* Waterbrook Press.
Luskin, Fred. 2002. *Forgive for Good.* San Francisco: HarperCollins.

Chapter Four

Being proactive
Collins, Jim. 2001. *Good to Great: Why Some Companies Make the Leap and Others Don't.* New York: HarperCollins.
Drucker, Peter F. 2006. *The Effective Executive: The Definitive Guide to Getting the Right Things Done.* New York: HarperCollins.
Drucker, Peter F. 2004. "What Makes an Effective Executive." *Harvard Business Review* June: 58-63.
Kouzes, James M. and Barry Z. Posner. 2002. *The Leadership Challenge, 3rd edition.* Jossey-Bass.

Establishing credibility
Hunter, James C. 2004. *The World's Most Powerful Leadership Principle: How to Become a Servant Leader.* Waterbrook Press.
Kouzes, James M. and Barry Z. Posner. 2004. "Leadership is a Relationship." In *Christian Reflections on The Leadership Challenge,* edited by James M. Kouzes and Barry Z. Posner, 119-126. Jossey-Bass.
Kouzes, James M. and Barry Posner. 2003. *Credibility: How Leaders Gain and Lose It, Why People Demand It.* Jossey-Bass.
Kouzes, James M. and Barry Z. Posner. 2002. *The Leadership Challenge, 3rd edition.* Jossey-Bass.

Building trust
Autry, James A. 2001. *The Servant Leader: How to Build a Creative Team, Develop Great Morale, and Improve Performance.* Roseville, CA: Prima Publishing.
Collins, Jim. 2001. *Good to Great: Why Some Companies Make the Leap and Others Don't.* New York: Harper Collins.
Covey, Stephen R. 1989. *The 7 Habits of Highly Effective People.* New York: Free Press.

Hunter, James C. 2004. *The World's Most Powerful Leadership Principle: How to Become a Servant Leader*. Waterbrook Press.
Kouzes, James M. and Barry Z. Posner. 2016. *Learning Leadership: The Five Fundamentals of Becoming an Exemplary Leader*. Wiley.
Kouzes, James M. and Barry Z. Posner. 2012. *The Leadership Challenge, 5th edition*. Jossey-Bass.
Kouzes, James, M. and Barry Z. Posner. 2010. *The Truth About Leadership*. Jossey-Bass.
Kouzes, James M. and Barry Z. Posner. 2002. *The Leadership Challenge, 3rd edition*. Jossey-Bass.
Maxwell, John C. 1998. *The 21 Irrefutable Laws of Leadership*. Nashville: Thomas Nelson.
Ortberg, Nancy. 2004. "Reflections on Enable Others to Act." In *Christian Reflections on The Leadership Challenge*, edited by James M. Kouzes and Barry Z. Posner, 85-98. Jossey-Bass.

Building networks
Ibarra, Herminia and Mark Lee Hunter. "Leveraging Your Links: Why Successful Leaders Network." https://www.criticaleye.com/inspiring/insights-servfile.cfm?id=2781. Accessed June 10, 2108.
Ibarra, Herminia and Mark Lee Hunter. 2007. "How Leaders Create and Use Networks." *Harvard Business Review* January: 40-47.
Kouzes, James M. and Barry Z. Posner. 2016. *Learning Leadership: The Five Fundamentals of Becoming an Exemplary Leader*. Wiley.
Slevin, Dennis P. 1989. *The Whole Manager: How to Increase Your Professional and Personal Effectiveness*. New York: American Management Association, AMACOM.

Empowering others to act
Collins, Jim. 2001. *Good to Great: Why Some Companies Make the Leap and Others Don't*. New York: HarperCollins.
Drucker, Peter F. 2006. *The Effective Executive: The Definitive Guide to Getting the Right Things Done*. New York: HarperCollins.
Hunter, James C. 2004. *The World's Most Powerful Leadership Principle: How to Become a Servant Leader*. Waterbrook Press.
Kouzes, James M. and Barry Z. Posner. 2012. *The Leadership Challenge, 5th edition*. Jossey-Bass.
Kouzes, James M. and Barry Z. Posner. 2004. "The Five Practices of Exemplary Leadership." In *Christian Reflections on The Leadership Challenge*, edited by James M. Kouzes and Barry Z. Posner, 7-38. Jossey-Bass.

Kouzes, James M. and Barry Z. Posner. 2002. *The Leadership Challenge, 3rd edition.* Jossey-Bass.

Maxwell, John C. 2007. *The 21 Irrefutable Laws of Leadership, 10th Anniversary Edition.* Nashville: Thomas Nelson.

Ortberg, Nancy. 2004. "Reflections on Enable Others to Act." In *Christian Reflections on The Leadership Challenge*, edited by James M. Kouzes and Barry Z. Posner, 85-98. Jossey-Bass.

Embracing change

Autry, James A. 2001. *The Servant Leader: How to Build a Creative Team, Develop Great Morale, and Improve Performance.* Roseville, CA: Prima Publishing.

Kouzes, James M. and Barry Z. Posner. 2012. *The Leadership Challenge, 5th edition.* Jossey-Bass.

Kouzes, James M. and Barry Z. Posner. 2004. "The Five Practices of Exemplary Leadership." In *Christian Reflections on The Leadership Challenge*, edited by James M. Kouzes and Barry Z. Posner, 7-38. Jossey-Bass.

Kouzes, James M. and Barry Z. Posner. 2002. *The Leadership Challenge, 3rd edition.* Jossey-Bass.

Lencioni, Patrick. 2004. "Reflections on Challenge the Process." In *Christian Reflections on The Leadership Challenge*, edited by James M. Kouzes and Barry Z. Posner, 71-81. Jossey-Bass.

Magalhaes, Ivan Luizio. Published January 25, 2015. "Peter Senge's 11 Laws of Systems Thinking." Accessed July 5, 2018. https://www.linkedin.com/pulse/peter-senges-11-laws-systems-thinking-ivan-luizio-magalhães/.

Robbins, Stephen P. and Timothy A. Judge. 2015. *Organizational Behavior, 16th edition.* Pearson Education.

Robbins, Stephen P. 2013. *The Truth About Managing People, 3rd edition.* FT Press.

Saaty, Thomas L. and Larry W. Boone. 1990. *Embracing the Future: Meeting the Challenge of Our Changing World.* New York: Praeger.

Sipe, James W. and Don M. Frick. 2009. *Seven Pillars of Servant Leadership: Practicing the Wisdom of Leading by Serving.* New York: Paulist Press.

Planning the future

Kouzes, James M. and Barry Z. Posner. 2012. *The Leadership Challenge Workbook, 3rd edition.* Jossey-Bass.

Kouzes, James M. and Barry Z. Posner. 2002. *The Leadership Challenge,*

3rd edition. Jossey-Bass.
Pickett, William L. 2007. *A Concise Guide to Pastoral Planning*. Notre Dame, IN: Ave Maria Press.
Robbins, Stephen P. and Mary Coulter. 2014. *Management, 12th edition*. Pearson.
Sipe, James W. and Don M. Frick. 2009. *Seven Pillars of Servant Leadership: Practicing the Wisdom of Leading by Serving*. Paulist Press.
Winseman, Albert L. 2007. *Growing an Engaged Church*. New York: Gallup Press.

Reflecting
Greenleaf, Robert K. 2002. *Servant Leadership: A Journey into the Nature of Legitimate Power & Greatness*. New York: Paulist Press.
"How Self-Reflection Can Make You a Better Leader." Kellogg Insight based on insights from Harry M. Kraemer. Accessed July 20, 2018. https://insight.kellogg.northwestern.edu/article/how-self-reflection-can-make-you-a-better-leader.
Hunter, James C. 2004. *The World's Most Powerful Leadership Principle: How to Become a Servant Leader*. Waterbrook Press.
Kouzes, James M. and Barry Z. Posner. 2012. *The Leadership Challenge, 5th edition*. Jossey-Bass.
Kouzes, James M. and Barry Z. Posner (eds.). 2004. *Christian Reflections on The Leadership Challenge*. Jossey-Bass.
Kouzes, James M. and Barry Z. Posner. 2002. *The Leadership Challenge, 3rd edition*. Jossey-Bass.
Saaty, Thomas L. and Larry W. Boone. 1990. *Embracing the Future: Meeting the Challenge of Our Changing World*. New York: Praeger.
Shepard, H.A. and J. A. Hawley. 1974. *Life Planning: Personal and Organizational*. Washington, D.C.: National Training and Development Service Press.
Sipe, James W. and Don M. Frick. 2009. *Seven Pillars of Servant Leadership: Practicing the Wisdom of Leading by Serving*. Paulist Press.
Spears, Larry C. 2004. "The Understanding and Practice of Servant Leadership." In *Practicing Servant Leadership: Succeeding Through Trust, Bravery, and Forgiveness*, edited by Larry C. Spears and Michelle Lawrence. San Francisco: Jossey-Bass.
Thiran, Roshan. August 29, 2017. "To Become and Effective Leader, You Need to Practise Self-Reflection." Accessed July 18, 2017. https://leaderonomics.com/leadership/practise-self-reflection.

Webster, Vicky and Martin Webster (eds.). "Why Self-Reflection Is the Key to Effective Leadership." Accessed July 18, 2018. https://www.leadershipthoughts.com/why-self-reflection-is-the-key-to-effective-leadership/.

Index

A

accepting, 10
accountability, 1, 10, 11, 12, 30, 40, 41, 98, 129, 130, 133, 143, 174, 178, 217
active listening, 59
Adair, John, 95
admitting mistakes, 43, 143
after-action reviews, 177
agenda, 75, 119, 123, 124, 217
asking questions, 62, 146, 170, 191, 215
assumptions, 205
attitudes, 1, 6, 15, 24, 28, 132, 133, 191, 214, 215
authenticity, 10, 11, 173
authority, 8, 9, 98, 100, 122
autocratic leadership, 3, 19, 40
autonomy, 14
Autry, James, 2, 10, 42, 133, 150, 179, 183
available, 45, 59, 153

B

behaviour modelling, 97
behavioural boundaries, 137
behavioural expectations, 4, 32
behavioural guidelines, 39, 142
behaviours, 1, 2, 4, 7, 10, 15, 18, 24, 25, 28, 70, 110, 132, 133, 134, 141, 159, 214, 215, 217

being optimistic, 147, 170, 189, 191, 217
beliefs, 31, 53
Bennis, Warren, 68, 80, 147
Blanchard, Ken, 1, 81, 133
brewing consensus, 44
broken promises, 143
bureaucratic leadership, 3

C

candid, 153
career growth, 12
celebrations, 50, 71, 86, 154
challenge the process, 66, 185, 188, 191
change, 140, 180, 189, 191, 199
change agent, 188
character, 17, 83, 132, 141, 149, 193, 212
characteristics of servant leaders, 5
charismatic leadership, 3, 21
circadian day, 107
climate, 41, 132, 133, 134, 172, 178, 180
closure, 129
coach, 11, 15, 42, 64, 139, 152, 160, 199, 217
coercive power, 14
collaboration, 1, 62, 132, 172
Collins, Jim, 49, 138, 157, 190
commitment, 2, 17, 24, 46, 50, 99, 141, 160, 172, 195, 206
common cause, 141

common good, 32, 94
common purpose, 57
common vision, 88
communication, 62, 100
community, 1, 4, 12, 24, 30, 39, 86, 133, 170, 179, 191, 198, 199, 214, 217
community-building, 7, 31, 49, 50, 52, 117, 118, 121
compassion, 153
compassionate collaborator, 83
compelling modesty, 157, 177
competence, 133, 153, 155, 174, 175
competent, 134, 141, 146, 148, 172, 218
confidence, 17, 134, 141, 144, 146, 150, 153, 171, 172, 174, 175, 178, 217
conflict resolution, 50
connect, 15, 134, 174
consensus, 24
consistency, 141, 142
contingency approach, 2
core values, 17
courage, 12, 17, 216
Covey, Stephen, 132, 135, 148
creativity, 2
credibility, 53, 134, 141, 142, 146, 147, 148, 150, 155, 172, 180, 197
culture, 68, 70, 81, 124
culture of inclusion, 155

D

De Pree, Max, 155
decision-making, 5, 149, 180, 212

deep listening, 64
delegation, 40, 97, 98, 176, 191, 217
democratic leadership, 3
development, 154, 172, 175, 177
dignity of work, 5, 173
diversity, 50
dreaded task, 116
Drucker, Peter, 44, 49, 96, 135, 136, 137, 140, 148

E

educate, 11, 15, 152, 156, 160, 199
embracing change, viii, 26, 135, 180, 183, 191, 192, 214, 218, 232
emotional healing, 12
empathetic listening, 58, 153
empathy, 179
empower, 1, 12, 40, 98, 99, 132, 134, 171, 176, 177, 182
empowering others to act, 26, 172, 174, 175, 180, 183
enabling others to act, 132
encouragement, 12, 171, 178
environment, 2, 15, 41, 84, 119, 132, 134, 135, 139, 148, 151, 154, 155, 157, 159, 160, 163, 172, 176, 177, 178, 179
example, 14
expectations, 38, 143, 217
experiment, 7

F

facilitate, 11, 15, 41, 100, 139, 144, 152, 160, 199
failure, 30
faith, 17, 32

feedback, 47, 62, 65, 158, 170, 177, 187, 191, 217
feel able, 180
filtering, 144
filtering out interruptions, 110
First Law of Leadership, 17, 55, 141
first to trust, 151, 159
flexibility, 195
focus areas, 202, 203, 206
foresight, 32, 196, 213, 214
forgiving, 12, 128, 130, 146, 156, 160, 191, 209, 217
formal authority, 15, 39
forthright, 153
forward-looking, 80, 134, 141, 145, 146, 147, 148, 172, 197, 199, 218

G

Gardner, Howard, 68, 70, 71
goals, 203
golden halo, 65
Good to Great, 49, 138, 157, 190
goodwill, 151
gossiping, 159
Greenleaf, Robert, 4, 6, 7, 8, 44, 57, 61, 213

H

hard truth, 143
heroes, 68, 70, 71, 124, 152, 215
Hesse, Hermann, 8
honesty, 129, 134, 141, 143, 144, 148, 151, 155, 156, 157, 160, 172, 188, 209, 218
hope, 9

humility, 7, 12, 17, 22, 42, 47, 155, 156, 160, 188, 216
humility and pain tolerance, 188
Hunter, James, 1, 59, 128, 131, 133, 143, 160, 177

I

I Have a Dream speech, 33, 93
I need help, 102, 155, 156, 162
Ibarra, Herminia and Mark Hunter, 162
ideas, values, emotional energy and edge, 69
identity stories, 70
inclusion, 154
influence, 149
informal conversations, 45, 84, 85, 146, 153, 170, 217
initiative, 70, 133, 134, 148, 216
innovation, 2, 24, 46
innovation board, 185
inspiring, 134, 141, 147, 148, 172, 215, 218
integrity, 7, 17, 129, 141, 173
interpersonal skills, 146
intuition, 213

J

job satisfaction, 46
joy, 173

K

kindness, 58
knowing oneself, 142
knowledge-builder role, 154

Kouzes, James and Barry Posner, 1, 17, 33, 44, 55, 74, 76, 80, 85, 87, 96, 132, 141, 145, 146, 148, 158, 165, 174, 180, 185, 189, 209, 211

L

laissez-faire leadership, 3
Law of Acceptance, 42
Law of Addition, 44, 178
Law of Connection, 179
Law of Empowerment, 2, 42, 132, 178
Law of Reproduction, 38
Law of Solid Ground, 149, 178
Law of the Inner Circle, 49
lead from the top, 10
leadership role models, 142
Leadership Skills Inventory, 177
leadership styles, 19
learning environment, 174, 176, 177, 216
legacy, 71, 217
legitimate power base, 40
Lencioni, Patrick, 188, 190
Level 5 leadership style, 138
listen first, 44, 46, 158
listen first and speak last, 44
listen first–and often, 44
listening, 4, 9, 32, 35, 43, 46, 47, 50, 57, 142, 146, 153, 158, 170, 174, 175, 177, 182, 185, 191, 198, 208, 209, 214, 217
listening deeply, 175
love, 4, 131
loyalty, 17, 24, 201
Luskin, Fred, 129

M

managing time, 52, 95, 146
Martin Luther King Jr., 33
Maxwell, John, 2, 38, 44, 49, 132, 149, 178
McAllister-Wilson, David, 32, 86
McGinnis, Alan Loy, 77
McKee, Robert, 71
meeting types, 117
members-engaged, not engaged, disengaged, 201
mentor, 12, 142, 161
metaphors, 72, 75, 90, 94
micromanage, 139
mission, 1, 12, 24, 40, 93, 104, 108, 132, 133, 136, 138, 182, 190, 196, 197, 198, 199, 206, 214
mistakes, 7, 134, 144, 155, 216
modesty, 139
moral authority, 83
motivation, 133, 148, 153, 173

N

net importers of ideas, 185
network building, 102
networking, 160, 162, 172, 175, 180, 216
networks, 101, 134, 214
networks-operational, personal, strategic, 161
neutral spaces, 85
non-judgmental listening, 153
not-for-profit organizations, 22

O

Onken, William and Donald Wass, 104
open-ended questions, 45, 62, 64
openness, 151, 157, 160
operational networking, 163
opportunities, 14, 139, 185
optimism, 9, 76, 77, 79, 80, 139, 146
organizational story, 93, 202
Ortberg, Nancy, 1, 38, 133, 149, 155, 173
other-centred, 7, 29
outsight, 185

P

pairing, 159
paradox of power, 40
participative leadership, 3
passion, 147
patience, 17, 160, 182, 217
peace, 129
people-growing, 52
performance, 1, 2, 10, 24, 133, 143, 150, 154, 159, 161, 164, 172, 198, 216, 217
performance art, 68, 75, 147
performance-based, 22
personal board of advisors, 161, 165, 166
personal networking, 165
personal transformation, 4
persuasion, 14
pillars, 83, 202, 205, 206
planning the future, viii, 26, 193, 218, 232

power, 5, 9, 12, 40, 214, 216
present, 10, 45
pride in accomplishment, 2
priorities, 97, 104, 108, 110, 197, 198, 199, 202, 206, 208
proactive, 133, 134, 135, 137, 138, 140, 180
productivity, 2, 46, 152
professional development, 12
progress, the art of, 180
psychological hardiness, 189, 190, 193, 196

Q

quality of service, 2

R

ready to suffer, 188, 189
reciprocal relationship, 141
referent power, 14, 40
reflecting, 61, 97, 108, 115, 135, 208, 209, 212, 214, 218
reflective listening, 58
relationship-based, 22
relationships, 1, 2, 7, 12, 24, 28, 49, 58, 62, 77, 99, 102, 130, 132, 133, 134, 148, 151, 160, 161, 169, 170, 179, 209, 216, 218
release others to do their work, 133
resentment, 128, 129
resistance to change, 183, 184, 189, 192, 214
respect, 4, 46, 50, 58, 64, 65, 151, 153, 154, 155, 157, 160, 178, 217

responsibility, 2, 30, 98, 135, 144, 150
right people on the bus, 190
Robbins, Stephen, 59
Rokeach, Milton, 53
rule-breaking, 91
running a meeting, 52, 117, 146, 217

S

satisfaction, 2, 24
say "we," not "I", 82
saying "No", 97, 103
self-awareness, 7, 15, 17, 135, 209
self-confidence, 15, 41, 99, 176
self-control, 217
self-determination, 133
self-disclosure, 155, 174
self-esteem, 46, 58, 189
self-examination, 210
self-improvement, 154, 158, 215
self-knowledge, 209
selfless, 160
self-reflection, 88
self-serving leaders, 15, 42, 47
self-sufficiency, 148
self-worth, 2, 132
Senge, Peter, 189
sense of direction, 145
servant leadership, 4, 7, 8, 15, 18, 24, 32, 86
service, 4, 15, 40, 47, 121
share the pain, 153
silence, 44, 214
Sipe, James and Don Frick, 32, 48, 58, 60, 83, 87, 181, 212
six degrees of separation, 167

skills, 1, 15, 24, 52, 132, 133, 191, 214, 215
Slevin, Dennis, 97
small wins, 181, 185, 187, 192, 216
social consciousness, 7
Spears, Larry, 5, 213
steering committee, 205, 206, 207
stewardship, 12
stories, 124, 142, 144, 152, 215
storytelling, 68, 69, 75, 146, 191
strategic networking, 168
stress management, 96, 114
structured listening, 198, 199
subsidiarity, 40, 41
suffer first, 82, 153, 154

T

talent radar, 217
talent scouts, 37
teamwork, 149, 159, 172
third places, 86
Tichy, Noel, 69, 71, 72, 74
time management, 95, 97, 160, 172, 217
timeline, 203
to-do list, 97, 114, 161
tolerance for errors, 156
train first, 154
traits, leadership, 18, 24
transactional leadership, 3, 21
transformational leadership, 3, 19
trust, 1, 7, 17, 38, 43, 46, 49, 58, 62, 99, 132, 133, 134, 141, 150, 153, 154, 155, 156, 157, 159, 163, 172, 174, 175, 176, 177, 180, 209, 214, 216
trustworthy, 17, 141

U

ultradian cycles, 107
unity, 30
useful, 10

V

values, 2, 4, 12, 15, 16, 30, 32, 36, 39, 40, 49, 51, 52, 53, 54, 62, 65, 68, 86, 93, 97, 104, 108, 134, 136, 138, 139, 141, 144, 150, 152, 160, 172, 173, 193, 196, 197, 198, 199, 200, 206, 208, 215
values statement, 30, 200
values-centred life, 116
virtues, 7, 16
vision, 1, 4, 11, 12, 15, 24, 31, 32, 34, 35, 39, 40, 44, 46, 49, 51, 65, 72, 73, 81, 86, 104, 108, 135, 139, 147, 154, 172, 182, 190, 196, 197, 198, 199, 202, 206, 208, 214, 215
vision and change, 181
vision formats, 34, 94
vision statement, 200
visioning, 33, 86, 92, 95, 137, 146, 163, 191, 193, 214
visioning journey, 87
visioning themes, 92
von Oech, Roger, 90
vulnerable, 10, 151, 179

W

walk the shop, 45, 50, 153
wear another hat, 91
when in doubt, invite, 154
Whitehead, Alfred North, 180
wisdom, 12, 17